The Giant Book of Dreams

The Giant Book of Dreams

Magpie Books, London

Constable & Robinson Ltd
3 The Lanchesters
162 Fulham Palace Road
London W6 9ER
www.constablerobinson.com

Previously published in the UK as
The World's Greatest Dreams by Magpie Books,
an imprint of Constable & Robinson Ltd 2004

This edition published by Magpie Books,
an imprint of Constable & Robinson Ltd 2005

A copy of the British Library Cataloguing in
Publication Data is available from the British Library

ISBN-10: 1-84529-544-7
ISBN-13: 978-1-84529-544-8

Printed and bound in the EU

3 5 7 9 10 8 6 4 2

Introduction

"We are such stuff
As dreams are made of, and our little life
Is rounded with a sleep."

Shakespeare's words could not be more true: not only are dreams an essential part of our lives and mental health, they are also a subject which has fascinated humanity since time immemorial.

Ancient civilizations placed great emphasis on the prophetic value of dreams. The ancient Egyptians believed that gods spoke through dreams, a view which was later adopted by the ancient Greeks. The Greeks made use of a practice known as incubation, in which ritually-induced dreams were afterwards interpreted by an oracle or priest. In classical Rome, dreams felt to be of importance were submitted to the Senate for consideration. Dreams appear throughout the Bible, as the quotations opening each letter of this book amply demonstrate.

In more recent times, there have been many examples of dreams conveying a prophesy. After the sinking of the ocean liner *Titanic*, there were a number of newspaper reports of passengers who had cancelled their reservations after dreaming of the sinking. One businessman had the same dream three times. Similar dreams were reported after the sinking of the *Lusitania* in 1915. On a more directly religious level, St Bernadette's visions of the Virgin Mary at Lourdes can be viewed as a kind of waking dream. The fascination with the link between dreaming and reality has remained undimmed, and has also been explored time and again by the arts, in forms as varied as the paintings of Goya and Dalí, the visionary poetry of Coleridge and Blake, and popular films such as *The Wizard of Oz*.

The nineteenth and early twentieth centuries saw dreams being brought into the sphere of science, with the birth of psychology and psychoanalysis. These new sciences saw dreams as expressions of what was going on within the dreamer's unconscious, and felt that their successful interpretation could be used to identify and treat psychological problems. The Austrian psychotherapist Sigmund Freud, in his book *The Interpretation of Dreams*, argued that dreams expressed either the unfulfilled wishes of the dreamer, or repressed emotions. Freud's work was followed by that of the Swiss Carl Gustav Jung, who believed that dreams expressed universal images, or archetypes, which lay within the mind of the dreamer. It is now recognized that dreams are essential to health, and that a good night's sleep includes dreaming.

Even if you do not remember your dreams, it is almost certain that you have them. If you would like to remember them, there are several steps that you can take. Try to keep a clear mind before you go to sleep. Avoid alcohol and drug consumption, as these are likely to result in an unnaturally heavy sleep, which will make recollection difficult. When you wake up, take a few minutes and try to to recall as much of what you have dreamed as you can. This is particularly important: dreams fade quickly once you wake up, and ninety per cent of the dream is lost after only five minutes awake. Then write down what you remember in a dream diary. In this way you can start to build up a picture of your dreams, to get an idea of any recurrent themes and a sense of when anything of particular significance occurs.

The aim of this book is to help you to unravel the secrets of your dreams. It contains thousands of dreams, with their most common interpretations, both in terms of what they predict for your future and of what they tell you about your inner life. Remember, though, that helpful as these interpretations are, you should also take into account your own emotions and circumstances at the time of the dream. If you dream about a lion the day before a visit to the zoo, the significance is patently obvious! Likewise, a recurrent dream of rushing for a train at a time when you are overloaded with work and deadlines is an obvious reflection of the anxiety in your waking life. If you are torn between several interpretations of a dream, go with your own gut feeling.

You will spend around one tenth of your life dreaming. We hope that this book will help you to explore this fascinating area of your life.

Happy dreaming!

A

'When he was set down on the Judgment seat, his wife sent unto him, saying, "Have thou nothing to do with that just man; for I have suffered many things this day in a dream, because of him."'

—Matthew xxvii, 19.

Abandon

To dream that you are abandoned denotes that you will have difficulty in framing your plans for future success.

To abandon others, you will see unhappy conditions around you.

If it is your house that you abandon, you may come to grief in experimenting with fortune.

If you abandon your sweetheart, you may fail to recover lost valuables, and friends may reject your favours.

If you abandon a mistress, you will unexpectedly come into a goodly inheritance.

If it is religion you abandon, you will come to grief through your attacks on prominent people.

To abandon children warns that you could lose your fortune by lack of calmness and judgment.

To abandon your business indicates distressing circumstances in which there will be quarrels and suspicion. (This dream may have a literal fulfilment if it is impressed on your waking mind, whether you abandon a person, or that person abandons you, or, as indicated, it denotes other worries.)

To see yourself or a friend abandon a ship suggests your possible entanglement in some business failure, but if you escape to shore your interests will remain secure.

Abbey

To see an abbey in ruins foretells that your hopes and schemes may not come to fruition.

To dream that a priest bars your entrance into an abbey denotes that you will be saved from a ruinous state by enemies mistaking your embarrassment for progress.

For a young woman to get into an abbey foretells illness. If she converses with a priest in an abbey, she will incur the censure of true friends for indiscretion.

Abbess

For a young woman to dream that she sees an abbess denotes that she will submit to authority only after unsuccessful rebellion.

To dream of an abbess smiling and benign denotes you will be surrounded by true friends and pleasing prospects.

Abbot

To dream that you are an abbot warns you that treacherous plots are being laid for your downfall.

If you see this pious man in devotional exercises, it forewarns you of smooth flattery and deceit pulling you a willing victim into the meshes of artful bewilderment.

For a young woman to talk with an abbot portends that she will yield to insinuating flatteries, and in yielding she may besmirch her reputation. If she marries one, she will uphold her name and honour despite poverty and temptation.

Abhor

To dream that you abhor a person denotes that you will entertain strange dislike for some person, and that your suspicions about his honesty will prove correct.

To think yourself held in abhorrence by others warns that your good intentions to others will subside into selfishness.

For a young woman to dream that her lover abhors her, foretells that she may love a man who is in no sense congenial.

Abject

To dream that you are abject denotes that you will be the recipient of gloomy tidings, which will cause a relaxation in your strenuous efforts to climb the heights of prosperity.

To see others abject, is a sign of bickerings and false dealings among your friends.

Abode

To dream that you can't find your abode warns that you may lose faith in the integrity of others.

If you have no abode in your dreams, you will be unfortunate in your affairs, and lose if you indulge in speculation.

To change your abode signifies hurried tidings and that hasty journeys will be made by you.

For a young woman to dream that she has left her abode is significant of slander and falsehoods being perpetrated against her.

See also **Home**.

Above

To see anything hanging above you, and about to fall, implies danger; if it falls upon you it indicates sudden disappointment. If it falls near, but misses you, it is a sign that you will have a narrow escape from loss of money.

Should the object be securely fixed above you, so as not to imply danger, your condition will improve after threatened loss.

Abroad

To dream that you are abroad, or going abroad foretells that you will soon, in company with a party, make a pleasant trip, and you will find it necessary to absent yourself from your native country for a sojourn in a different climate.

Absence

To grieve over the absence of anyone in your dreams denotes that repentance for some hasty action will be the means of securing you life-long friendships.

If you rejoice over the absence of friends, it denotes that you will soon be well rid of an enemy.

Abscess

To dream that you have an abscess which seems to have reached a chronic stage, you will be overwhelmed with misfortune of your own; at the same time your deepest sympathies will be enlisted for the sorrows of others.

Absinthe

To come under the influence of absinthe in dreams denotes that you will lead a merry and foolish pace with innocent companions, and waste your inheritance in prodigal lavishness on the siren, selfish fancy.

For a young woman to dream that she drinks absinthe with her lover warns her to resist his persuasions to illicit consummation of their love. If she dreams she is drunk, she will yield up her favours without strong persuasion. (This dream typifies that you are likely to waste your energies in pleasure.)

Abundance

To dream that you are possessed with an abundance foretells that you will have no occasion to reproach Fortune, and that you will be independent of her future favours; but your domestic happiness may suffer under the strain you are likely to put upon it by your infidelity.

Abuse

To dream of abusing a person warns that you will be unfortunate in your affairs, losing good money through overbearing persistence in business relations with others.

To feel yourself abused, you may be molested in your daily pursuits by the enmity of others.

For a young woman to dream that she hears abusive language foretells that she will fall under the ban of some person's jealousy and envy. If she uses the language herself, she will meet with unexpected rebuffs, that may fill her with mortification and remorse for her past unworthy conduct toward friends.

Abyss

To dream of looking into an abyss means that you may be confronted by threats of seizure of property, and that there may be quarrels and reproaches of a personal nature.

For a woman to be looking into an abyss foretells that she will burden herself with unwelcome cares. If she falls into the abyss her disappointment will be complete; but if she succeeds in crossing, or avoiding it, she will reinstate herself.

To dream recurrently of falling into an abyss signifies that you will suffer from depression or enduring anxiety.

See also **Pit, Precipice**.

Academy

To visit an academy in your dreams denotes that you will regret opportunities that you have let pass through sheer idleness and indifference.

To think you own, or are an inmate of one, you may find that you are to meet easy defeat of aspirations. You will take on knowledge, but be unable to rightly assimilate and apply it.

For a young woman or any person to return to an academy, after having finished there, signifies that demands will be made which the dreamer may find himself or herself unable to meet.

Accepted

For a business man to dream that his proposition has been accepted foretells that he will succeed in making a trade, which heretofore looked as if it would prove a failure.

For a lover to dream that he has been accepted by his sweetheart denotes that he will happily wed the object of his own and others' admiration.

Accident

To dream of an accident is a warning to avoid any mode of travel for a short period as it may well be unsafe.

For an accident to befall stock, denotes that you will struggle with all your might to gain some object and then see some friend lose property of the same value in aiding your cause.

Accordion

To dream of hearing the music of an accordion denotes that you will engage in amusement which will win you from sadness and retrospection. You will by this means be enabled to take up your burden more cheerfully.

For a young woman to dream that she is playing an accordion portends that she will win her lover by some sad occurrence; but, notwithstanding which, the same will confer lasting happiness upon her union. If the accordion gets out of tune, she will be saddened by the illness or trouble of her lover.

Accounts

To dream of having accounts presented to you for payment, you will be in a dangerous position. You may have recourse to law to disentangle yourself. If you pay the accounts, you will soon effect a compromise in some serious dispute.

To hold accounts against others foretells that disagreeable contingencies will arise in your business, marring the smoothness of its management.

For a young woman bookkeeper to dream of footing up accounts denotes that she will have trouble in business, and in her love affairs; but some worthy person will persuade her to account for his happiness. She will be much respected by her present employers.

Accuse

To dream that you accuse anyone of a mean action, denotes that you will have quarrels with those under you, and that your dignity may be thrown from a high pedestal.

If you are accused, you are in danger of being guilty of distributing scandal in a sly and malicious way.

Aches

Dreams of aches are usually due to physical causes and have little significance.

To dream that you have aches denotes that you are halting too much in your business, and that some other person is profiting by your ideas.

For a young woman to dream that she has a heartache, foretells that she will be in sore distress over the laggardly way her lover prosecutes his suit. If it is a backache, she may encounter illness through careless exposure. If she has a headache, there will be much disquietude of mind for the risk she has taken to rid herself of rivalry.

Acid

To drink any acid is an adverse dream, bringing you much anxiety.

For a woman to drink aciduous liquors denotes that she may ensnare herself with compromising situations; even health may be involved.

To see poisonous acids, some treachery against you may be discovered.

Acorn

Seeing acorns in dreams is portent of pleasant things ahead, and much gain is to be expected.

To pick them from the ground foretells success after weary labours.

For a woman to eat them denotes that she will rise from a station of labour to a position of ease and pleasure.

To shake them from the trees denotes that you will rapidly attain your wishes in business or love.

To see green-growing acorns, or to see them scattered over the ground, affairs will change for the better. Decayed or blasted acorns have import of disappointments and reverses.

To pull them green from the trees, you will injure your interests by haste and indiscretion.

Acquaintance

To meet an acquaintance, and converse pleasantly with him foretells that your business will run smoothly, and there will be but little discord in your domestic affairs.

If you seem to be disputing, or engaged in loud talk, humiliations and embarrassments will whirl seethingly around you.

If you feel ashamed of meeting an acquaintance, or meet him at an inopportune time, it denotes that you will be guilty of illicitly conducting yourself, and other parties will let the secret out.

For a young woman to think that she has an extensive acquaintance signifies that she will be the possessor of vast interests, and her love will be worth winning. If her circle of acquaintances is small, she will be unlucky in gaining social favours.

After dreaming of acquaintances, you may see or hear from them.

Acquit

To dream that you are acquitted of a crime denotes that you are about to come into possession of valuable property, but there is danger of a lawsuit before obtaining possession.

To see others acquitted, foretells that your friends will add pleasure to your labours.

Acrobat

To dream of seeing acrobats denotes that you will be prevented from carrying out hazardous schemes by the foolish fears of others.

To see yourself acrobating, you will have a sensation to answer for, and your existence will be made almost unendurable by the guying of your enemies.

To see women acrobating denotes that your name may be maliciously and slanderously handled. Also your business interests may be hindered.

For a young woman to dream that she sees acrobats in tights signifies that she will court the favour of men.

To dream of acrobats performing dangerous feats signifies that you will need to have greater courage.

Actor and Actress

To see in your dreams an actress denotes that your present state will be one of unbroken pleasure and favour.

To see one in distress, you will gladly contribute your means and influence to raise a friend from misfortune and indebtedness.

If you think yourself one, you will have to work for subsistence, but your labours will be pleasantly attended.

If you dream of being in love with one, your inclination and talent will be allied with pleasure and opposed to downright toil.

To dream of others acting while you look on signifies that you place others in too high a position in relation to yourself.

To see an amateur actor on the stage denotes that you will see your hopes pleasantly and satisfactorily fulfilled. If they play a tragedy, evil may be disseminated through your happiness. If the images in your dream are distorted or indistinct, you are likely to meet with quick and decisive defeat in some enterprise other than your regular business.

To see a dead actor, or actress, your good luck will be overwhelmed in violent and insubordinate misery.

To see them wandering and penniless foretells that your affairs will undergo a change from promise to threatenings of failure. To those enjoying domestic comforts, it is a warning of revolution and faithless vows.

For a young woman to dream that she is engaged to an actor, or about to marry one warns that her fancy will bring remorse after the glamour of pleasure has vanished.

If a man dreams that he is sporting with an actress, it foretells that private broils with his wife, or sweetheart, will bring him more misery than enjoyment.

Adam and Eve

To dream of Adam and Eve foretells that some eventful occasion will rob you of the hope of success in your affairs.

To see them in the garden, Adam dressed in his fig leaf, but Eve perfectly nude save for an Oriental coloured serpent ornamenting her waist and abdomen, warns that treachery and ill faith may combine to overthrow your fortune.

To see or hear Eve conversing with the serpent foretells that artful women will reduce you to the loss of fortune and reputation.

See also Eve.

Adder

To dream of seeing an adder strike, and a friend, who is dead but seems to be lying down and breathing, rises partly to a sitting position when the adder strikes at him, and then both disappear into some bushes nearby, denotes that you may be greatly distressed over the ill luck of friends, and a loss threatened to yourself.

For a young woman to see an adder warns that a deceitful person is going to cause her trouble. If it runs from her, she will be able to defend her character in attacks made on her.

Addition

To dream of pondering over addition denotes that you will have a struggle to overcome difficult situations, which will soon prominently assume formidable shapes in your business transactions.

To find some error in addition shows that you will be able to overcome enemies by fortunately discerning their intention before they have executed their design.

To add figures with a machine foretells that you will have a powerful ally who will save you from much oppression.

If you fail to read the figures, you will lose fortune by blind speculation.

Adieu

To dream of bidding cheerful adieus to people denotes that you will make pleasant visits and enjoy much social festivity; but if they are made in a sad or doleful strain, you will endure loss and bereaving sorrow.

If you bid adieu to home and country, you will travel in the nature of an exile from fortune and love.

To throw kisses of adieu to loved ones, or children, foretells that you will soon have a journey to make, and there will be no unpleasant accidents or happenings attending your trip.

See also **Farewell**.

Admire

To dream that you are an object of admiration denotes that you will retain the love of former associates, though your position will take you above their circle.

Admonish

To admonish your child, or son, or some young person, denotes that your generous principles will keep you in favour, and that fortune will be added to your gifts.

Adopted

To see an adopted child, or parent, in your dreams, indicates that you will amass fortune through the schemes and speculations of strangers.

To dream that you or others are adopting a child warns that you will make an unfortunate change in your abode.

Adulation

To dream that you seek adulation foretells that you will pompously fill unmerited positions of honour.

If you offer adulation you will expressly part with some dear belonging in the hope of furthering material interests.

Advancement

To dream of advancing in any engagement denotes your rapid ascendency to preferment and the consummation of affairs of the heart.

To see others advancing foretells that friends will hold positions of favour near you.

Adversary

To dream that you meet or engage with an adversary denotes that you will promptly defend any attacks on your interest. Sickness may also threaten you after this dream.

If you overcome an adversary, you will escape the effect of some serious disaster.

Adventurer

To dream that you are victimized by an adventurer suggests that you will be an easy prey for flatterers and designing villains.

For a woman to dream of an adventurer signifies that harmonious creativity and balanced extroversion are on their way.

For a young woman to think she is an adventuress portends that she will be too wrapped up in her own conduct to see that she is being flattered into throwing away her favours.

Adversity

To dream that you are in the clutches of adversity warns you to beware of failure and bad prospects.

To see others in adversity portends gloomy surroundings; the illness of someone may produce grave fears over the successful working of plans.

Advertisement

To dream that you are taking out advertisements denotes that you will have to resort to physical labour to promote your interest, or establish your fortune.

To read advertisements, warns that enemies may overtake you, and defeat you in rivalry.

Advice

To dream that you receive advice denotes that you will be enabled to raise your standard of integrity, and strive by honest means to reach independent competency and moral altitude.

To dream that you seek legal advice foretells that there will be some transactions in your affairs which will create doubt as to their merits and legality.

Advocate

To dream that you advocate any cause denotes that you will be faithful to your interests, and endeavour to deal honestly with the public, as your interests affect it, and be loyal to your promises to friends.

Aeroplanes

To dream of seeing an aeroplane foretells that you will make satisfactory progress in your future speculations. To see one failing to work foretells poor returns for much disturbing and stressful planning.

To dream that you are piloting an aeroplane signifies that you will travel towards a spiritual domain. Difficulties in piloting mean that the journey will be a turbulent one. Dreaming that someone else is piloting the plane denotes that you will have a spiritual guide on your journey.

Dreaming that you are in a plane which suddenly plummets towards the earth signifies that you will need to curb your ambition before it runs away from you.

Affliction

To dream that affliction lays a heavy hand upon you and calls your energy to a halt, warns you to take steps to avoid an approaching disaster.

To see others afflicted, warns that you may be surrounded by ills and misfortunes.

Affluence

To dream that you are in affluence foretells that you will make fortunate ventures, and will be pleasantly associated with people of wealth.

See also **Opulence, Riches, Wealth.**

Affront

This is a bad dream. The dreamer is sure to shed tears and weep. For a young woman to dream that she is affronted denotes that some unfriendly person will take advantage of her ignorance to place her in a compromising situation with a stranger, or to jeopardize her interests with a friend.

Afraid

To dream that you are afraid, portends that you may suffer injury to yourself in an accident.

To feel that you are afraid to proceed with some affair, or continue a journey, denotes that you will find trouble in your household, and enterprises will be unsuccessful.

To see others afraid denotes that a friend will be deterred from performing some favour for you because of his own difficulties. Such dreams occur when sleep is disturbed.

For a young woman to dream that she is afraid of a dog suggests that there will be a possibility of her doubting a true friend.

Africa

To dream that you are in Africa warns that you may be oppressed by enemies and quarrelsome persons.

For a woman to dream of African scenes warns that journeys will prove lonesome and devoid of pleasure or profit.

16

Afternoon

For a woman to dream of an afternoon, denotes she will form friendships which will be lasting and entertaining. A cloudy, rainy afternoon, implies disappointment and displeasure.

Agate

To see agate in a dream signifies a slight advancement in business affairs.

Age

To dream of old age portends failures in any kind of undertaking.

To dream of your own age indicates that perversity of opinion will bring down upon you the indignation of relatives.

For a young woman to dream of being accused of being older than she is denotes that she will fall into bad companionship, and her denial of stated things will be brought to scorn. To see herself looking aged intimates possible sickness, or unsatisfactory ventures. If it is her lover she sees aged, she will be in danger of losing him.

Agony

This dream portends worry and pleasure intermingled, more of the former than of the latter.

To be in agony over the loss of money, or property, denotes that disturbing and imaginary fears will rack you over the critical condition of affairs, or the illness of some dear relative.

Ague

A sickly condition of the dreamer is sometimes implied by this dream. To dream that you are shaking with an ague warns that you may suffer from some physical disorder, and that fluctuating opinions of your own affairs may bring you to the borders of prostration.

To see others thus affected denotes that you will offend people by your supreme indifference to the influences of others.

Air

This dream denotes a withering state of things, and bodes no good to the dreamer.

To dream of breathing hot air suggests that you will be influenced to evil by oppression.

To feel cold air denotes discrepancies in your business, and incompatibility in domestic relations.

To feel oppressed with humidity, ill luck may close down on your optimistical views of the future.

Alabaster

To dream of alabaster foretells success in marriage and all legitimate affairs. To break an alabaster figure or vessel denotes sorrow and repentence.

Alarm Bell

To hear an alarm bell in your sleep denotes that you are likely to have cause for anxiety.

Album

To dream of an album denotes you will have success and true friends.

For a young woman to dream of looking at photographs in an album foretells that she will soon have a new lover who will be very agreeable to her.

Alcoholic Drink

To dream of buying alcohol denotes selfish usurpation of property upon which you have no legal claim. If you sell it, you will be criticised for niggardly benevolence.

To drink some, you will come into doubtful possession of wealth, but your generosity will draw around you convivial friends, and women will seek to entrance and hold you.

To see alcoholic drink in barrels denotes prosperity, but is an unfavourable tendency against making home pleasant.

If in bottles, fortune will appear in a very tangible form.

For a woman to dream of handling, or drinking alcohol, foretells for her a happy Bohemian kind of existence. She will be good-natured but shallow-minded. she will be generous to rivals, and the indifference of lovers or husband will not seriously offset her pleasures or contentment.

Alley

To dream of an alley, denotes your fortune will not be so pleasing or promising as it formerly was. Many vexing cares may present themselves to you.

For a young woman to wander through an alley after dark, warns her of disreputable friendships and a stigma on her character.

Alligator

To dream of an alligator, is a dream of caution.
See also **Crocodile**.

Almanac

To dream of an almanac suggests variable fortunes and illusory pleasures. To be studying the signs foretells that you will be harassed by small matters taking up your time.

Almonds

This is a good omen. It has wealth in store. However, sorrow will go with it for a short while. If the almonds are defective, your disappointment in obtaining a certain wish will be complete until new conditions are brought about.

Alms

Alms will bring evil if given or taken unwillingly. Otherwise, a good dream.

Altar

To dream of seeing a priest at the altar denotes quarrels and unsatisfactory states in your business and home.

An altar would hardly be shown you in dream, except to warn you against the commission of error. Repentance is also implied.

Aluminium

To dream of aluminium denotes contentment with any fortune, however small. For a woman to see her aluminium ornaments or vessels tarnished warns that a loss may befall her.

Ambush

To dream that you are ambushed and attacked denotes that you have lurking secretly near you a danger, which will soon set upon and overthrow you if you are heedless of warnings.

If you lie in ambush to revenge yourself on others, you will unhesitatingly stoop to debasing actions to defraud your friends.

America

High officials dreaming of America should be careful of State affairs; others will do well to look after their own person, as some trouble is at hand after this dream.

Amethyst

Amethyst, seen in a dream, represents contentment with fair business.

For a young woman to lose an amethyst warns of broken engagements and slights in love.

Ammonia

Ammonia, seen in a dream, means displeasure will be felt by the dreamer at the conduct of a friend. Quarrels and disruptions of friendships may follow this dream.

For a young woman to see clear bottles of ammonia warns that she may be deceived in the character and intentions of some person whom she considers friendly.

Ammunition

To dream of ammunition foretells the undertaking of some work, which promises fruitful completion. To dream your ammunition is exhausted denotes fruitless struggles and endeavours.

Amorous

To dream you are amorous warns you against personal desires and pleasures, which are threatening to engulf you in scandal.

For a young woman it portends illicit engagements, unless she chooses staid and moral companions. For a married woman, it foreshadows discontent and desire for pleasure outside the home.

To see others amorous portends that you may well be persuaded to neglect your moral obligations.

Anchor

To dream of an anchor is favourable to sailors, if seas are calm. To others it portends separation from friends, change of residence, and foreign travel. Sweethearts are soon to quarrel if either sees an anchor.

Andirons

Andirons seen in a dream denote good will among friends, if the irons support burning logs; if they are in an empty fireplace, misfortune and loss of property are signified.

Anecdote

To dream of relating an anecdote signifies that you will greatly prefer frivolous companionship to that of intellect, and that your affairs will prove as unstable as yourself.

For a young woman to hear anecdotes related denotes that she will be one of a merry party of pleasure-seekers.

Angels

To dream of angels is prophetic of disturbing influences in the soul. It brings a changed condition of the person's lot. If the dream is unusually pleasing, you will hear of the good health of friends, and receive a legacy from unknown relatives.

If the dream comes as a token of warning, the dreamer may expect threats of scandal about love or money matters. To wicked people, it is a demand to repent; to good people it should be a consolation.

To dream of a black angel signifies that the course of your life will undergo a major change as the result of a decision that you have taken. This is a very rare dream.

Anger

To dream of anger denotes that difficulty awaits you. Disappointments in loved ones, and broken ties, or enemies may make new attacks upon your property or character.

To dream that friends or relatives are angry with you, while you meet their anger with composure, denotes that you will mediate between opposing friends, and gain their lasting favour and gratitude.

See also **Rage**.

Angling

To dream of catching fish is good. If you fail to catch any, it will be bad for you.

Annoyance

This dream denotes that you have enemies who are at work against you. Annoyances experienced in dreams are apt to find speedy fulfilment in the trifling incidents of the following day.

Antelope

Seeing antelopes in a dream foretells your ambitions will be high, but may be realized by putting forth great energy.

For a young woman to see an antelope miss its footing and fall from a height warns that the love she aspires to will prove her undoing.

Ants

The dreamer of ants should expect many petty annoyances during the day; chasing little worries, and finding general dissatisfaction in all things.

Anvil

To see hot iron, with sparks flying, is significant of a pleasing work; to the farmer, an abundant crop; favourable indeed to women. Cold, or small, favours may be expected from those in power. The means of success is in your power, but in order to obtain it you will have to labour under difficulty. If the anvil is broken, it foretells that you have, through your own neglect, thrown away promising opportunities that cannot be recalled.

Anxiety

A dream involving anxiety is a warning to stop procrastinating and get on with a project that you need to complete. A dream of this kind is very common, and the degree of anxiety is often out of proportion with the situation in real life. Occasionally it is a good omen, denoting, after threatening states, success and rejuvenation of mind

Apes

This dream warns of danger to some dear friend.

To see a small ape clinging to a tree warns the dreamer to beware; a false person is close to you and will cause unpleasantness in your circle. Deceit goes with this dream.

Apparel

See also **Clothing**.

Apparition

See also **Ghost**.

Apples

This is a very good dream for the majority of people.

To see red apples on trees with green foliage is exceedingly propitious to the dreamer.

To eat them is not as good, unless they are faultless. A friend who interprets dreams says: 'Ripe apples on a tree, denotes that the time has arrived for you to realize your hopes; think over what you intend to do, and go fearlessly ahead. Ripe on the top of the tree, warns you not to aim too high. Apples on the ground imply that false friends, and flatterers are working you harm. Decayed apples typify hopeless efforts.'

Apprentice

To dream that you serve as an apprentice foretells you will have a struggle to win a place among your companions.

Apricot

Dreams of seeing apricots growing denote that the future, though seemingly rosy holds masked bitterness and sorrow for you.

To eat them warns of the near approach of calamitous influences. If others eat them, your surroundings will be unpleasant and disagreeable to your fancies. A friend says: 'Apricots denote that you have been wasting time over trifles or small things of no value.'

April

To dream of the month of April signifies that much pleasure and profit will be your allotment. If the weather is miserable, it is a sign of passing ill luck.

Apron

To dream of an apron signifies a zigzag course, for a young woman. For a schoolgirl to dream that her apron is loosened, or torn, implies bad lessons, and lectures in propriety from parents and teachers.

Arch

An arch, in a dream, denotes your rise to distinction and the gaining of wealth by persistent effort. To pass under one foretells that many will seek you who formerly ignored your position.

For a young woman to see a fallen arch warns that she will be miserable in a new situation.

Archbishop

To dream of seeing an archbishop foretells you will have many obstacles to resist in your attempt to master fortune or rise to public honour. To see one in the everyday dress of a common citizen denotes you will have aid and encouragement from those in prominent positions and will succeed in your enterprises.

For a young woman to dream that an archbishop is kindly directing her foretells she will be fortunate in forming her friendships.

Architect

Architects drawing plans in your dreams denotes a change in your business, which will be likely to result in loss to you.

For a young woman to see an architect foretells she will meet rebuffs in her aspirations and manoeuvres to make a favourable marriage.

Arm

To dream of seeing an arm cut warns of separation or divorce. Mutual dissatisfaction will occur between husband and wife. Beware of deceitfulness and fraud.

Armour

To dream that you are wearing armour signifies that you lack self-confidence.

Army

To dream of two armies fighting denotes that you are suffering from inner conflict, which you need to resolve before you can go on with your life.

For a woman to have a threatening dream of an army implies a fear of being emotionally crushed by other people with stronger personalities.

See also **Soldiers**.

Aroma

For a young woman to dream of a sweet aroma denotes she will soon be the recipient of some pleasure or present.

Arrested

To see respectable-looking strangers arrested foretells that you desire to make changes, but that new speculations will be subordinated by the fear of failure. If they resist the officers, you will have great delight in pushing the new enterprise to completion.

Arrow

Pleasure follows this dream. Entertainments, festivals and pleasant journeys may be expected. Suffering will cease.

An old or broken arrow portends disappointments in love or business.

Art Gallery

To visit an art gallery portends unfortunate unions in domestic circles. You will struggle to put forth an appearance of happiness, but will secretly care for other associations.

Ascent

If you reach the extreme point of ascent, or the top of steps, without stumbling, it is good; otherwise, you will have obstacles to overcome before the good of the day is found.

Asceticism

To dream of asceticism denotes that you will cultivate strange principles and views, rendering yourself fascinating to strangers, but unattractive to friends.

Ashes

Dreaming of ashes is a sign of change for the worse, and warns of sorrow to come. Farmers should take care as there is a high risk of poor harvests, and traders should beware of unsuccessful deals. Parents may derive trouble from wayward children.

Asia

To dream of visiting Asia is assurance of change, but no material benefits from fortune will follow.

Asparagus

To dream of asparagus signifies prosperous surroundings and obedience from servants and children. To eat it denotes interrupted success.

Assassin

If you are the one to receive the assassin's blow, you will not surmount all your trials.

To see another, with the assassin standing over him with blood stains, portends that misfortune may come to the dreamer.

To see an assassin under any condition is a warning that losses may befall you through secret enemies.

Assistance

Giving assistance to anyone in a dream, foretells you will be favoured in your efforts to rise to higher position.

If anyone assists you, you will be pleasantly situated, and loving friends will be near you.

Atlas

To dream you are looking at an atlas denotes that you will carefully study interests before making changes or journeys.

Atonement

This dream means joyous communing with friends, and speculators need not fear any drop in stocks. Courting among the young will meet with happy consummation.

The sacrifice or atonement of another for your waywardness is portentous of the humiliation of self or friends through your open or secret disregard of duty. A woman after this dream is warned of approaching disappointment.

Attic

To dream that you are in an attic denotes that you are entertaining hopes which will fail to materialize. Climbing upstairs towards an attic signifies that you will embark on a solitary spiritual quest.

For a young woman to dream that she is sleeping in an attic foretells that she will fail to find contentment in her present occupation.

Auction

To dream of an auction, in a general way, is good. If you hear the auctioneer crying his sales, it means bright prospects and fair treatment from business ventures.

To dream of buying at an auction signifies close deals to tradesmen, and good luck in livestock to the farmer. Plenty, to the housewife, is the omen for women. If there is a feeling of regret about the dream, you are warned to be careful of your business affairs.

August

To dream of the month of August denotes unfortunate deals, and misunderstandings in love affairs.

For a young woman to dream that she is going to be married in August, is an omen of sorrow in her early wedded life.

Augur

To see augurs in your dreams is a forecast of labour and toil.

Aunt

For a young woman to dream of seeing her aunt denotes that she will receive sharp censure for some action, which will cause her much distress.

If this relative appears smiling and happy, slight difference will soon give way to pleasure.

Aura

To dream of discussing any subject relating to an aura, denotes that you will work to discover the power which influences you from within.

Author

For an author to dream that his manuscript has been rejected by the publisher denotes some doubt at first, but finally his work will be accepted as authentic and original.

To dream of seeing an author over his work, perusing it with anxiety, denotes that you will be worried over some literary work either of your own or some other person.

Automobile

See also **Car**.

Autumn

For a woman to dream of Autumn denotes she will obtain property through the struggles of others. If she thinks of marrying in Autumn, she will be likely to contract a favourable marriage and possess a cheerful home.

Avalanche

To dream of an avalanche indicates that you feel overwhelmed by events in your waking life.

Awake

To dream that you are awake denotes that you may experience strange happenings which throw you into gloom.

To pass through green, growing fields, and look upon landscape, in your dreams, and feel that it is an awakening experience, signifies that there is some good and brightness in store for you, but there will be disappointments intermingled between the present and that time.

Axe

Seeing an axe in a dream foretells that what enjoyment you may have will depend on your struggles and energy. To see others using an axe foretells that your friends will be energetic and lively, making existence a pleasure when near them.

For a young woman to see one portends her lover will be worthy, but not possessed with much wealth. A broken or rusty axe indicates illness and loss of money and property.

See also **Hatchet**.

B

'God came to Abimelech in a dream by night, and said to him,
"Behold, thou art but a dead man, for the woman thou hast taken; for
she is a man's wife." '

—Genesis xx, 3.

Baby

To dream of seeing a newly born baby denotes that pleasant surprises
are awaiting you. For a young woman to dream that she has a baby
warns that she may be accused of immorality.

To see a baby swimming portends a fortunate escape from some
entanglement.

To dream of crying babies warns of of ill health and disappointments.

A bright, clean baby denotes love requited and many warm friends.
Walking alone, it is a sure sign of independence and a total ignoring of
smaller spirits. If a woman dream she is nursing a baby, she should
beware of deception from by the one she trusts most.

Bachelor

For a man to dream that he is a bachelor is a warning for him to keep
clear of women.

For a woman to dream of a bachelor denotes love not born of
purity. Justice goes awry. Politicians lose honour.

Back

To dream of seeing a nude back denotes loss of power. Lending advice
or money is dangerous. Sickness often attends this dream.

To see a person turn his back on you and walk away, you may be sure envy and jealousy are working against you.

To dream of your own back bodes no good to the dreamer.

Backbiting

Conditions will change from good to bad if you are joined with others in backbiting.

For your friends to backbite you indicates worriment by servants and children.

Backgammon

To dream of playing backgammon denotes that you will, while visiting, meet with unfriendly hospitality, but will unconsciously win friendships which will endure much straining.

If you are defeated in the game, you will be unfortunate in bestowing your affections, and your affairs will remain in an unsettled condition.

Bacon

To dream of eating bacon is good, if someone is eating with you and hands are clean.

Rancid bacon warns that dullness of perception and unsatisfactory states will worry you.

To dream of curing bacon is bad, if not clear of salt and smoke. If clear, it is good.

Badger

To dream of a badger is a sign of luck after battles with hardships.

Bagpipes

This is not a bad dream, unless the music is harsh and the player in rags.

Bail

If the dreamer is seeking bail, unforeseen troubles will arise; accidents are likely to occur; unfortunate alliances may be made.

If you stand bail for another, about the same conditions, though hardly as bad.

Bailiff

Shows a striving for a higher place, and a deficiency in intellect. If the bailiff comes to arrest, or make love, false friends are trying to work for your money.

Bakery

To dream of a bakery demands caution in making changes in one's career. Pitfalls may reveal themselves on every hand.

For a young woman to dream that she is in a bakery portends that her character will be assailed. She should exercise great care in her social affairs.

Baking

Baking is unpropitious for a woman. Ill health and the care of many children, meanness and poverty of supporters are indicated.

Balcony

For lovers to dream of making sad adieus on a balcony, long and perhaps final separation may follow. Balcony also denotes unpleasant news of absent friends.

Bald

To see a bald-headed man denotes that sharpers are to make a deal adverse to your interests, but that by keeping wide awake, you will outwit them.

For a man to dream of a bald-headed woman ensures have a vixen for a wife.

A bald hill, or mountain, indicates shortages of that which will take various forms.

For a woman to dream that she has suddenly gone bald denotes her dread of losing her beauty, power and youthful dynamism.

For a young woman to dream of a bald-headed man is a warning to her to use her intelligence when listening to her next marriage offer.

Bald-headed babies signify a happy home, a loving companion, and obedient children.

Ball

A very satisfactory omen, if beautiful and gaily-dressed people are dancing to the strains of entrancing music. If you feel gloomy and distressed at the inattention of others, a portent of bad news.

Ballet

Warns of marital infidelity; also failures in business, and quarrels and jealousies among sweethearts.

Balloon

To dream of balloons rising into the air signifies a desire to lift yourself above the mire of current problems and difficulties.

To ascend in a balloon denotes an unfortunate journey.

A balloon which falls to the ground or is punctured foretells blighted hopes and adversity.

To see children blowing up balloons warns that your expectations will fail to bring you much comfort.

Banana

To dream of bananas warns that you may be mated to an uninteresting and an unloved companion.

To eat them foretells a tiresome venture in business, and self-inflicted duty.

To see them decaying, you may soon fall into some disagreeable enterprise.

To trade in them, non-productive interests will accumulate around you.

Bandits

For a man to dream of a bandit can foretell internal conflict and danger.

For a woman to dream of a bandit indicates that she is seeking to free her creativity and realize her full potential.

Banjo

To dream of a banjo denotes that pleasant amusements will be enjoyed.

For a young woman to see banjo players warns that she may fail in some anticipated amusement. She may have misunderstandings with her lover.

Bank

To see vacant counters foretells business losses. Giving out gold money denotes carelessness; receiving it, great gain and prosperity.

To see silver and bank notes accumulated, increase of honour and fortune. You will enjoy the highest respect of all classes.

Bankrupt

A warning to leave speculations alone.

Banner

To see one's country's banner floating in a clear sky denotes triumph over foreign foes. To see it battered is significant of wars and loss of military honours on land and sea.

Banquet

It is good to dream of a banquet. Friends will wait to do you favours. To dream of yourself, together with many gaily-attired guests, eating from costly plate and drinking wine of fabulous price and age, foretells enormous gain in enterprises of every nature, and happiness among friends.

To see inharmonious influences, strange and grotesque faces or empty tables, is ominous of grave misunderstandings or disappointments.

Bantam

To see bantams in your dream denotes your fortune will be small, yet you will enjoy contentment. If they appear sickly, or exposed to wintry storms, your interests will be impaired.

See also **Chickens, Poultry**.

Baptism

To dream of baptism signifies that your character needs strengthening by the practice of temperance in advocating your opinions to the disparagement of your friends.

To dream that you are an applicant signifies that you will humiliate your inward self for public favour.

To dream that you see John the Baptist baptizing Christ in the Jordan denotes that you will have a desperate mental struggle between yielding yourself to labour in meagre capacity for the sustenance of others, or following desires which might lead you into wealth and exclusiveness.

To see the Holy Ghost descending on Christ is significant of resignation to duty and abnegation of self.

Bar

To dream of tending a bar denotes that you are capable of resorting to some questionable mode of advancement.

Seeing a bar denotes activity in communities, quick uplifting of fortunes, and the consummation of illicit desires.

See also **Public House**.

Barber

To dream of a barber denotes that success will come through struggling and close attention to business. For a young woman to dream of a barber foretells that her fortune will increase, though meagrely.

Barefoot

Wandering barefoot in the night, with torn garments, warns that your expectations are likely to be dashed and your every effort met with discouragement.

Barley Field

The dreamer will obtain his highest desires, and every effort will be crowned with success. Decay in anything denotes loss.

Barmaid

For a man to dream of a barmaid, denotes that he will scorn purity.

For a young woman to dream that she is a barmaid foretells that she will be attracted to fast men, and disdain propriety.

Barn

If well filled with ripe and matured grain, and perfect ears of corn, with fat stock surrounding it, it is an omen of great prosperity. If empty, the reverse may be expected.

Barometer

To see a barometer in a dream foretells a change that will soon take place in your affairs, which will prove profitable to you. If it is broken, you will find displeasing incidents in your business, arising unexpectedly.

Barrel

To see one filled denotes prosperous times and feastings. If empty, a warning that life may be joyless and lacking consolation from outside influences.

Barrister

To see a barrister at the bar denotes that disputes of a serious nature will arise between parties interested in worldly things. Enemies may be stealing up on you, making false claims. If you see a barrister defending you, your friends will assist you in coming trouble, but they will cause you more trouble than your enemies.

Baseball

To see a baseball in your dream denotes you will be easily contented, and your cheerfulness will make you a popular companion.

For a young woman to dream that she is playing baseball, means much pleasure for her, but no real profit or comfort.

Basement

To dream that you are in a basement portends that you will see prosperous opportunities abating, and that with them, pleasure will dwindle into trouble and care.
*See also **Cellar**.*

Basin

For a young woman to dream of bathing in a basin foretells that her womanly graces will win her real friendships and elevations.

Basket

To dream of seeing or carrying a basket signifies that you will meet unqualified success, if the basket is full; but empty baskets indicate discontent and sorrow.

Bass Voice

To dream that you have a bass voice denotes you will detect some discrepancy in your business, brought about by the deceit of someone in your employ. For the lover, this foretells estrangements and quarrels.

Baste

To dream of basting meats while cooking denotes that you will undermine your own expectations by folly and selfishness. For a woman to baste her sewing omens much vexation owing to her extravagance.

Bath

Dealings of all kinds should be carried on with discretion after a dream of having a bath.

For a young person to dream of taking a bath means much solicitude for one of the opposite sex, fearing to lose his good opinion through the influence of others.

To go in bathing with others means that evil companions should be avoided or defamation of character is likely to follow. If the water is muddy, enemies are near you.

A warm bath is generally significant of evil. A cold, clear bath is the forerunner of joyful tidings and a long period of excellent health.

Bathing in a clear sea denotes expansion of business and satisfying research after knowledge.

Bathroom

To see white roses in a bathroom, and yellow ones in a box, denote that sickness will interfere with pleasure; but more lasting joys will result from this disappointment.

For a young woman to dream of a bathroom signifies that her inclinations tend too much towards light pleasures and frivolities.

Bats

To dream of a bat denotes that there are dark forces at work within the dreamer. At worst, the dreamer is trapped in a dark night of the soul and feels incapable of escape.

Battle

Battle signifies striving with difficulties, but a final victory over the same.

If you are defeated in battle, it denotes that bad deals made by others will mar your prospects

Bayonet

To dream of a bayonet signifies that enemies are capable of holding you in their power, unless you get possession of the bayonet.

Bay Tree

A palmy leisure awaits you in which you will meet many pleasing varieties of diversions. Much knowledge will be reaped in the rest from work. It is generally a good dream for everybody.

Beacon Light

For a sailor to see a beacon light portends fair seas and a prosperous voyage.

For persons in distress, warm and unbroken attachments will arise among the young.

To the sick, speedy recovery and continued health. Business will gain new impetus. To see it go out in time of storm or distress, indicates reverses at the time when you thought Fortune was deciding in your favour.

Beads

To dream of beads foretells attention from those in elevated positions will be shown you. To count beads portends immaculate joy and contentment. To string them, you will obtain the favour of the rich.

To scatter them signifies loss of status among your acquaintances.

Beans

This is a bad dream. To see them growing, omens worries and sickness among children.

Dried beans mean much disappointment in worldly affairs. Care should be taken to prevent contagious diseases from spreading.

To dream of eating them implies the misfortune or illness of a well-loved friend.

Bear

A bear is significant of overwhelming competition in pursuits of every kind. To dream of a bear can also warn of the unforeseeable, of capricious violence and wildness.

To kill a bear portends extrication from former entanglements.

A young woman who dreams of a bear will have a threatening rival or some misfortune.

*See also **Polar Bear**.*

Beard

To dream of seeing a beard denotes that some uncongenial person will oppose his will against yours, and there will be a fierce struggle for mastery; you are likely to lose some money in the combat.

A grey beard signifies hard luck and quarrels.

A white beard signifies wisdom and, often, old age.

A thick, luxuriant beard denotes vigour and strength.

To see beards on women warns of unpleasant associations and illness.

For someone to pull your beard denotes that you will run a narrow risk if you do not lose property.

For someone to cut or shave off your beard signifies a fear of separation and powerlessness.

To comb and admire it shows that your vanity will grow with prosperity, making you detestable in the sight of many of your former companions.

For a young woman to admire a beard intimates her desire to leave celibacy – but she is threatened with an unfortunate marriage.

Beat

It bodes no good to dream of being beaten by an angry person; family jars and discord are signified.

Beauty

Beauty in any form is pre-eminently good. A beautiful woman brings pleasure and profitable business. A well formed and beautiful child indicates love reciprocated and a happy union.

Beaver

To dream of seeing beavers foretells that you will obtain comfortable circumstances by patient striving. If you dream of killing them for their skins, you will be accused of fraud and improper conduct towards the innocent.

Bed

A bed, clean and white, denotes a peaceful end to worries. For a woman to dream of making a bed signifies a new lover and pleasant occupation.

To dream of being in bed, if in a strange room, unexpected friends will visit you. If a sick person dreams of being in bed, a development in the illness is signified.

To dream that you are sleeping on a bed in the open air foretells that you will have delightful experiences and opportunity for improving your fortune. For you to see strangers passing by your bed denotes exasperating circumstances arising, which will interfere with your plans.

To see a friend looking very pale, lying in bed, signifies that strange and woeful complications will oppress your friends, bringing discontent to yourself.

For a mother to dream that her child wets a bed foretells unusual anxiety. For persons to dream that they wet the bed, warns of sickness, or interference with their daily routine of business.

Bedbugs

Seen in your dreams, they indicate continued sickness and unhappy states.

Bedfellow

To dream that you do not like your bedfellow foretells that some person who has claims upon you will censure and make your surroundings generally unpleasant.

If you have a strange bedfellow, your discontent will worry all who come near you. If you think you have any kind of animal in bed with you, ill luck is overhanging you.

Bedroom

To see one newly furnished, a happy change for the dreamer. Journeys to distant places, and pleasant companions.

Beef

Beef properly served, under pleasing surroundings, denotes harmonious states in love and business; if otherwise, evil is foreboded, though it may be of a trifling nature.

Beer

Fateful of disappointments if drinking from a bar. To see others drinking, work of designing intriguers will displace your fairest hopes.

To habitués of this beverage, harmonious prospectives are foreshadowed, if pleasing, natural and cleanly conditions survive. The dream occurrences frequently follow in the actual.

Bees

Bees signify pleasant and profitable engagements.

For an officer, it brings obedient subjects and healthy environments.

To a preacher, many new members and a praying congregation.

To business people, increase in trade. To parents, much pleasure from dutiful children. If one stings, loss or injury will bear upon you from a friendly source.

Beetles

To dream of seeing them on your person, warns of poverty and small ills. Getting rid of them is good.

Beetroot

To see beetroot growing abundantly, harvest and peace will obtain in the land; eating it with others is full of good tidings.

If it is served in soiled or impure dishes, distressful awakenings threaten to disturb you.

Beggar

To see an old, decrepit beggar is a sign of bad management; unless you are economical, you will lose much property. Scandalous reports will prove detrimental to your fame.

To give to a beggar denotes dissatisfaction with present surroundings.

To dream that you refuse to give to a beggar is altogether bad.

For a woman to dream of beggars, she may meet with disagreeable interferences in her plans for betterment and enjoyment.

Beheading

To dream of being beheaded, overwhelming defeat or failure in some undertaking is likely to follow.

This dream appears at times of deep disappointments.

Bellows

Working a bellows denotes a struggle, but a final triumph over poverty and fate by energy and perseverance.

To dream of seeing a bellows, distant friends are longing to see you.

To hear one, occult knowledge will be obtained by the help of powerful means. One fallen into disuse portends you have wasted energies under misguiding impulses.

Bell-Ringer

Fortune is hurrying after you. Questions of importance will be settled amicably among disputants. To see one looking sad denotes that some sorrowful event or misfortune may soon follow.

Bells

To hear bells tolling in your dreams, death of distant friends may occur, and intelligence of wrong may worry you.

Joyous pealing of bells bells indicates a joyous victory over an opponent.

Belly

To see your belly in a dream foretells that you will have great expectations, but you must curb hard-headedness and redouble your energies if you are to achieve your ambition.

To see anything moving on the belly, prognosticates humiliation and hard labour.

To see a healthy belly, denotes wild desires.

Belt

To dream that you have a new-style belt denotes you are soon to meet and make engagements with a stranger, which will demoralize your prosperity. If it is out of date, you will be meritedly censured for rudeness.

Bench

Distrust debtors and confidants if you dream of sitting on one.

If you see others doing so, happy reunions between friends who have been separated through misunderstandings are suggested.

Bequest

After this dream, pleasures of consolation from the knowledge of duties well performed, and the health of the young is assured.

Bereavement

To dream of the bereavement of a child warns you that your plans will meet with quick frustration, and that where you expect success there will be failure.

Bereavement of relatives, or friends, denotes disappointment in well matured plans and a poor outlook for the future.

Bet

To dream of making a bet signifies that you may resort to dishonest means to forward your schemes.

If you lose a bet, you may sustain injury.

To win one reinstates you in favour with fortune.

Betting on races warns you to beware of engaging in new undertakings. Enemies are trying to divert your attention from legitimate business.

Betting at gaming tables denotes that immoral devices may be used to wring money from you.

Bhagavad Gita

To dream of the Bhagavad Gita foretells for you a season of seclusion; also rest to the exhausted faculties. A pleasant journey for your advancement will be planned by your friends. Little financial advancement is promised in this dream.

Bible

To dream of the Bible foretells that innocent and disillusioned enjoyment will be proffered for your acceptance.

To dream that you villify the teachings of the Bible forewarns you that you are about to succumb to resisted temptations through the seductive persuasiveness of a friend.

Bicycle

Dreams of bicycles in general signify harmony.

To dream of riding a bicycle uphill signifies bright prospects. Riding it downhill, if the rider is a woman, calls for care regarding her good name and health: misfortune hovers near.

Bigamy

For a man to commit bigamy denotes loss of manhood and failing mentality. To a woman, it predicts that she will suffer dishonour unless very discreet.

Billiards

Billiards foretell coming troubles to the dreamer. Lawsuits and contentions over property. Slander may work to your detriment. If you see table and balls idle, deceitful comrades are undermining you

Bill-poster

To dream that you are a bill-poster denotes that you may undertake some unpleasant and unprofitable work.

To see bill-posters at work foretells disagreeable news.

Birds

It is a favourable dream to see birds of beautiful plumage. A wealthy and happy partner is near if a woman has dreams of this nature.

A white bird signifies simplification and internal harmony.

Moulting and songless birds denote merciless and inhuman treatment of the outcast and fallen by people of wealth.

To see a wounded bird is fateful of deep sorrow caused by erring offspring.

To dream of a flock of birds foretells that you will undergo an important inner transformation.

To see flying birds is a sign of prosperity to the dreamer. All disagreeable environments will vanish before the wave of prospective good.

To catch birds is not at all bad. To hear them speak is owning one's inability to perform tasks that demand great clearness of perception.

To kill them with a gun warns of disaster from dearth of harvest.

Birth

To dream of birth, or similar events such as eggs hatching and baby animals, indicates that a major change or opportunity will be coming into your life.

For a woman to dream of giving birth, great joy and a handsome legacy are foretold. If she is pregnant, this dream indicates fortunate circumstances and the safe delivery of a healthy child.

Birthday

To dream of a birthday is a warning of poverty and falsehood to the young; to the old, long trouble and desolation.

Birthday Presents

Receiving happy surprises, means a multitude of high accomplishments. Working people will advance in their trades.

Giving birthday presents denotes small deferences, if given at a fête or reception.

Biscuits

Eating or baking them indicates ill health and family peace ruptured over silly disputes.

Bishop

To dream of a bishop, teachers and authors risk suffering great mental worries, caused from delving into intricate subjects.

To the tradesman, foolish buying, in which he is likely to incur loss of good money.

For one to see a bishop in his dreams, hard work will be his patrimony, with chills and ague as attendant. If you meet the approval of a much admired bishop, you will be successful in your undertakings in love or business.

Bite

This dream omens ill.

It implies a wish to undo work that is past undoing. You are also likely to suffer losses through some enemy.

Bits

To see bridle bits in your dreams foretells you will subdue and overcome any obstacle opposing your advancement or happiness. If they break or are broken you will be surprised into making concessions to enemies.

Black

To dream of the colour black indicates hope which one day will be realized.

To see yourself, or others, dressed in black, portends quarrels, disappointments and disagreeable companions; if the dream refers to business, the business will fall short of expectations.

For a young woman to dream of being attired in a gauzy black costume warns her to beware lest she meet with chastening sorrow and disappointment.

Blackberries

To dream of blackberries denotes many ills. To gather them is unlucky. Eating them denotes losses.

Blackboard

To see in your dreams writing in white chalk on a blackboard warns of ill tidings of some person prostrated with some severe malady, or that your financial security will be swayed by the panicky condition of commerce.

Blacksmith

To see a blacksmith in a dream means that laborious undertakings will soon work to your advantage.

Blanket

Blankets in your dream means treachery if soiled. If new and white, success where failure is feared, and a dangerous illness will be avoided through unseen agencies.

Blasphemy

Blasphemy denotes an enemy creeping into your life, who under assumed friendship will do you great harm.

To dream you are cursing yourself means evil fortune. To dream you are cursed by others signifies relief through affection and prosperity.

Bleating

To hear young animals bleating in your dreams foretells that you will have new duties and cares, though not necessarily unpleasant ones.

Bleeding

To dream of bleeding warns of malicious reports about you. Fortune may turn against you.

Blind

To dream of being blind warns of a sudden loss of affluence.

To see others blind denotes that some worthy person will call on you for aid.

Blindfold

For a woman to dream that she is blindfolded mean that disturbing elements are rising around to distress and trouble her. Disappointment may be felt by others through her.

Blind Man's Buff

To dream that you are playing at blind man's buff warns that you are about to engage in some weak enterprise which will likely humiliate you, besides losing money for you.

Blood

Blood-stained garments indicate that enemies seek to tear down a successful career that is opening up before you.

The dreamer should beware of strange friendships.

To see blood flowing from a wound, physical ailments and worry. Bad business caused from disastrous dealings with foreign combines.

To see blood on your hands, immediate bad luck, if not careful of your person and your own affairs.

Bloodhound

To dream that a bloodhound is tracking you, you run the risk of falling into some temptation, in which there is much danger of your downfall.

See also **Dogs**.

Bloodstone

To dream of seeing a bloodstone denotes that you are likely to be unfortunate in your engagements. For a young woman to receive one as a gift denotes she will suffer estrangement from one friend, but will, by this, gain one more worthy of her.

Blossoms

To dream of seeing trees and shrubs in blossom denotes that a time of pleasing prosperity is nearing you.

Blotting Paper

To dream of using blotting paper signifies you may be deceived into the betrayal of secrets which will seriously involve a friend.

To see worn blotting paper denotes continued disagreements in the home or among friends.

Blows

Denotes injury to yourself. If you defend yourself, a rise in business will follow.

Blue

To dream of, or in, blue denotes that you are looking beyond the physical plane of life to the spiritual, metaphysical plane. You are looking as far ahead as you can, perhaps to the point of infinity itself.

To dream of blue apparel signifies carrying forward your aspirations to victory, through energetic, insistent efforts. Friends will support you loyally.

Bluebird

To dream of a bluebird foretells hope, happiness and rebirth.

Blushing

For a young woman to dream of blushing denotes that she will be worried and humiliated by false accusations. If she sees others blush, she will be given to flippant railery which will make her unpleasing to her friends.

Boa Constrictor

To dream of this indicates stormy times and disenchantment with humanity ahead.

Boarding House

To dream of a boarding house foretells that you may suffer entanglement and disorder in your enterprises, and are likely to change your residence.

Boasting

To hear boasting in your dreams, you will sincerely regret an impulsive act, which will cause trouble to your friends. To boast to a competitor, foretells that you will be unjust, and will use dishonest means to overcome competition.

Boat

Boats forecast bright prospects, if upon clear water. Crossing a river by boat signifies inner transformation. If the water is unsettled and turbulent, cares and unhappy changes threaten the dreamer. If with a gay party you board a boat without an accident, many favours will be showered upon you. Unlucky the dreamer who falls overboard while sailing upon stormy waters.

See also **Ship, Vessels.**

Bobbin

To dream of bobbins denotes that important work will devolve on you, and that your interests will be adversely affected if you are negligent in dispatching the same work.

Bog

Bogs denote burdens under whose weight you feel that endeavours to rise are useless. Illness and other worries may oppress you.

Boiler

To dream of seeing a boiler out of repair signifies that you may suffer from bad management or disappointment. For a woman to dream that she goes into a cellar to see about a boiler warns that sickness and losses will surround her.

Boils

To dream of a boil running pus and blood, you probably have unpleasant things to meet in your immediate future. The insincerity of friends may cause you great inconvenience.

To dream of boils on your forehead is significant of the sickness of someone near you.

Bolts

To dream of bolts signifies that formidable obstacles will oppose your progress.

If the bolts are old or broken, your expectations will be eclipsed by failures.

Bombshell

To dream of bombshells foretells anger and disputes, ending in lawsuits. Many displeasing incidents follow this dream.

Bones

To see your bones protruding from the flesh warns that treachery is working to ensnare you.

Bonnet

A bonnet denotes much gossiping and slanderous insinuations, from which a woman should carefully defend herself.

For a man to see a woman tying her bonnet denotes unforeseen good luck nearby. His friends will be faithful and true.

A young woman is likely to engage in pleasant and harmless flirtations if her bonnet is new and of any colour except black.

Black bonnets denote false friends of the opposite sex.

See also **Hat**.

Book

Pleasant pursuits, honour and riches are signified if you dream of studying them. For an author to dream of his works going to press, is a dream of caution; he will have much trouble in placing them before the public.

To dream of spending great study and time in solving some intricate subjects, and the hidden meaning of learned authors, is significant of honours well earned.

Finding yourself ploughing hopelessly through a reference book indicates a need to find an answer to a pressing question.

Being unable to determine what a book means, or being unable to read the print, indicates a need to improve your concentration and increase your general awareness.

To see children at their books denotes the harmony and good conduct of the young.

To dream of old books is a warning to shun evil in any form.

Bookcase

To see a bookcase in your dreams signifies that you will associate knowledge with your work and pleasure. Empty bookcases imply that you will be put out because of lack of means or facility for work.

Bookshop

To visit a bookshop in your dream foretells you will be filled with literary aspirations, which will interfere with your other works and labours.

Boots

To see your boots on another, your place will be usurped in the affections of your sweetheart.

To wear new boots, you will be lucky in your dealings. Breadwinners will command higher wages.

Old and torn boots indicate sickness and snares before you.

Borrowing

Borrowing is a sign of loss and meagre support. For a banker to dream of borrowing from another bank, a run on his own will leave him in a state of collapse, unless he accepts this warning. If another borrows from you, help in time of need will be extended or offered to you. True friends will attend you.

Bottles

Bottles are good to dream of if well filled with transparent liquid. You will overcome all obstacles in affairs of the heart, prosperous engagements will ensue. If empty, coming trouble will envelop you in meshes of sinister design, from which you will be forced to use strategy to disengage yourself.

Bouquet

To dream of a bouquet beautifully and richly coloured denotes a legacy from some wealthy and unknown relative; also, pleasant, joyous gatherings among young folks.

To see a withered bouquet warns of illness.

For a young woman to receive a bouquet of mixed flowers foretells that she will have many admirers.

Bow and Arrow

To see a bow and arrow in a dream denotes great gain reaped from the inability of others to carry out plans.

To make a bad shot means disappointed hopes in carrying forward successfully business affairs.

Bowling

To dream that you go bowling denotes that you are foolishly wasting your energy and opportunities. You should be careful in the selection of companions. All phases of this dream are bad.

See also **Tenpin Bowling**.

Box

Boxes in dreams often signify mystery and the search for a secret.

Opening a goods box in your dream signifies untold wealth and that delightful journeys to distant places may be made with happy results. If the box is empty disappointment in works of all kinds will follow.

Boxer

For a young woman to see a boxer foretells that she will take a good deal of pleasure in her social life, to the extent that her friends may worry about her reputation.

Boxing

To watch boxing in your dreams warns that you may have trouble in controlling your affairs.

Bracelet

To see in your dreams a bracelet encircling your arm, the gift of lover or friend, is assurance of an early marriage and a happy union.

If a young woman loses her bracelet she will meet with sundry losses and vexations.

To find one, good property will come into her possession.

Brain

To see your own brain in a dream denotes that uncongenial surroundings will irritate and dwarf you into an unpleasant companion.

To see the brains of animals foretells that you will suffer mental trouble. If you eat them, you will gain knowledge, and profit unexpectedly.

Brambles

To dream of brambles entangling you is a portent of ill luck. Lawsuits will most likely go against you. Take care of your and your family's health.

Branch

It betokens, if full of fruit and green leaves, wealth, many delightful hours with friends. If dried, sorrowful news of the absent.

Brandy

To dream of brandy foretells that while you may reach heights of distinction and wealth, you will lack that innate refinement which wins true friendship from people whom you most wish to please.

Brass

To dream of brass denotes that you will rise rapidly in your profession, but while of apparently solid elevation you will secretly fear a downfall of fortune.

Bread

For a woman to dream of eating bread denotes that she will be afflicted with children of stubborn will, for whom she is likely to spend many days of useless labour and worry.

To dream of breaking bread with others indicates an assured competence through life.

To see a lot of impure bread, want and misery will burden the dreamer. If the bread is good and you have access to it, it is a favourable dream.

See also **Loaves.**

Break

Breakage is a bad dream. To dream of breaking any of your limbs denotes bad management and probable failures. To break furniture denotes domestic quarrels and an unquiet state of the mind.

Breakfast

Is favourable to persons engaged in mental work. To see a breakfast of fresh milk and eggs and a well filled dish of ripe fruit indicates hasty, but favourable changes.

If you are eating alone, it means you will fall into your enemies' trap. If you are eating with others it is good.

Breastfeeding

For a woman to dream of breastfeeding her baby denotes pleasant employment.

For a young woman to dream of breastfeeding a baby foretells that she will occupy positions of honour and trust.

For a man to dream of seeing his wife or partner breastfeeding their baby denotes harmony in their pursuits.

To see a baby feeding denotes that contentment and favourable conditions are unfolding for you.

Breath

To come close to a person in your dreaming with a pure and sweet breath, commendable will be your conduct, and a profitable consummation of business deals will follow.

Breath, if fetid, indicates sickness and snares.

Losing one's breath warns of signal failure where success seemed assured.

Breeze

To dream of soft breezes denotes that you will sacrifice fortune to obtain the object of your affection and will find reciprocal affection in your wooing

If a young woman dreams that she is saddened by the whisperings of the breeze she will have a season of disquietude caused by the enforced absence of her lover.

Brewing

To dream of being in a vast brewery means unjust persecution by public officials, but you will eventually prove your innocence and will rise far above your persecutors.

Brewing in any way in your dreams denotes anxiety at the outset, but usually ends in profit and satisfaction.

Briars

To see yourself caught among briars, black enemies are weaving cords of calumny and perjury intricately around you and will cause you great distress, but if you succeed in disengaging yourself from the briars, loyal friends will come to your assistance in every emergency.

Brick

Brick in a dream indicates unsettled business and disagreements in love affairs. To make them, you are likely to fail in your efforts to amass great wealth.

Bride

For a young woman to dream that she is a bride foretells that she will shortly come into an inheritance which will please her exceedingly, if she is happy to be wed. If displeasure is felt she will suffer disappointments in her anticipations.

To dream that you kiss a bride denotes a happy reconciliation between friends. For a bride to kiss others foretells for you many friends and pleasures; to kiss you, denotes you will enjoy health and find that your sweetheart will inherit unexpected fortune.

To kiss a bride and find that she looks careworn and ill denotes you will be displeased with your success and the action of your friends.

If a bride dreams that she is indifferent to her husband, it foretells that many circumstances may pollute her pleasures.

See also **Wedding**.

Bridge

To see a long bridge dilapidated, and mysteriously winding into darkness, profound melancholy over the loss of dearest possessions and dismal situations will fall upon you. To the young and those in love, disappointment in the heart's fondest hopes, as the loved one will fall below your ideal.

Bridges in dreams foretell transition.

To cross a bridge safely, a final surmounting of difficulties, though the means seem hardly safe to use. Any obstacle or delay denotes disaster.

To see a bridge give way before you, beware of treachery and false admirers. Affluence comes with clear waters. Sorrowful returns of best efforts are experienced after looking upon or coming in contact with muddy or turbid water in dreams.

Bridle

To dream of a bridle denotes you will engage in some enterprise which will afford much worry, but will eventually terminate in pleasure and gain. If it is old or broken you will have difficulties to encounter, and the probabilities are that you will go down before them.

Brimstone

To dream of brimstone foretells that discreditable dealings will lose you many friends, if you fail to rectify the mistakes you are making.

Bronchitis

To dream that you are affected with bronchitis warns that you will be detained from pursuing your views and plans by unfortunate complications of sickness in your home.

To suffer with bronchitis in a dream denotes that discouraging prospects of winning desired objects will soon loom up before you.

Bronze

For a woman to dream of a bronze statue signifies that she is likely to fail in her efforts to win the person she has determined on for a husband.

If the statue simulates life, or moves, she will be involved in a love affair, but no marriage will occur. Disappointment to some person may follow the dream.

To dream of bronze serpents or insects foretells you will be pursued by envy or bad luck. To see bronze metals denotes that your fortune will be uncertain and unsatisfactory.

Broom

To dream of brooms denotes thrift and rapid improvement in your fortune, if the brooms are new. If they are seen in use, you will lose in speculation. For a woman to lose a broom foretells that she will prove a disagreeable and slovenly wife and housekeeper.

Broth

Broth denotes the sincerity of friends. They will uphold you in all instances. If you need pecuniary aid it will be forthcoming. To lovers, it promises a strong and lasting attachment.

To make broth, you will rule your own and others' fate.

See also **Soup**.

Brothel

To dream of being in a brothel denotes you will encounter disgrace through your material indulgence.

Brothers

To see your brothers, while dreaming, full of energy, you will have cause to rejoice at your own, or their good fortune; but if they are poor and in distress, or begging for assistance, you are warned of some dire loss to you or them.

Brush

To dream of using a hairbrush denotes you will suffer misfortune from your mismanagement. To see old hairbrushes denotes sickness and ill health.

To see clothes brushes indicates a heavy task is pending over you.

If you are busy brushing your clothes, you will soon receive reimbursement for laborious work. To see miscellaneous brushes foretells a varied line of work yet, withal, rather pleasing and remunerative.

Buckle

To dream of buckles foretells that you will be beset with invitations to places of pleasure, and that your affairs will be in danger of chaotic confusion.

Buffalo

If a woman dreams that she kills a lot of buffaloes, she will undertake a stupendous enterprise, but by enforcing willpower and leaving off material pleasures, she will win commendation, from men and may receive long-wished for favours. Buffalo, seen in a dream, augurs obstinate and powerful but stupid enemies. They will boldly declare against you but by diplomacy you will escape much misfortune.

Bugle

To hear joyous blasts from a bugle, prepare for some unusual happiness, as a harmony of good things for you is being formed by unseen powers.

Blowing a bugle denotes fortunate dealings.

Bugs

To dream of bugs denotes that some disgustingly revolting complications will rise in your daily life. Families will suffer from the carelessness of outside parties, and illness may follow.

Buildings

To see large and magnificent buildings, with green lawns stretching out before them, is significant of a long life of plenty, and travels and explorations into distant countries.

Small and newly built houses denote happy homes and profitable undertakings; but, if old and filthy buildings, ill health and decay of love and business will follow.

To dream of a building that is in need of repair warns you to take care of your health.

Bull

To see one pursuing you, business trouble, through envious and jealous competitors, will harass you.

If a young woman meets a bull, she will have an offer of marriage, but, by declining this offer, she will better her fortune.

To see a bull goring a person, misfortune from unwisely using another's possessions will overtake you.

To dream of a white bull denotes that you will lift yourself up to a higher plane of life than those who persist in making material things their God. It usually denotes gain.

Bulldog

To dream of entering strange premises and having a bulldog attack you, you will be in danger of transgressing the laws of your country by using perjury to obtain your desires.

If one meets you in a friendly way, you will rise in life, regardless of adverse criticisms and seditious interference of enemies.

See also **Dog**.

Bullock

Denotes that kind friends will surround you, if you are in danger from enemies. Good health is promised you.

Burden

To dream that you carry a heavy burden signifies that you will be tied down by oppressive weights of care and injustice, caused from favouritism shown to your enemies by those in power. But to struggle free from it, you will climb to the topmost heights of success.

Bureaucracy

To dream of being obstructed by bureaucracy is a warning to the dreamer to plan projects more carefully in future, so as not to be held up unnecessarily.

Burglars

To dream that they are searching your person, you may have danger-ous enemies to contend with; practise extreme carefulness in your dealings with strangers.

If you dream of your home, or place of business, being burgled, your good standing in business or society will be assailed, but courage in meeting these difficulties will defend you. Accidents may happen to the careless after this dream.

Burial

To attend the burial of a relative, if the sun is shining on the procession, is a sign of the good health of relations, and that perhaps the happy marriage of one of them is about to occur. But if rain and dismal weather prevails, bad news of the absent is likely, and depres-sions in business circles will be felt.

A burial where there are sad rites performed, or sorrowing faces, is indicative of adverse surroundings or their speedy approach.

See also **Funeral**.

Buried Alive

To dream that you are buried alive warns that you are about to make a great mistake, which your opponents will quickly turn to your injury. If you are rescued from the grave, your struggle will eventually correct your misadventure.

Burns

Burns stand for tidings of good. To burn your hand in a clear and flowing fire denotes purity of purpose and the approbation of friends. To burn your feet in walking through coals, or beds of fire, denotes your ability to accomplish any endeavour, however impossible it may be to others. Your usual good health will remain with you, but, if you are overcome in the fire, it represents that your interests will suffer through treachery of supposed friends.

Burr

To dream of burrs denotes that you will struggle to free yourself from some unpleasant burden, and will seek a change of surroundings.

Bus

To dream that you are being drive through the streets in a bus foretells misunderstandings with friends, and unwise promises made by you.

Business Partner

To dream of seeing your business partner with a basket of crockery on his back and, letting it fall, gets it mixed with other crockery, warns that your business may sustain a loss through the indiscriminate dealings of your partner. If you reprimand him for it, you will, to some extent, recover the loss.

Butcher

To see a butcher cutting meat, your character will be dissected by society to your detriment. Take care when writing letters or documents.

Butter

To dream of eating fresh, golden butter is a sign of good health and plans well carried out; it will bring you possessions, wealth and knowledge.

To eat rancid butter denotes competence acquired through the struggles of manual labour.

To sell butter denotes small gain.

Butterfly

To see a butterfly among flowers and green grasses indicates prosperity and fair attainments.

To see them flying about denotes news from absent friends by letter, or from someone who has seen them. To a young woman, a happy love, culminating in a life union.

Buttermilk

Drinking buttermilk denotes that sorrow will follow some worldly pleasure, and some imprudence will impair the general health of the dreamer.

To give it away, or feed it to pigs, is bad still.

To dream that you are drinking buttermilk made into oyster soup denotes that you will be called on to do some very repulsive thing, and that ill luck will confront you. There are quarrels brewing and friendships threatened. If you awaken while you are drinking it, by discreet manoeuvring you may effect a pleasant understanding of disagreements.

Buttons

To dream of sewing bright shining buttons on a uniform betokens to a young woman the warm affection of a fine-looking and wealthy partner in marriage. To a youth, it signifies admittance to military honours and a bright career.

Dull, or cloth, buttons denote disappointments and systematic losses and ill health.

The loss of a button, and the consequent anxiety as to losing a garment, denotes prospective losses in trade.

Buzzard

To dream that you hear a buzzard talking foretells that some old scandal may arise and work you injury by your connection with it.

To see one sitting on a railway line warns that some accident or loss is likely to descend upon you. To see them fly away as you approach foretells that you will be able to smooth over some scandalous disagreement among your friends, or even appertaining to yourself.

To see buzzards in a dream portends salacious gossip, or that unusual scandal will disturb you.

C

'And the Angel of God spake unto me in a dream, saying, Jacob; and I said, here am I.'

—Genesis xxxi, II.

Cabbage

It is bad to dream of cabbage. Disorders may run riot in all forms. To dream of seeing cabbage green warns of unfaithfulness in love.

To cut heads of cabbage denotes that you are tightening the cords of calamity around you by lavish expenditure.

Cabin

The cabin of a ship is rather unfortunate to be in a dream. Some mischief is brewing for you. You will most likely be engaged in a lawsuit, which you may lose owing to the instability of your witness.

For log cabin, see house.

Cable

To dream of a cable foretells the undertaking of a decidedly hazardous task, which, if successfully carried to completion, will abound in riches and honour to you.

To dream of receiving a cable denotes that a message of importance will reach you soon, and may cause disagreeable comments.

See also **Telegram**.

Cackle

To hear the cackling of hens denotes a sudden shock produced by bad news.

Café

To see or visit a café in your dreams foretells that you may unwisely entertain friendly relations with persons known to be your enemies. Manipulative women may scheme against your morality and possessions.

Cage

In your dreaming, if you see a cageful of birds, you will be the happy possessor of immense wealth and many beautiful and charming children. To see only one bird, you will contract a desirable and wealthy marriage. No bird indicates a member of the family lost, either by elopement or death.

To see wild animals caged denotes that you will triumph over your enemies and misfortunes. If you are in the cage with them, it warns of accidents while travelling.

Cakes

To dream of sweet cakes means gain for hard workers and a favourable opportunity for the enterprising. Those in love will prosper.

Pound cake is significant of much pleasure either from society or business. For a young woman to dream of her wedding cake is the only bad luck cake in the category. Baking them is not so good an omen as seeing them or eating them.

Calendar

To dream of keeping a calendar indicates that you will be very orderly and systematic in habits throughout the year.

To see a calendar denotes disappointment in you calculations.

Called

To hear your name called in a dream by strange voices warns that your business may fall into a precarious state, and that strangers may lend you assistance, or you may fail to meet your obligations.

Lovers hearing the voice of their affianced should heed the warning. If they have been negligent in attention they should make amends. Otherwise they may suffer separation from misunderstanding.

To hear the voice of the dead may be a warning of your own serious illness or that some business worry from bad judgment may ensue. The voice is an echo thrown back from the future on the subjective mind, taking the sound of your ancestor's voice from coming in contact with that part of your ancestor which remains with you. A certain portion of mind matter remains the same in lines of family descent.

Calm

To see calm seas denotes a successful ending to a doubtful undertaking.

To feel calm and happy is a sign of a long and well-spent life and a vigorous old age.

Calves

To dream of calves peacefully grazing on a velvety lawn foretells, to the young, happy, festive gatherings and enjoyment. Those engaged in seeking wealth will see it rapidly increasing.

See also **Cattle**.

Camels

To see this beast of burden signifies that you will exhibit great patience and fortitude at a time of almost unbearable anguish and failures that will seemingly sweep every vestige of hope from you.

To own a camel is a sign that you will possess rich mining property.

To see a herd of camels on the desert denotes assistance when all human aid seems at a low ebb, and of sickness from which you will arise, contrary to all expectations.

See also **Dromedary**.

Camera

To dream of a camera signifies that changes may bring undeserved environments. For a young woman to dream that she is taking pictures with a camera warns that her immediate future may be displeasing and that a friend may subject her to acute disappointment.

Cameo Brooch

To dream of a cameo brooch denotes that some sad occurrence may soon claim your attention.

Camp

To dream of camping in the open air, you may expect a change in your affairs; also, prepare to make a long and wearisome journey.

To see a camping settlement, many of your companions will move away and your own prospects will appear gloomy.

For a young woman to dream that she is in a camp denotes that her lover will have trouble in getting her to name a day for their wedding, and that he will prove a kind husband. If in a military camp she will marry the first time she has a chance.

A married woman after dreaming of being in a soldier's camp is in danger of having her husband's name sullied, and divorce courts may be her destination.

Campaign

To dream of running a political campaign signifies your opposition to approved ways of conducting business, and that you will set up original plans for yourself regardless of enemies working against you. Those in power will lose.

If it is a religious people conducting a campaign against sin, it denotes that you will be called upon to contribute from your private means to sustain charitable institutions.

For a woman to dream that she is interested in a moral campaign denotes that she will surmount obstacles and prove courageous in time of need.

Canal

To see the water of a canal muddy and stagnant-looking portends sickness and disorders of the stomach, and dark designs of enemies. But if its waters are clear a placid life and the devotion of friends is before you.

For a young woman to glide in a canoe across a canal denotes a chaste life and an adoring husband. If she crosses the canal on a bridge over clear water and gathers ferns and other greens on the banks, she will enjoy a life of ceaseless rounds of pleasure and attain to high social distinction. But if the water be turbid she will often find herself tangled in meshes of perplexity and will be the victim of nervous troubles.

Canary Birds

To dream of this sweet songster denotes unexpected pleasures. For a young person to dream of possessing a beautiful canary denotes high-class honours and a successful passage through the literary world, or a happy termination of love's young dream.

To dream one is given you indicates a welcome legacy. To give away a canary warns that you may suffer disappointment in your dearest wishes.

To dream that one dies denotes the unfaithfulness of dear friends.

Advancing, fluttering, and singing canaries, in luxurious apartments, denotes feasting and a life of exquisite refinement, wealth, and satisfying friendships. If the light is weird or unnaturally bright, it augurs that you are entertaining illusory hopes. Your over-confidence is your worst enemy. A young woman after this dream should beware, lest flattering promises react upon her in disappointment. Fairy-like scenes in a dream are peculiarly misleading and treacherous to women.

Candles

Candles generally signify spiritual comprehension and wisdom. To see them burning with a clear and steady flame denotes the constancy of those about you and a well-grounded fortune.

For a maiden to dream that she is moulding candles denotes that she will have an unexpected offer of marriage and a pleasant visit to distant relatives. If she is lighting a candle, she will meet her lover clandestinely because of parental objections.

To see a candle wasting in a draught, enemies are circulating detrimental reports about you.

If the candle is extinguished, you need to make the effort to acquire knowledge about something or someone important.

To snuff a candle warns of news.

Candlestick

To see a candlestick bearing a whole candle denotes that a bright future lies before you filled with health, happiness and loving companions. If empty, the reverse.

Cane

To see cane growing in your dream foretells that favourable advancement will be made towards fortune. To see it cut warns of failure in a variety of undertakings.

Cannon

This dream denotes that one's home and country are in danger of foreign intrusion, from which our youth will suffer from the perils of war.

For a young woman to hear or see cannons denotes she will be a soldier's wife and will have to bid him goodbye as he marches in defence of her and honour.

The reader will have to interpret dreams of this character by the influences surrounding him, and by the experiences stored away in his subjective mind. If you have thought about cannons a great deal and you dream of them when there is no war, they are most likely to warn you against struggle and probable defeat. Or if business is manipulated by yourself successful engagements after much worry and ill luck may ensue.

Cannon ball

This means that secret enemies are uniting against you. For a maid to see a cannonball denotes that she is likely to have a soldier sweetheart. For a youth to see a cannonball denotes that he is likely to be called upon to defend his country.

Canoe

To paddle a canoe on a calm stream denotes your perfect confidence in your own ability to conduct your business in a profitable way.

To row with a sweetheart means an early marriage and fidelity. To row on rough waters, you will have to tame your partner before you attain connubial bliss. Affairs in the business world will prove disappointing after you dream of rowing in muddy waters. If the waters are shallow and swift, a hasty courtship or stolen pleasures, from which there can be no lasting good, are indicated.

Shallow, clear and calm waters in rowing signifies happiness of a pleasing character, but of short duration.

Water is typical of futurity in the dream realms. If a pleasant immediate future awaits the dreamer he will come in close proximity with clear water. Or if he emerges from disturbed watery elements into waking life the near future is filled with obstacles for him.

Canopy

To dream of a canopy, or of being beneath one, denotes that false friends are influencing you to undesirable ways of securing gain. You will do well to protect those in your care.

Cap

For a woman to dream of seeing a cap signifies that she will be invited to take part in some festivity.

For a girl to dream that she sees her sweetheart with a cap on denotes that she will be bashful and shy in his presence.

To see a prisoner's cap denotes that your courage is failing you in time of danger.

To see a miner's cap, you will inherit a substantial income.

Captain

To dream of seeing a captain of any company denotes your noblest aspirations will be realized. If a woman dreams that her lover is a captain, she will be much harassed in mind from jealousy and rivalry.

Captive

To dream that you are a captive denotes that you may have treachery to deal with and, if you cannot escape, that injury and misfortune will befall you.

To dream of taking anyone captive, you will join yourself to pursuits and persons of lowest status.

For a young woman to dream that she is a captive denotes that she will have a husband who will be jealous of her confidence in others; or she may be censured for her indiscretion.

Car

To dream that you are riding in a car denotes that you will be restless under pleasant conditions and will make changes in your affairs. There is a grave danger of imprudent conduct intimated through a dream of this nature.

If a car breaks down while you are in it, the enjoyment of a pleasure will not extend to the heights you contemplate.

To find yourself escaping from the path of one signifies that you will do well to avoid some rival as much as you reasonably can.

For a young woman to look for a car suggests that she will be disappointed in her aims to entice someone into her favour.

Cardboard

To dream of cardboard denotes that unfaithful friends may deceive you concerning important matters. To cut cardboard, you will throw aside difficulties in your struggle to reach eminent positions.

Cardinal

It is unlucky to dream of seeing a cardinal in his robes. You are in danger of meeting such misfortunes as may even necessitate your removal to distant or foreign lands to begin anew your ruined fortune. For a woman to dream this is a sign of her downfall through false promises. If priest or preacher is a spiritual adviser and his services are supposed to be needed, especially in the hour of temptation, then we find ourselves dreaming of him as a warning against approaching evil.

Cards

If playing them in your dreams with others for social pastime, you will meet with fair realization of hopes that have long buoyed you up. Small ills will vanish. But playing for stakes will involve you in difficulties of a serious nature.

If you lose at cards you will encounter enemies. If you win you will justify yourself in the eyes of the law, but will have trouble in so doing.

If a young woman dreams that her sweetheart is playing at cards, she will have cause to question his good intentions.

In social games, seeing diamonds indicate wealth; clubs, that your partner in life will be exacting, and that you may have trouble in explaining your absence at times; hearts denote fidelity and cosy surroundings; spades signify that you will be encumbered with a large estate.

Carnival

To dream that you are participating in a carnival portends that you are soon to enjoy some unusual pleasure or recreation. A carnival when masks are used, or when incongruous or clownish figures are seen, implies discord in the home; business may be unsatisfactory and love unrequited.

Carpenter

To see carpenters at their labour foretells you will engage in honest endeavours to raise your fortune, to the exclusion of selfish pastime or so-called recreation.

Carpet

To see a carpet in a dream denotes profit, and wealthy friends to aid you in need.

To walk on a carpet, you will be prosperous and happy.

To dream that you buy carpets denotes great gain. If selling them, you will have cause to go on a pleasant journey, as well as a profitable one.

For a young woman to dream of carpets shows that she will own a beautiful home and servants will wait upon her.

Carriage

To see a carriage implies that you will be gratified, and that you will make visits.

To ride in one, you will have a sickness that will soon pass, and you will enjoy health and advantageous positions.

To dream that you are looking for a carriage, you will have to labour hard, but will eventually be possessed with reasonable ability.

Carrot

To dream of carrots, portends prosperity and health. For a young woman to eat them, denotes that she will contract an early marriage and be the mother of several hardy children.

Cart

To dream of riding in a cart, constant work will employ your time if you would keep supplies for your family.

To see a cart warns of bad news from kindred or friends.

To dream of driving a cart, you will meet with merited success in business and other aspirations.

For lovers to ride together in a cart, they will be true in spite of the machinations of rivals.

Cartridge

To dream of cartridges foretells unhappy quarrels and dissensions.

Some untoward fate threatens you or someone closely allied to you.

If they are empty, there will be foolish variances in your associations.

Carving

To dream of carving a fowl indicates that you will be poorly off in a worldly way. Companions will cause you vexation from continued ill temper.

Carving meat denotes bad investments, but, if a change is made, prospects will be brighter.

Cash

To dream that you have plenty of cash, but that it has been borrowed, portends that you will be looked upon as a worthy man, but that those who come in close contact with you will find that you are mercenary and unfeeling.

For a young woman to dream that she is spending borrowed money foretells that she will be found out in her practice of deceit, and through this lose a prized friend.

See also Money.

Cash Box

To dream of a full cash box, denotes that favourable prospects will open around you. If empty, you will experience meager reimbursements.

Cashier

To see a cashier in your dream denotes that others will claim your possessions. If you owe anyone, you will practice deceit in your designs upon some wealthy person.

Castle

These are important symbols which frequently appear in dreams, and which can signify many things. For a child to dream of a castle often denotes nobility, difficult enterprise and nostalgia. For an adult, yearning for greatness that has gone astray, regret.

To dream of being in a castle, you will be possessed of sufficient wealth to make life as you wish. You have prospects of being a great traveller, enjoying contact with people of many nations.

To dream of having to prove your identity to enter a castle signifies that you will achieve inner nobility, but that you must maintain vigilance and spiritual strength.

To see an old and vine-covered castle, you are likely to become romantic in your tastes, and care should be taken that you do not contract an undesirable marriage or engagement. Business is depressed after this dream.

To dream that you are leaving a castle, you risk being robbed of your possessions.

Castor Oil

To dream of castor oil denotes that you will seek to overthrow a friend who is secretly abetting your advancement.

Cats

To dream of a cat, denotes ill luck, if you do not succeed in befriending it.

If the cat attacks you, you will have enemies who will go to any extreme to blacken your reputation and to cause you loss of property. But if you succeed in befriending it, you will overcome great obstacles and rise in fortune and fame.

If you meet a thin, mean and dirty-looking cat, you may have bad news.

To hear the mewing of a cat, some false friend is using all the words and work at his command to do you harm.

To dream that a cat scratches you, an enemy will succeed in wrenching from you the profits of a deal that you have spent many days making.

If a young woman dreams that she is holding a cat, or kitten, she may be influenced into some impropriety through the treachery of others.

To dream of a clean white cat denotes entanglements which, while seemingly harmless, may prove a source of sorrow and loss of wealth.

When a merchant dreams of a cat, he should put his best energies to work, as his competitors are about to succeed in demolishing his standard of dealing, and he will be forced to other measures if he undersells others and still succeeds.

To dream of seeing a cat and snake on friendly terms signifies the beginning of an angry struggle. It denotes that an enemy is being entertained by you with the intention of using him to find out some secret which you believe concerns yourself; uneasy of his confidences given, you will endeavour to disclaim all knowledge of his actions, as you are fearful that things divulged, concerning your private life, may become public.

In interpreting dreams of cats, however, the dreamer's own attitude towards these animals, and the context of the dream, must also be considered. Positive dreams about cats can signify wisdom.

Catechism

To dream of the catechism foretells that you will be offered a lucrative position, but the strictures will be such that you will be worried as to accepting it.

Caterpillar

To see a caterpillar in a dream denotes that low and hypocritical people are in your immediate future, and that you will do well to keep clear of deceitful appearances. You may suffer a loss in love or business.

To dream of a caterpillar indicates that you will be placed in embarrassing situations, and there will be small honour or gain to be expected.

Cathedral

To dream of a vast cathedral with its domes rising into space denotes that you will be possessed with an envious nature and unhappy longings for the unattainable, both mental and physical; but if you enter you will be elevated in life, having for your companions the learned and wise.

Cattle

To dream of seeing good-looking and fat cattle contentedly grazing in green pastures denotes prosperity and happiness through a congenial and pleasant companion.

To see cattle lean and shaggy, and poorly fed, you will be likely to toil unnecessarily because of misspent energy and dislike of details of work. Correct your habits after this dream.

To see cattle stampeding means that you will have to exert all the powers of command you have to keep your career in a profitable channel.

To see a herd of cows at milking time, you will be the successful owner of wealth that many have worked to obtain. To a young woman this means that her affections will not suffer from the one of her choice.

To dream of milking cows with udders well filled, great good fortune is in store for you. If the calf has stolen the milk, it signifies that you are is danger of losing your lover by slowness to show your reciprocity, or your property from neglect of business.

To see young calves in your dream, you will become a great

favourite in society and win the heart of a loyal person. For business, this dream indicates profit from sales. For a lover, the entering into bonds that will be respected. If the calves are poor, look for about the same, except that the object sought will be much harder to obtain.

Long-horned and dark, vicious cattle, denote enemies.

See also **Calves, Cows, Ox**.

Cauliflower

To dream of eating it, you will be taken to task for neglect of duty. To see it growing, your prospects will brighten after a period of loss.

For a young woman to see this vegetable in a garden denotes that she will marry to please her parents and not herself.

Cavalry

To dream that you see a division of cavalry denotes personal advancement and distinction. Some little sensation may accompany your elevation.

Cavern or Cave

To dream of seeing a cavern yawning in the weird moonlight before you, many perplexities will assail you, and doubtful advancement because of adversaries. Work and health is threatened.

To be in a cave foreshadows change. You will probably be estranged from those who are very dear to you.

For a young woman to walk in a cave with her lover or friend denotes she may fall in love with a villain and suffer the loss of true friends.

Cedars

To dream of seeing them green and shapely denotes pleasing success in an undertaking.

To see them dead or blighted signifies despair. No object will be attained from seeing them thus.

Celery

To dream of seeing fresh, crisp stalks of celery, you will be prosperous and influential beyond your highest hopes.

To eat it, boundless love and affection will be heaped upon you.

For a young woman to eat it with her lover denotes she will come into rich possessions.

Cellar

To dream of the cellar of the house indicates that the dreamer is seeing the foundation of his personality.

To dream of being in a cold, damp cellar, you will be oppressed by doubts. You will lose confidence in all things and suffer gloomy forebodings from which you will fail to escape unless you control your will. It also warns of loss of property.

To see a cellar stored with wines and table stores, you will be offered a share in profits coming from a doubtful source. If a young woman dreams of this she may have an offer of marriage from a speculator or gambler.

See also **Basement, Wine Cellar.**

Cemetery

To dream of being in a beautiful and well-kept cemetery, you will have unexpected news of the recovery of one whom you had mourned as dead, and you will regain the title to lands occupied by usurpers.

For young people to dream of wandering through the silent avenues of the dead foreshows they will meet with tender and loving responses from friends, but will have to meet sorrows that friends are powerless to avert.

For a mother to carry fresh flowers to a cemetery, indicates she may expect the continued good health of her family.

For a young widow to visit a cemetery means she will soon throw aside her weeds for robes of matrimony. If she feels sad and depressed, she is likely to have new cares and regrets.

Old people dreaming of a cemetery indicates that they will soon make pleasant journeys where they will find perfect rest.

To see little children gathering flowers and chasing butterflies among the graves denotes prosperous changes and no graves of any of your friends to weep over. Good health will hold high carnival.
See also **Churchyard**.

Chaff

To see chaff denotes an empty and fruitless undertaking and ill health causing great anxiety.

Women dreaming of piles of chaff portends many hours spent in useless and degrading gossip, bringing them into notoriety and causing them to run the risk of losing husbands who would have maintained them without work on their part.

Chains

To dream of being bound in chains denotes that unjust burdens are about to be thrown upon your shoulders; but if you succeed in breaking them you will free yourself from some unpleasant business or social engagement.

To see chains warns of calumny and treacherous designs by the envious.

Seeing others in chains denotes bad fortunes for them.

Chair

To see a chair in your dream denotes failure to meet some obligation. If you are not careful you will also vacate your most profitable places.

To see a friend sitting on a chair and remaining motionless, warns of bad news about him.

Chair Maker

To dream of seeing a chair maker denotes that worry from apparently pleasant labour will confront you.

Chairman

To dream that you see the chairman of any public body foretells that you will seek elevation and be recompensed by receiving a high position of trust. To see one looking out of humour, you are threatened with unsatisfactory states.

If you are a chairman, you will be distinguished for your justice and kindness to others.

Chalk

To dream of using chalk on a board, you will attain public honours.
To hold hands full of chalk, disappointment is foretold.

Chalice

To dream of a chalice denotes that pleasure will be gained by you to the sorrow of others. To break one foretells your failure to obtain power over some friend.

Challenge

If you are challenged to fight a duel, you will become involved in a social difficulty wherein you will be compelled to make apologies or else lose friendships.

To accept a challenge of any character denotes that you will bear many ills yourself in your endeavour to shield others from dishonour.

Chamber

See also **Room**.

Chambermaid

To see a chambermaid denotes bad fortune; decided changes will be made.

For a man to dream of making love to a chambermaid shows he is likely to find himself an object of derision on account of indiscreet conduct and want of tact.

Chameleon

To dream of seeing your sweetheart wearing a chameleon chained to her warns that she may prove faithless to you if by changing she can better her fortune. Ordinarily chameleons signify deceit and self-advancement, even if others suffer.

Champion

To dream of a champion denotes that you will win the warmest friendship of some person by your dignity and moral conduct.

Chandelier

To dream of a chandelier portends that unhoped-for success will make it possible for you to enjoy pleasure and luxury at your caprice.

To see a broken or ill-kept one denotes that unfortunate speculation will depress your seemingly substantial fortune. To see the light in one go out warns that sickness and distress may cloud a promising future.

Chapel

To dream of a chapel denotes dissension in social circles and unsettled business.

To be in a chapel denotes disappointment and change of business.

For young people to dream of entering a chapel implies false loves and enemies. Unlucky unions may entangle them.

Charcoal

To dream of charcoal unlighted warns of miserable situations and unhappiness. If it is burning with glowing coals, there are prospects of great enhancement of fortune, and possession of unalloyed joys.

Chariot

To dream of riding in a chariot foretells that favourable opportunities will present themselves resulting in your good if rightly used by you.

To fall, or to see others fall from one, denotes displacement from high positions.

Charity

To dream of giving charity denotes that you will be harassed with supplications for help from the poor and your business will grind to a halt.

To dream of giving to charitable institutions, your right of possession to paying property will be disputed. Worries and ill health will threaten you.

For young persons to dream of giving charity foreshows that they will be annoyed by deceitful rivals.

To dream that you are an object of charity omens that you will succeed in life after hard times with misfortunes.

Chastise

To dream of being chastised indicates that you have not been prudent in conducting your airs.

To dream that you administer chastisement to another signifies that you will have an ill-tempered partner either in business or marriage.

For parents to dream of chastising their children indicates they will be loose in their manner of correcting them, but they will succeed in bringing them up honourably.

Cheated

To dream of being cheated in business, you will meet designing people who will seek to close your avenues to fortune.

For young persons to dream that they are being cheated in games portends that they lose their sweethearts through quarrels and misunderstandings.

Cheese

To dream of eating cheese denotes great disappointments and sorrow. No good of any nature can be hoped for. Cheese is generally a bad dream.

The only exception to this is dreaming of Swiss cheese, which foretells that you will come into possession of substantial property, and that healthy amusements will be enjoyed.

Cheques

To dream of palming off false cheques on your friends denotes that you will resort to subterfuge in order to carry forward your plans.

To receive cheques, you will be able to meet your payments and will inherit money.

To dream that you pay out cheques denotes depression and loss in business.

Cherries

To dream of cherries denotes that you will gain popularity by your amiability and unselfishness. To eat them portends possession of some much desired object. To see green ones indicates approaching good fortune.

Cherubs

To dream you see cherubs foretells you will have some distinct joy, which will leave an impression of lasting good upon your life.

To see them looking sorrowful or reproachful warns that distress will come unexpectedly upon you.

Chess

To dream of playing chess warns of stagnation of business, dull companions, and poor health.

To dream that you lose at chess, worries from mean sources will ensue; but if you win, disagreeable influences may be surmounted.

Chestnuts

To dream of handling chestnuts foretells losses in a business way, but indicates an agreeable companion through life.

Eating them denotes sorrow for a time, but final happiness.

For a young woman to dream of eating or trying her fortune with them, she will have a well-to-do lover and comparative plenty.

Chickens

To dream of chickens denotes pleasant family reunions with added members.

To dream of seeing a brood of chickens denotes worry from many cares, some of which will prove to your profit.

Young or half grown chickens signify fortunate enterprises, but to make them so you will have to exert your physical strength.

To see chickens going to roost, enemies are planning to work you evil.

To eat them denotes that selfishness will detract from your otherwise good name. Business and love will remain in precarious states.

See also **Bantam, Fowl, Poultry**.

Chicks

To see a fowl with her chicks denotes that, if you are a woman, your cares will be varied and irksome. Many children will be in your care, and some of them will prove wayward and unruly.

Chicks to others, denote accumulation of wealth.

Chilblain

To dream of suffering with chilblains denotes that you will be driven into some bad dealing through over-anxity of a friend or partner. This dream also warns of your own illness or an accident.

Childhood

To dream of childhood is a warning to look to the future instead of remaining trapped by rose-tinted memories of the past.

If the childhood is lonely and despairing, you will need to face and resolve an issue from that part of your life.

Children

'Dream of children sweet and fair,
To you will come suave debonair,
Fortune robed in shining dress,
Bearing wealth and happiness.'

To dream of your own children denotes cheerfulness and the merry voices of neighbours and children.

To dream of seeing many beautiful children is portentous of great prosperity and blessings.

For a mother to dream of seeing her child sick from slight cause, she may see it enjoying robust health, but trifles of another nature may harass her.

To see children working or studying denotes peaceful times and general prosperity.

To dream of seeing disappointed children denotes trouble from enemies, and anxious forebodings from underhanded work of seemingly friendly people.

To romp and play with children denotes that all your speculating and love enterprises will prevail.

Seeing children in dreams often indicates that an essential aspect of the dreamer is about to be lost, or is in the process of being lost.

Chimes

To dream of Christmas chimes denotes fair prospects for business people and farmers.

For the young, happy anticipations fulfilled. Ordinary chimes denote that some small anxiety will soon be displaced by news of distant friends.

Chimney

To dream of seeing chimneys warns that a very displeasing incident will occur. A tumbledown chimney denotes sorrow. To see one overgrown with ivy or other vines foretells that happiness will result from sorrow.

To see a fire burning in a chimney denotes much good is approaching you. To hide in a chimney corner denotes distress and doubt will assail you. Business will appear gloomy.

For a young woman to dream that she is going down a chimney foretells she will be guilty of some impropriety which will cause consternation among her associates. To ascend a chimney shows that she will escape trouble which will be planned for her.

China

For a woman to dream of painting or arranging her china foretells she will have a pleasant home and be a thrifty and economical matron.

Chocolate

To dream of chocolate denotes that you will provide abundantly for those who are dependent on you. To see chocolates indicates agreeable companions and employments. If sour, illness or other disappointments may follow. To drink chocolate foretells you will prosper after a short period of unfavourable reverses.

Choir

To dream of a choir foretells that you may expect cheerful surroundings to replace gloom and discontent. For a young woman to sing in a choir denotes that she will be miserable over the attention paid others by her lover.

Christ

To dream of beholding Christ, the young child, worshipped by the Wise Men, denotes many peaceful days, full of wealth and knowledge, abundant with joy, and content.

If in the garden of Gethsemane, sorrowing adversity will fill your soul, great longings for change and absent objects of love will be felt.

To see him in the temple scourging the traders denotes that evil enemies will be defeated and honest endeavours will prevail.

Christmas Tree

To dream of a Christmas tree denotes joyful occasions and auspicious fortune. To see one dismantled foretells that some painful incident will follow occasions of festivity.

Chrysanthemum

To dream that you gather white chrysanthemums signifies loss and great perplexity; coloured ones betoken pleasant engagements.

To see them in bouquets denotes that love will be offered you, but a foolish ambition will cause you to put it aside. To pass down an avenue of white chrysanthemums, with here and there a yellow one showing among the white, foretells a strange sense of loss and sadness, from which the sensibilities will expand and take on new powers. While looking on these white flowers as you pass, and you suddenly feel your spirit leave your body and a voice shouts aloud 'Glory to God, my Creator,' foretells that a crisis is pending in your near future. If some of your friends pass out, and others take up true ideas in connection with spiritual and earthly needs, you will enjoy life in its deepest meaning.

Church

To enter a church signifies a movement towards spirituality, and even a spiritual transition.

To come out of a church signifies that you will emerge safely from an inner renewal.

To dream of seeing a church in the distance denotes disappointment in pleasures long anticipated.

To enter one wrapped in gloom, dull prospects of better times are portended.

Churchyard

To dream of walking in a churchyard, if in winter, denotes that you are to have a long and bitter struggle with poverty, and you will reside far from the home of your childhood, and friends will be separated from you; but if you see the signs of springtime, you will walk up into pleasant places and enjoy the society of friends.

For lovers to dream of being in a churchyard means they are unlikely to marry each other.

See also **Cemetery**.

Churning

To dream of churning, you will have difficult tasks set you, but by diligence and industry you will accomplish them and be very prosperous. To the farmer, it denotes profit from a plenteous harvest; to a young woman, it denotes a thrifty and energetic husband.

Cider

To dream of cider denotes that fortune may be won by you if your time is not squandered upon material pleasure. To see people drinking it, you will be under the influence of unfaithful friends.

Circle

To dream of a circle denotes that your affairs will deceive you in their proportions of gain. For a young woman to dream of a circle warns her of indiscreet involvement to the exclusion of marriage.

Cistern

To dream of a cistern denotes you are in danger of trespassing upon the pleasures and rights of your friends. To draw from one foretells that you will indulge in your pastime and enjoyment in a manner which may be questioned by propriety.

To see an empty one foretells despairing change from happiness to sorrow.

City

To dream that you are in a strange city denotes that you may have sorrowful occasion to change your abode or mode of living.

See also **Town.**

Clairvoyance

To dream of being a clairvoyant and seeing yourself in the future warns of signal changes in your present occupation, followed by a series of unhappy conflicts with designing people.

To dream of visiting a clairvoyant warms of unprosperous commercial states and unhappy unions.

Clams

To dream of clams denotes that you will have dealings with an obstinate but honest person. To eat them foretells that you will enjoy another's prosperity.

For a young woman to dream of eating baked clams with her sweetheart foretells that she will enjoy his money as well as his confidence.

Claret

To dream of drinking claret denotes you will come under the influence of ennobling association. To dream of seeing broken bottles of claret portends you will be induced to commit immoralities by the false persuasions of deceitful persons.

*See also **Wine**.*

Clarinet

To dream of a clarinet foretells that you will indulge in frivolity beneath your usual dignity. If it is broken, you will incur the displeasure of a close friend.

Classroom

To dream of a classroom denotes that you are longing for the past and feel pessimistic about the future.

Clay

To dream of clay denotes isolation of interest and probable insolvency. To dig in a clay bank foretells you may well submit to extraordinary demands from enemies. If you dig in an ash bank and find clay, unfortunate surprises will combat progressive enterprises or new work. Your efforts are likely to be misdirected after this dream.

Women will find this dream unfavourable in love, social and business states; misrepresentations are likely to overwhelm them.

Clergyman

To dream that you send for a clergyman to preach a funeral sermon denotes that evil influences are likely to prevail in spite of your earnest endeavours.

If a young woman marries a clergyman in her dream, she may be the object of much mental distress, and the wayward hand of fortune may lead her into adversity.

*See also **Minister, Preacher, Priest, Vicar**.*

Climbing

To dream of climbing up a hill or mountain and reaching the top, you will overcome the most formidable obstacles between you and a prosperous future; but if you should fail to reach the top, your dearest plans will most likely be wrecked.

To climb a ladder to the last rung, you will succeed in business; but if the ladder breaks, you will be plunged into unexpected straits, and accidents may happen to you.

To see yourself climbing the side of a house in some mysterious way in a dream, and to have a window suddenly open to let you in, foretells that you will make or have made extraordinary ventures against the approbation of friends, but success will eventually crown your efforts, though there will be times when despair will almost enshroud you.

See also ***Ascent, Hill, Ladder*** *and* ***Mountain.***

Cloak

To dream that you are using a cloak to disguise yourself signifies that you will need to reveal more of yourself and your emotions to others, and face up to reality.

Clock

To dream that you see a clock denotes danger from a foe. To hear one strike, you will receive unpleasant news.

To see the hands of a clock turning unnaturally quickly indicates that you are afraid of your own feelings.

Cloister

To dream of a cloister omens dissatisfaction with present surroundings, and you will soon seek new environments. For a young woman to dream of a cloister foretells that her life will be made unselfish by the chastening of sorrow.

Clothing

Dreams of clothing denote that enterprises will be successes or failures, depending on whether the garments are whole and clean, or soiled and threadbare.

To dream of the loss of any article of clothing denotes disturbances in your business and love affairs.

To see clothing which is fine, but out of date, foretells that you will have fortune, but you will scorn progressive ideas.

If you reject out-of-date costumes, you will outgrow present environments and enter into new relations, new enterprises and new loves, which will transform you into a different person.

To see multicoloured clothing foretells swift changes, and intermingling of good and bad influences on your future.

To dream of poorly-fitting apparel intimates crosses in your affections, and that you are likely to make a mistake in some enterprise.

To see old or young people appropriately dressed denotes that you will undertake some engagement for which you will have no liking, and which will give rise to many cares.

For a woman to dream that she is displeased with her clothing foretells that she will have many vexatious rivalries in her quest for social distinction.

For a woman to dream that she is admiring the clothing of others suggests that she may have jealous fears of her friends.

The dreamer interpreting dreams of clothing should be careful to note whether the objects are looking natural. If the faces are distorted and the light unearthly, though the colours are bright, beware: the miscarriage of some worthy plan may do you harm.

Clouds

To dream of seeing dark heavy clouds portends misfortune and bad management. If rain is falling, it warns of troubles and illness.

To see bright transparent clouds with the sun shining through them, you will be successful after trouble has been your companion.

To see them with the stars shining denotes fleeting joys and small advancements.

Cloven Foot

To dream of a cloven foot portends that some unusual ill luck is threatening you, and you will do well to avoid the friendship of strange persons.

Clover

Walking through fields of fragrant clover is a propitious dream. It brings all objects desired into the reach of the dreamer. Fine crops are portended for the farmer and wealth for the young. Blasted fields of clover brings harrowing and regretful sighs.

To dream of clover foretells prosperity will soon enfold you. For a young woman to dream of seeing a snake crawling through blossoming clover foretells she may be early disappointed in love, and her surroundings may be gloomy and discouraging, though to her friends she seems peculiarly fortunate.

Club

To dream of being approached by a person bearing a club denotes that you will be assailed by your adversaries, but you will overcome them and be unusually happy and prosperous; but if you club anyone, you will undergo a rough and profitless journey.

Coach

To dream of riding in a coach warns of continued losses and depressions in business. Driving one implies removal or business changes.

Coal

To dream of coal warns that affliction and discord may enter your near future.

Coal Mine

To dream of being in a coal mine, and seeing miners, denotes that some evil will try to assert its power for your downfall; but if you dream of holding a share in a coal mine, it denotes your safe investment in some deal.

For a young woman to dream of mining coal foreshows she may become the wife of an estate agent or a dentist.

See also **Mine**.

Coals

To see bright coals of fire denotes pleasure and many pleasant changes.

To dream you handle them yourself denotes unmitigated joy. To see dead coals implies trouble and disappointments.

Coal-Scuttle

To dream of a coal scuttle denotes that grief will be likely to fill a vacancy made by reckless extravagance. To see your neighbour carrying in a coal scuttle foretells that your surroundings are likely to be decidedly distasteful and inharmonious.

Coat

To dream of wearing another's coat signifies that you will ask some friend to stand security for you. To see your coat torn denotes the loss of a close friend and dreary business.

To see a new coat portends some literary honour for you.

To lose your coat, you will have to rebuild your fortune lost through being over-confident in speculations.

Coat of Arms

To dream of seeing your coat of arms is a dream of ill luck. You will never possess a title.

Cockade

This dream denotes that foes will bring disastrous suits against you. Beware of titles.

Cockerel

To dream of a cockerel foretells that you will be very successful and rise to prominence, but that you must take care not to let yourself become conceited over your fortunate rise.

To dream of hearing a cock crowing in the morning is significant of good. If you are single, it denotes an early marriage and a luxurious home.

To hear one at night denotes despair and cause for tears.

To dream of seeing cocks fight, you may leave your family because of quarrels and infidelity. This dream usually announces some unexpected and sorrowful events. The cock warned the Apostle Peter when he was about to perjure himself. It may also warn you in a dream when the meshes of the world are swaying you from 'the straight line' of spiritual wisdom.

Cocktail

To drink a cocktail while dreaming denotes that you may deceive your friends as to your inclinations and enjoy the companionship of fast men and women while posing as a serious student and staid home-lover. For a woman, this dream portends fast living and an ignoring of moral and set rules.

Coca-Cola

For a woman to dream that she is drinking coca-cola signifies that she will lose health and a chance for marrying a wealthy man by her abandonment to material delights.

Cocoa

To dream of cocoa denotes that you are willing to cultivate distasteful friends for your own advancement and pleasure.

Coconut

Coconuts in dreams warn you of a shortfall in your expectations, as sly enemies are encroaching upon your rights in the guise of ardent friends. Dead coconut trees are a sign of loss and sorrow.

Code

To dream of reading code indicates that you are interested in literary researches, and that by constant study you will become well acquainted with the habits and lives of the ancients.

Coffee

To dream of drinking coffee denotes the disapproval of friends towards your marriage intentions. If married, disagreements and frequent quarrels are implied.

To dream of dealing in coffee portends business failures. If selling, sure loss. Buying it, you may with ease retain your credit.

For a young woman to see or handle coffee, she needs to be discreet in her actions.

To dream of roasting coffee, for a young woman, denotes escape from evil by luckily marrying a stranger.

To see ground coffee foretells successful struggles with adversity. Parched coffee warns you of the evil attentions of strangers.

Green coffee denotes you have bold enemies who will show you no quarter, but will fight for your overthrow.

Coffee Mill

To see a coffee mill in your dreams warns that you are approaching a critical danger, and that all your energy and alertness will have to stand up with obduracy to avert its disastrous consequences. To hear it grinding signifies that you will just manage to overthrow some evil pitted against your interest.

Coffin

This dream is generally unlucky. You must, if you are a farmer, take particular care of your crops and livestock, as they are likely to be more vulnerable than usual. To businesspeople it warns of debts whose accumulation will be hard to avoid. To the young it warns of unhappy unions.

To see your own coffin in a dream warns of business and domestic difficulties. If you are sitting on a coffin in a moving hearse, this indicates illness, though not a fatal one, for yourself or someone close to you.

Quarrels with the opposite sex are also indicated. Take care in how you behave towards a friend, as you may later regret it.

Coins

To dream of gold coins denotes great prosperity and much pleasure derived from sight-seeing and ocean voyages.

Silver coin is unlucky to dream about. Dissensions will arise in the most orderly families.

For a maiden to dream that her lover gives her a silver coin signifies she is likely to be jilted by him.

Copper coins denote despair and physical burdens. Nickel coins imply that work of the lowest nature will devolve upon you.

If silver coins are your ideal of money, and they are bright and clean, or seen distinctly in your possession, the dream will be a propitious one.

Coke Oven

To see coke ovens burning foretells some unexpected good fortune will result from failure in some enterprise.

Cold

To dream of suffering from a cold warns you to look well to your affairs. There are enemies at work to destroy you. Your health is also menaced.

Collar

To dream of wearing a collar, you will have high honours thrust upon you that you will hardly be worthy of. For a woman to dream of collars, she will have many admirers, but no sincere ones. She will be likely to remain single for a long while.

College

To dream of a college denotes you are soon to advance to a position long sought after. To dream that you are back in college foretells you will receive distinction through some well-favoured work.

Collision

To dream of a collision, you may meet with an accident of a serious type and disappointments in business.

For a young woman to see a collision denotes that she will be unable to decide between lovers, and will be the cause of wrangles.

Colonel

To dream of seeing or being commanded by a colonel denotes you will struggle to reach any prominence in social or business circles.

To dream you are a colonel denotes you will contrive to hold position above those of friends or acquaintances.

Combat

To dream of engaging in combat, you will find yourself seeking to ingratiate your affections into the life and love of someone whom you know to be another's, and you will run great risks of losing your good reputation in business. It denotes struggles to keep on firm ground.

For a young woman to dream of seeing combatants signifies that she will have choice between lovers, both of whom love her and would face death for her.

Combing

To dream of combing one's hair portends news of illness or death. Decay of friendship and loss of property is also indicated by this dream.

See also **Hair**.

Comedy

To dream of being at a light play denotes that foolish and short-lived pleasures will be indulged in by the dreamer.

To dream of seeing a comedy is significant of light pleasures and pleasant tasks.

Comet

To dream of this heavenly awe-inspiring object sailing through the skies, you will have trials of an unexpected nature to beset you, but by bravely combating these foes you will rise above the mediocre in life to heights of fame.

For a young person, this dream portends sorrow.

Comic Songs

To hear comic songs in dreams foretells that you will disregard opportunity to advance your affairs and enjoy the companionship of the pleasure-loving. To sing one proves that you will enjoy much pleasure for a time, but difficulties will overtake you.

Command

To dream of being commanded denotes that you will be humbled in some way by your associates for scorn shown to your superiors.

To dream of giving a command, you will have some honour conferred upon you. If this is done in a tyrannical or boastful way, disappointments will follow.

To dream of receiving commands foretells that you will be unwisely influenced by persons of stronger will than your own.

Commerce

To dream that you are engaged in commerce denotes that you will handle your opportunities wisely and advantageously. To dream of failures and gloomy outlooks in commercial circles denotes trouble and ominous threatening of failure in real business life.

Committee

To dream of a committee foretells that you will be surprised into doing some distasteful work. For one to wait on you foretells that some unfruitful labour will be assigned you.

Companion

To dream of seeing a wife or husband signifies small anxieties and possible illness.

To dream of social companions denotes that fight and frivolous pastimes will engage your attention, hindering you from performing your duties.

Compass

To dream of a compass denotes that you will be forced to struggle in narrow limits, thus making elevation more toilsome but fuller of honour.

108

To dream of the compass or mariner's needle foretells that you will be surrounded by prosperous circumstances and that honest people will favour you.

To see one pointing awry foretells threatened loss and deception.

Completion

To dream of completing a task or piece of work denotes that you will have acquired competence early in life, and that you can spend your days as you like and wherever you please.

For a young woman to dream that she has completed a garment denotes that she will soon decide on a husband.

To dream of completing a journey, you will have the means to make one whenever you like.

Complexion

To dream that you have a beautiful complexion is lucky. You will pass through pleasing incidents.

To dream that you have a bad complexion warns of disappointment and sickness.

Concert

To dream of a concert of a high musical order denotes delightful seasons of pleasure, and literary work to the author. To the business man it portends successful trade, and to the young it signifies un-alloyed bliss and faithful loves.

Confectionery

To dream of impure confectionary denotes that an enemy in the guise of a friend will enter your privacy and discover secrets of moment to your opponents.

Confetti

To dream of confetti obstructing your view in a crowd of merry-makers denotes that you will lose much by first seeking enjoyment, and later fulfilling tasks set by duty.

Conflagration

To dream of a conflagration, denotes, if no lives are lost, changes in the future which will be beneficial to your interests and happiness. *See also* **Fire**.

Conjuror

To dream of a conjuror denotes unpleasant experience will beset you in your search for wealth and happiness.

Conscience

To dream that your conscience censures you for deceiving someone denotes that you will be tempted to commit wrong and should be constantly on your guard.

To dream of having a quiet conscience denotes that you will stand in high repute.

Conspiracy

To dream that you are the object of a conspiracy foretells that you will make a wrong move in the directing of your affairs.

Contempt

To dream of being in contempt of court denotes that you have committed business or social indiscretion and that it is unmerited.

To dream that you are held in contempt by others, you will succeed in winning their highest regard, and will find yourself prosperous and happy. But if the contempt is merited, your exile from business or social circles is intimated.

Convent

To dream of seeking refuge in a convent denotes that your future will be signally free from care and enemies, unless on entering the building you encounter a priest. If so, you will seek often and in vain for relief from worldly cares and mind worry.

For a young girl to dream of seeing a convent, her virtue and honestly will be questioned.

Convention

To dream of a convention denotes unusual activity in business affairs and final engagement in love. An inharmonious or displeasing convention brings you disappointment.

Convicts

To dream of seeing convicts denotes disasters and sad news. To dream that you are a convict indicates that you will worry over some affair; but you will clear up all mistakes.

For a young woman to dream of seeing her lover in the garb of a convict indicates that she will have cause to question the character of his love.

Cook

To cook a meal denotes that some pleasant duty will devolve on you. Many friends will visit you in the near future. If there is discord or a lack of cheerfulness you may expect harassing and disappointing events to happen.

Cooker

To see a cooker in a dream denotes that much unpleasantness will be modified by your timely interference. For a young woman to dream of using a cooker foretells she will be too hasty in showing her appreciation of the attention of some person and thereby may lose a closer friendship.

Copper

To dream of copper denotes oppression from those above you in station.

Copper Plate

Copper plate, seen in a dream, is a warning of discordant views causing unhappiness between members of the same household.

Coppersmith

To dream of a coppersmith denotes small returns for labour, but withal contentment.

Copying

To dream of copying denotes unfavourable workings of well-tried plans.

For a young woman to dream that she is copying a letter denotes that she will be prejudiced into error by her love for a certain class of people.

Coral

To dream of coral is momentous of enduring friendship which will know no weariness in alleviating your trouble. (Coloured coral is meant in this dream.)

White coral warns of unfaithfulness in love.

Cornet

A cornet seen or heard in a dream denotes kindly attentions from strangers.

Coronation

To dream of a coronation foretells that you will enjoy acquaintances and friendships with prominent people. For a young woman to be participating in a coronation foretells that she will come into some surprising favour with distinguished personages. But if the coronation presents disagreeable incoherence in her dreams, then she may expect unsatisfactory states growing out of anticipated pleasure.

Cords See Rope

Cork

To dream of drawing corks at a banquet signifies that you will soon enter a state of prosperity, in which you will revel in happiness of the most select kind.

To dream of medicine corks denotes sickness and wasted energies.

To dream of seeing a fishing cork resting on clear water denotes success. If the water is disturbed you will be annoyed by unprincipled persons.

To dream that you are corking bottles denotes a well-organized business and system in your living.

For a young woman to dream of drawing champagne corks indicates she will have a gay and handsome lover who will lavish much attention and money on her. She should look well to her reputation and listen to the warning of parents after this dream.

Corkscrew

To dream of seeing a corkscrew indicates an unsatisfied mind. The dreamer should heed this as a warning to curb his desires, for it is likely they are on dangerous grounds.

113

To dream of breaking a corkscrew while using it indicates perilous surroundings to the dreamer. He should use force of will to abandon unhealthful inclinations.

Corn and Corn Field

To dream of husking ears of corn denotes that you will enjoy varied success and pleasure. To see others gathering corn foretells you will rejoice in the prosperity of friends or relatives.

To dream of passing through a green and luxurious corn field, and seeing full ears hanging heavily, denotes great wealth for the farmer. It denotes fine crops and rich harvest and harmony in the home. To the young it promises much happiness and true friends, but to see the ears blasted denotes disappointments and bereavements.

To see young corn newly ploughed denotes favour with the powerful and coming success. To see it ripe denotes fame and wealth. To see it gathered in signifies that your highest desires will be realized.

To see shelled corn denotes wealthy combines and unstinted favours.

To dream of eating green corn denotes harmony among friends and happy unions for the young.

Corner

This is an unfavourable dream if the dreamer is frightened and secretes himself in a corner for safety.

To see persons talking in a corner, enemies are seeking to destroy you. The chances are that someone whom you consider a friend will prove a traitor to your interest.

Cornmeal

To see cornmeal foretells the consummation of ardent wishes. To eat it made into bread denotes that you will unwittingly throw obstructions in the way of your own advancement.

Corns

To dream that your corns hurt your feet denotes that some enemies are undermining you, and that you will have much distress; but if you succeed in clearing your feet of corns, you will inherit a large estate from some unknown source.

For a young woman to dream of having corns on her feet indicates that she will have to bear many crosses and be coldly treated by her sex.

Corpse

To dream of a corpse indicates sorrowful tidings and gloomy business prospects. The young will suffer many disappointments and pleasure will vanish.

To see a corpse placed in its coffin warns of immediate troubles to the dreamer.

To see a battlefield strewn with corpses indicates war and general dissatisfaction between countries and political factions.

To see the corpse of an animal denotes unhealthy situation, both as to business and health.

To put money on the eyes of a corpse in your dreams denotes that you will see unscrupulous enemies robbing you while you are powerless to resent injury. If you only put it on one eye you will be able to recover lost property after an almost hopeless struggle. For a young woman this dream denotes distress and loss by unfortunately giving her confidence to designing persons.

For a young woman to dream that the proprietor of the shop in which she works is a corpse, and she sees while sitting up with him that his face is clean-shaven, foretells that she will fall below the standard of perfection in which she was held by her lover. If she sees the head of the corpse falling from the body, she is warned of secret enemies who, in harming her, will also detract from the interest of her employer. Seeing the corpse in the shop foretells that loss and unpleasantness will offset all concerned. There are those who are not conscientiously doing the right thing. There will be a gloomy outlook for peace and prosperous work.

Corset

To dream of a corset denotes that you will be perplexed as to the meaning of attentions won by you. If a young woman is vexed over undoing or fastening her corset, she will be strongly inclined to quarrel with her friends under slight provocations.

Cossack

To dream of a Cossack denotes humiliation of a personal character, brought about by dissipation and wanton extravagance.

Cot

To dream of a cot warns of some affliction, either through sickness or accident. Cots in rows signify you will not be alone in trouble, as friends will be afflicted also.

Cotton

To dream of young growing cotton fields denotes great business and prosperous times. To see cotton ready for gathering denotes wealth and abundance for farmers.

For manufacturers to dream of cotton means that they will be benefited by the advancement of this article. For merchants, it denotes a change for the better in their line of business.

To see cotton in bales is a favourable indication for better times.

To dream that cotton is advancing denotes an immediate change from low to high prices, and all will be in better circumstances.

Cotton Cap

It is a good dream, denoting many sincere friends.

Cotton Cloth

To see cotton cloth in a dream denotes easy circumstances. No great changes follow this dream.

For a young woman to dream of weaving cotton cloth denotes that she will have a thrifty and enterprising husband. To the married it denotes a pleasant yet a humble abode.

Cotton Gin

To dream of a cotton gin foretells that you will make some advancement towards fortune which will be very pleasing and satisfactory. To see a broken or dilapidated gin signifies that misfortune and trouble will overthrow success.

Couch

To dream of reclining on a couch indicates that false hopes will be entertained. You should be alert to every change of your affairs, for only in this way will your hopes be realized.

Cough

To dream that you are aggravated by a constant cough indicates a state of low health, but one from which you will recuperate if care is observed in your habits.

To dream of hearing others cough indicates unpleasant surroundings from which you will ultimately emerge.

Council

To dream of a town council foretells that your interests will clash with public institutions and there will be discouraging outlooks for you.

Counsellor

To dream of a counsellor, you are likely to be possessed of some ability yourself, and you will usually prefer your own judgment to that of others. Be guarded in executing your ideas of right.

Countenance

To dream of a beautiful and ingenuous countenance, you may safely look for some pleasure to fall to your lot in the near future; but to behold an ugly and scowling visage portends unfavourable transactions.

Counter

To dream of counters foretells that active interest will debar idleness from infecting your life with unhealthy desires. To dream of empty and soiled counters foretells unfortunate engagements which will bring great uneasiness of mind lest your interest will be wholly swept away.

Counterfeit Money

To dream of counterfeit money warns that may have trouble with some unruly and worthless person. This dream always omens evil, whether you receive the money or pass it.

Counterpane

A counterpane is very good to dream of, if clean and white, denoting pleasant occupations for women; but if it be soiled you may expect harassing situations. Sickness often follow this dream.

Counting

To dream of counting your children, if they are merry and sweet-looking, denotes that you will have no trouble in controlling them, and that they will attain honourable places.

To dream of counting money, you will be lucky and always able to pay your debts; but to count out money to another person, you will meet with loss of some kind. Such will be the case, also, in counting other things. If for yourself, good; if for others, usually bad luck will attend you.

Country

To dream of being in a beautiful and fertile country, where abound rich fields of grain and running streams of pure water, denotes the very acme of good times is at hand. Wealth will pile in upon you, and you will be able to reign in state in any country. If the country is dry and bare, you will see and hear of troublous times. Famine and sickness will be in the land.

Courtship

The woman who dreams of being courted as will often think that now he will propose, but often she will be disappointed. Disappointments are likely to follow illusory hopes and fleeting pleasures.

For a man to dream of courting implies that he is not worthy of a companion.

Cousin

Dreaming of one's cousin denotes disappointments and afflictions. Saddened lives are predicted by this dream.

To dream of an affectionate correspondence with one's cousin warns of a rift between families.

Cows

To dream of seeing cows waiting for the milking hour promises abundant fulfilment of hopes and desires.

See also **Cattle**.

Cowslip

To dream of gathering cowslips warns of unhappy ending of seemingly close and warm friendships; but seeing them growing denotes a limited competency for lovers. This is a sinister dream.

To see them in full bloom denotes a crisis in your affairs. The breaking up of happy homes may follow this dream.

Crabs

To dream of crabs indicates that you will have many complicated affairs, for the solving of which you will be forced to exert the soundest judgment. This dream portends to lovers a long and difficult courtship.

Cradle

To dream of a cradle, with a beautiful infant occupying it, portends prosperity and the affections of beautiful children.

To rock your own baby in a cradle warns of illness in the family.

For a young woman to dream of rocking a cradle warns her to beware of gossiping.

To dream that you are in a cradle denotes that you need to face and purge your longing for your past before you can go on with your life.

Crane

To dream of seeing a flight of cranes heading north indicates gloomy prospects for business. To a woman, it is significant of disappointment; but to see them flying south prognosticates a joyful meeting of absent friends, and that lovers will remain faithful.

To see them fly to the ground, events of unusual moment are at hand.

Crawl

To dream that you are crawling on the ground, and have hurt your hand, you may expect humiliating tasks to be placed on you.

To crawl over rough places and stones indicates that you have not taken proper advantage of your opportunities. A young woman, after dreaming of crawling, if not very careful of her conduct, will lose the respect of her lover.

To crawl in a mire with others denotes depression in business and loss of credit. Your friends may have cause to censure you.

Crayfish

Deceit is likely to assail you in your affairs of the heart, if you are young, after dreaming of this backward-going thing.

Cream

To dream of seeing cream served denotes that you will be associated with wealth if you are engaged in business other than farming.

To the farmer, it indicates fine crops and pleasant family relations. To drink cream yourself denotes immediate good fortune. To lovers, this is a happy omen, as they will soon be united.

Credit

To dream of asking for credit denotes that you will have cause to worry, although you may be inclined sometimes to think things look bright.

To credit another warns you to be careful of your affairs, as you are likely to trust those who will eventually work you harm.

Creek

To dream of a creek denotes new experiences and short journeys. If it is overflowing, you will have sharp trouble, but of brief period.

If it is dry, disappointment will be felt by you, and you will see another obtain the things you intrigued to secure.

Crepe

To dream of seeing crepe hanging from a door denotes that you will hear of a sudden death.

To see a person dressed in crepe indicates that sorrow, other than death, will possess you. It is bad for business and trade. To the young, it implies lovers' disputes and separations.

Crew

To dream of seeing a crew getting ready to leave port, some unforeseen circumstance is likely to cause you to give up a journey from which you would have gained much.

To see a crew working to save a ship in a storm warns of disaster on land and sea. To the young, this dream bodes evil.

Cricket

To hear a cricket in one's dream indicates melancholy news.

To see them indicates hard struggles with poverty.

Cries

To hear cries of distress denotes that you will be engulfed in serious troubles, but by being alert you will finally emerge from these distressing straits and gain by this temporary gloom.

To hear a cry of surprise, you will receive aid from unexpected sources.

To hear the cries of wild beasts denotes an accident of a serious nature.

To hear a cry for help from relatives, or friends, denotes that they may be sick or in distress.

Criminal

To dream of associating with a person who has committed a crime denotes that you will be harassed by unscrupulous persons, who will try to use your friendship for their own advancement.

To see a criminal fleeing from justice denotes that you will come into the possession of the secrets of others, and will therefore be in danger, for they will fear that you will betray them, and consequently will seek your removal.

Crimson

To dream of crimson clothing foretells that you will escape formidable enemies by a timely change in your expressed intention.

For a young woman to dream that she meets another young woman attired in a crimson dress, with a crepe mourning veil on her face, warns that she may be outrivalled by someone she hardly considers her equal, and that the experience may cause her to become embittered towards other women.

Crochet Work

To dream of doing crochet work foretells your entanglement in some silly affair growing out of a too great curiosity about other people's business. Beware of talking too frankly with over-confidential women.

Crockery

To dream of having an abundance of nice, clean crockery denotes that you will be a tidy and economical housekeeper.

To be in a crockery shop indicates, if you are a merchant or business person, that you will look well to the details of your business and thereby experience profit. To a young woman, this dream denotes that she will marry a sturdy and upright man. An untidy shop, with empty shelves, implies loss.

Crocodile

To dream of this creature warns that you may be deceived by friends. Enemies will assail you at every turn. It is also a warning to you to seek out those people whom you feel to be malign destroyers of your personality.

To dream of stepping on a crocodile's back, you may expect to fall into trouble, from which you will have to struggle mightily to extricate yourself. Heed this warning when dreams of this nature visit you. Avoid giving your confidence even to friends.

See also **Alligator**.

Cross

To dream of seeing a cross indicates trouble ahead for you. Shape your affairs accordingly.

To dream of seeing a person bearing a cross, you will be called on by missionaries to aid in charities.

Crossbones

To dream of a crossbones foretells that you will be troubled by the evil influence of others, and prosperity will assume other than promising aspects.

To see a crossbones as a monogram on an invitation to a funeral, which was sent out by a secret order, denotes that unnecessary fears will be entertained for some person, and events will transpire seemingly harsh, but of good import to the dreamer.

Crossroads

To dream of a crossroads always signifies that something highly important will take place in your life.

If you are undecided which road to take, you are likely to let unimportant matters irritate you in a distressing manner. You will be better favoured by fortune if you decide on your route. It may be that after this dream you will have some important matter of business or love to decide.

Croup

To dream that your child has the croup denotes slight illness, but useless fear for its safety. This is generally a good omen of health and domestic harmony.

Crow

To dream of a crow presages the coming of news; this maybe of death and disaster, or equally may be excellent tidings. To hear crows cawing, you will be influenced by others to make a bad disposal of property. To a young man, it is indicative of his succumbing to the wiles of designing women.

Crowd

To dream of a large, handsomely dressed crowd of people at some entertainment denotes pleasant association with friends; but anything occurring to mar the pleasure of the guests denotes distress and loss of friendship, and unhappiness will be found where profit and congenial intercourse was expected. It also denotes dissatisfaction in government and family dissensions.

To see a crowd in a church denotes that a death will be likely to affect you, or some slight unpleasantness may develop.

To see a crowd in the street indicates unusual briskness in trade and a general air of prosperity will surround you.

To try to be heard in a crowd foretells that you will push your interests ahead of all others.

To see a crowd is usually good, if too many are not wearing black or dull costumes.

Crown

To dream of a crown prognosticates a change in the habit of one's life. The dreamer will travel a long distance from home and form new relations. Serious illness may also be the sad omen of this dream.

To dream that you wear a crown may signify loss of personal property.

To dream of crowning a person denotes your own worthiness.

To dream of talking with the President of the United States denotes that you are interested in affairs of state, and sometimes show a great longing to be a politician.

Crucifix

To see a crucifix in a dream is a warning of distress approaching, which will involve others beside yourself. To kiss one foretells that trouble will be accepted by you with resignation.

For a young woman to possess one foretells she will observe modesty and kindness in her deportment, and thus win the love of others and better her fortune.

Crucifixion

If you chance to dream of the crucifixion, you risk seeing your opportunities slip away, tearing your hopes from your grasp, and leaving you wailing over the frustration of desires.

Cruelty

To dream of cruelty being shown to you foretells you may have trouble and disappointment in some dealings. If it is shown to others, there will be a disagreeable task set for others by you, which may contribute to your own loss.

Crust

To dream of a crust of bread warns of incompetence, and threatened misery through carelessness in appointed duties.

Crutches

To dream that you go on crutches denotes that you are likely to depend largely on others for your support and advancement.

To see others on crutches denotes unsatisfactory results from labours.

Crying

To dream of crying is a forerunner of illusory pleasures, which will subside into gloom, and distressing influences having a bad effect on business engagements and domestic affairs.

To see others crying forbodes unexpected calls for aid from you.

See also **Tears, Weeping**.

Crystal

To dream of crystal in any form is a sign of coming depression either in social relations or business transactions. Electrical storms often attend this dream, doing damage to town and country.

For a woman to dream of seeing a dining-room furnished in crystal, even to the chairs, she will have cause to believe that those whom she holds in high regard no longer deserve this distinction, but she will find out that there were others in the crystal-furnished room, who were implicated also in this dream.

Cuckoo

This dream often denotes the dreamer's feelings of guilt and inferiority.

To dream of a cuckoo, warns of the downfall of a dear friend.

To dream that you hear a cuckoo presages the illness of some absent loved one, or an accident to someone in your family.

Cucumber

This is a dream of plenty, denoting health and prosperity. For the sick to dream of serving cucumbers denotes their speedy recovery. For the married, a pleasant change.

Cuff-links

To dream of cuff-links foretells that you will struggle to humour your pride, and will usually be successful. If they are diamonds, you will enjoy wealth, or have an easy time, surrounded by congenial friends.

Cunning

To dream of being cunning denotes that you will assume happy cheerfulness to retain the friendship of prosperous and amusing people. If you are associating with cunning people, it warns you that deceit is being practised upon you in order to use your means for their own advancement.

Cup

Dreams of cups evoke truth and love. If the cup is full, it signifies fulfilment; if empty and the dreamer is thirsty, an emptiness in the dreamer's emotional life.

Cupboard

To see a cupboard in your dream is significant of pleasure and comfort, or penury and distress, depending on whether the cupboard is clean and full of shining ware, or empty and dirty.

Dreaming that you are locked in a cupboard indicates that you feel stifled by a family member, or imprisoned by your own emotions or anxieties.

Currycomb

To dream of a currycomb foretells that great labours must be endured in order to obtain wealth and comfort.

Currycombing a Horse

To dream of currycombing a horse signifies that you will have a great many hard licks to make both with brain and hand before you attain to the heights of your ambition; but if you successfully currycomb him you will attain that height, whatever it may be.

This dream denotes that you will not neglect your business interests for frivolous pleasures.

Curtains

To dream of curtains warns that unwelcome visitors may cause you worry and unhappiness. Soiled or torn curtains seen in a dream means disgraceful quarrels and reproaches.

Cushion

To dream of reclining on silken cushions foretells that your ease will be procured at the expense of others; but to see the cushions denotes that you will prosper in business and love-making.

For a young woman to dream of making silken cushions implies that she will be a bride before many months.

Custard

For a married woman to dream of making or eating custard indicates she will be called upon to entertain an unexpected guest. A young woman will meet a stranger who will in time become a warm friend. If the custard has a sickening sweet taste, or is insipid, sorrow will intervene where you had expected a pleasant experience.

Custom House

To dream of a custom house denotes that you will have rivalries and competition in your labours.

To enter a custom house foretells that you will strive for, or have offered to you, a position which you have long desired.

To leave one signifies loss of position or trade, or failure of securing some desired object.

Cut

To dream of a cut denotes sickness, or that the treachery of a friend will frustrate your cheerfulness.

Cymbal

Hearing a cymbal in your dreams warns of the death of a very aged person of your acquaintance.

D

'God came to Laban, the Syrian, by night, in a dream, and said unto him, take heed that thou speak not to Jacob, either good or bad.'
—Genesis xxxi, 24.

Dagger

If seen in a dream, denotes threatening enemies. If you wrench the dagger from the hand of another, it denotes that you will be able to counteract the influence of your enemies and overcome misfortune.

To dream of someone stabbing you with a dagger warns that secret enemies may cause you uneasiness of mind.

If you attack any person with one of these weapons, you will unfortunately suspect your friends of unfaithfulness.

Dreaming of daggers, generally, omens bad luck.

Dahlia

To see dahlias in a dream, if they are fresh and bright, signifies good fortune to the dreamer.

Dairy

Dairy is a good dream to everyone.

Daisy

To dream of a bunch of daisies implies sadness, but if you dream of being in a field where these lovely flowers are in bloom, with the sun shining and birds singing, happiness, health and prosperity will vie each with the other to lead you through the pleasantest avenues of life.

To dream of seeing them out of season, you risk being assailed by evil in some guise.

Damson

This is a peculiarly good dream if one is so fortunate as to see these trees lifting their branches loaded with rich purple fruit and dainty foliage; one may expect riches compared with his present estate.

To dream of eating them at any time forebodes grief.

Dance

Dreams of dancing are always important.

To dream of seeing a crowd of merry children dancing, signifies to the married, loving, obedient and intelligent children and a cheerful and comfortable home. To young people, it denotes easy tasks and many pleasures.

To see older people dancing denotes a brighter outlook for business.

To dream of dancing yourself, some unexpected good fortune will come to you.

Dancing Master

To dream of a dancing master foretells that you will neglect important affairs to pursue frivolities. For a young woman to dream that her lover is a dancing master portends that she will have a friend in accordance with her views of pleasure and life.

Dandelion

Dandelions blossoming in green foliage foretell happy unions and prosperous surroundings.

Danger

To dream of being in a perilous situation, with death seeming iminent, denotes that you will emerge from obscurity into places of distinction and honour; but if you should not escape the impending danger, and suffer death or a wound, you are likely to lose in business and be annoyed in your home, and by others. If you are in love, your prospects will grow discouraging.

Darkness

To dream of darkness overtaking you on a journey augurs ill for any work you may attempt, unless the sun breaks through before the journey ends, in which case faults will be overcome.

To lose your friend, or child, in the darkness, portends many provocations to wrath. Try to remain under control after dreaming of darkness, for trials in business and love will beset you.

Dates

To dream of seeing them on their parent trees signifies prosperity and happy union; but to eat them as prepared for commerce, they are omens of want and distress.

Daughter

To dream of your daughter signifies that many displeasing incidents will give way to pleasure and harmony. If in the dream, she fails to meet your wishes, through any cause, you will suffer vexation and discontent.

Daughter-in-law

To dream of your daughter-in-law indicates that some unusual occurence will add to happiness, or disquiet, depending on whether she is pleasant or unreasonable.

David

To dream of David, of Bible fame, denotes divisions in domestic circles, and unsettled affairs, which may cause you a great deal of stress.

Day

To dream of the day denotes improvement in your situation, and pleasant associations. A gloomy or cloudy day warns of loss and ill success in new enterprises.

Daybreak

To watch the day break in a dream omens successful undertakings, unless the scene is indistinct and weird; then it may imply disappointment when success in business or love seems assured.

Dead

To dream of the dead is usually a dream of warning. To dream of a departed sibling, or other relatives or friends, denotes that you may be called on for charity or aid within a short time.

To dream of seeing the dead, living and happy, signifies you are letting wrong influences into your life, which will bring material loss if not corrected by the assumption of your own will force.

To dream that you are conversing with a dead relative, and that relative endeavours to extract a promise from you, warns you of coming distress, unless you follow the advice given you. Disastrous consequences could often be averted if minds could grasp the inner workings and sight of the higher or spiritual self. The voice of relatives is only that higher self taking form to approach more distinctly the mind that lives near the material plane. There is so little congeniality between common or material natures that persons should depend upon their own subjectivity for true contentment and pleasure.

Deadly Nightshade

Strategic moves will bring success in commercial circles. Women will find rivals in society; vain and fruitless efforts will be made for places in men's affections.

Taking it denotes misery and failure to meet past debts.

Death

To dream of seeing any of your people dead warns of coming dissolution or sorrow. Disappointments always follow dreams of this nature.

To hear of any friend or relative being dead, you are soon likely to have bad news from some of them.

Dreams relating to death or dying, unless they are due to spiritual causes, are misleading and very confusing to the novice in dream lore when he attempts to interpret them. A person who thinks intensely fills his aura with thought or subjective images active with the passions that gave them birth; by thinking and acting on other lines, he may supplant these images with others possessed of a different form and nature. In his dreams he may see these images dying, dead or their burial, and mistake them for friends or enemies. In this way he may, while asleep, see himself or a relative die, when in reality he has been warned that some good thought or deed is to be supplanted by an evil one. To illustrate: if it is a dear friend or relative whom he sees in the agony of death, he is warned against immoral or other improper thought and action, but if it is an enemy or some repulsive object dismantled in death, he may overcome his evil ways and thus give himself or friends cause for joy. Often the end or beginning of suspense or trials are foretold by dreams of this nature. They also frequently occur when the dreamer is controlled by imaginary states of evil or good. A person in that state is not himself, but is what the dominating influences make him. He may be warned of approaching conditions or his extrication from the same. In our dreams we are closer to our real self than in waking life. The hideous or pleasing incidents seen and heard about us in our dreams are all of our own making, they reflect the true state of our soul and body, and we cannot flee from them unless we drive them out of our being by the use of good thoughts and deeds.

Dreaming of death is rarely predictive and more often than not will signify an exciting or necessary change, sometimes of a deeply psychological nature. Recurrent dreams about death may well signal a need for the dreamer's conscious mind to try to accept what is inevitable.

See also **Dying**.

Debt

Debt is rather a bad dream, foretelling worries in business and love, and struggles for an income; but if you have plenty to meet all your obligations, your affairs will assume a favourable turn.

December

To dream of December foretells accumulation of wealth, but loss of friendship. Strangers will occupy the position in the affections of some friend which was formerly held by you.

Deck

To dream of being on a ship and that a storm is raging you risk meeting with great disasters and unfortunate alliances, but if the sea is calm and the light distinct, your way is clear to success. For lovers, this dream augurs happiness.

Decorate

To dream of decorating a place with bright-hued flowers for some festive occasion is significant of favourable turns in business and, to the young, of continued rounds of social pleasures and fruitful study.

To see the graves or caskets of the dead decorated with white flowers is unfavourable to pleasure and worldly pursuits.

To be decorating, or see others decorate for some heroic action, foretells that you will be worthy, but that few will recognize your ability.

Deed

To dream of seeing or signing deeds portends a lawsuit, to gain which you should be careful in selecting your counsel, as you are likely to be the loser. To dream of signing any kind of a paper is a bad omen for the dreamer.

Deer

This is a favourable dream, denoting pure and deep friendships for the young and a quiet and even life for the married.

To kill a deer denotes that you will be hounded by enemies. For farmers, or businesspeople, to dream of hunting deer warns of failure in their respective pursuits.

See also **Fawn, Stag**.

Delay

To be delayed in a dream warns you of the scheming of enemies to prevent your progress.

Delight

To dream of experiencing delight over any event signifies a favourable turn in affairs. For lovers to be delighted with the conduct of their sweethearts denotes pleasant greetings.

To feel delight when looking on beautiful landscapes prognosticates to the dreamer very great success and congenial associations.

Demand

To dream that a demand for charity comes in upon you denotes that you will be placed in embarrassing situations, but that by your persistence you will fully restore your good standing. If the demand is unjust, you will become a leader in your profession. For a lover to make unhelpful demands implies his, or her, leniency.

Dentist

To dream of a dentist working on your teeth denotes that you will have occasion to doubt the sincerity and honour of some person with whom you have dealings.

To see him at work on a young woman's teeth denotes that you will soon be shocked by a scandal in circles near you.

Department Store

To dream of finding yourself in a department store foretells that much pleasure will be derived from various sources of profit.

To sell goods in one, your advancement will be accelerated by your energy and the efforts of friends.

See also Shop.

Departure

To dream of someone going away indicates a fear of being abandoned by that person.

To dream of oneself going away suggests a desire to leave someone or something.

Derrick

Derricks seen in a dream indicate strife and obstruction in your way to success.

Desert

To dream of wandering through a gloomy and barren desert warns of uprisings, and great loss of life and property.

For a young woman to find herself alone in a desert, her health and reputation is being jeopardized by her indiscretion. She should be more cautious.

Desk

To be using a desk in a dream denotes that unforeseen ill luck will rise before you. To see money on your desk brings you unexpected extrication from private difficulties.

Despair

To be in despair in dreams denotes that you are likely to have many and cruel vexations in the working world.

To see others in despair, foretells the distress and unhappy position of some relative or friend.

Detective

To dream of a detective keeping in your wake when you are innocent of charges preferred denotes that fortune and honour are drawing nearer to you each day; but if you feel yourself guilty, you are likely to find your reputation at stake, and friends will turn from you. For a young woman, this is not a fortunate dream.

Devil

For farmers to dream of the devil warns him to take particular care of his crops and livestock. Sporting people should heed this dream as a warning to be careful of their affairs, as they are likely to venture beyond the laws of their state. For a preacher, this dream is undeniable proof that he is over-zealous, and should forebear worshiping God by tongue-lashing his neighbour.

To dream of the devil as being a large, imposingly dressed person, wearing many sparkling jewels on his body and hands, trying to persuade you to enter his abode, warns you that unscrupulous persons are seeking your ruin by the most ingenious flattery. Young and innocent women should seek the stronghold of friends after this dream, and avoid strange attentions, especially from married men. Women of low character are likely to be robbed of jewels and money by seeming strangers.

Beware of associating with the devil, even in dreams. He is always the forerunner of despair. If you dream of being pursued by his majesty, you will fall into snares set for you by enemies in the guise of friends. To a lover, this denotes that he will be won away from his allegiance by a wanton.

See also **Satan**.

Devotion

For a farmer to dream of showing his devotion to God, or to his family, denotes plenteous crops and peaceful neighbours. To business-people, this is a warning that nothing is to be gained by deceit.

For a young woman to dream of being devout implies her chastity and an adoring husband.

Dew

To feel the dew falling on you in your dreams warns that you may be attacked by fever; but to see the dew sparkling through the grass in the sunlight, great honours and wealth are about to be heaped upon you. If you are single, a wealthy marriage will soon be your portion.

Diadem

To dream of a diadem denotes that some honour will be tendered you for acceptance.

Diamonds

To dream of owning diamonds is a very propitious dream, signifying great honour and recognition from high places.

To dream of burying a diamond in your garden is a warning that you are wasting your potential.

For a young woman to dream of her lover presenting her with diamonds foreshows that she will make a great and honourable marriage, which will fill her people with honest pride; but to lose diamonds, and not find them again, is the most unlucky of dreams, foretelling disgrace and want.

For a sporting woman to dream of diamonds, foretells for her many prosperous days and magnificent presents. For a speculator, it denotes prosperous transactions. To dream of owning diamonds portends the same for sporting men or women.

Diamonds are omens of good luck, unless stolen from the bodies of dead persons, when they foretell that your own unfaithfulness will be discovered by your friends.

Dice

To dream of dice is indicative of unfortunate speculations, and consequent misery and despair. It also warns of contagious illness.

For a girl to dream that she sees her lover throwing dice indicates his unworthiness.

Dictionary

To dream that you are referring to a dictionary signifies you will depend too much upon the opinion and suggestions of others for the clear management of your own affairs, which could be done with proper dispatch if your own will was given play.

Difficulty

This dream signifies temporary embarrassment for business men of all classes, including soldiers and writers. But to extricate yourself from difficulties foretells your prosperity.

For a woman to dream of being in difficulties denotes that she is threatened with ill health or enemies. For lovers, this is a dream of contrariety, denoting pleasant courtship.

Digging

Dreams of digging often symbolize a search for the truth, or for an answer to some difficulty in waking life; alternatively, the dreamer may be trying to hide something or is burying aspects of himself which he considers undesirable.

To dream of digging denotes that you will never be in want, but life will be an uphill affair.

To dig a hole and find any glittering substance, denotes a favourable turn in fortune; but to dig and open up a vast area of hollow mist, you will be harrassed with real misfortunes and be filled with gloomy forebodings. Water filling the hole that you dig denotes that in spite of your most strenuous efforts things will not bend to your will.

Dinner

To dream that you eat your dinner alone denotes that you will often have cause to think seriously of the necessities of life.

For a young woman to dream of taking dinner with her lover is indicative of a lovers' quarrel or a rupture, unless the affair is one of harmonious pleasure, when the reverse may be expected.

To be one of many invited guests at a dinner denotes that you will enjoy the hospitalities of those who are able to extend to you many pleasant courtesies.

Dirt

To see your clothes soiled with unclean dirt, you will be forced to save yourself from contagious diseases by leaving your home or submitting to the strictures of the law.

To dream that someone throws dirt upon you denotes that enemies will try to injure your character.

Disaster

Dreams of disaster are so frequent that they can only be really understood by careful examination of their context. Often they are a sign of the dreamer's anxiety and fear of powerlessness. Such dreams must never be ignored; they can precede a state of depression.

To dream of being in any disaster from public conveyance, you are in danger of losing property or of becoming ill.

For a young woman to dream of a disaster in which she is a participant, warns of the loss of her lover.

To dream of a disaster at sea denotes unhappiness to sailors and loss of their gains. To others, it signifies loss; but if you dream that you are rescued, you will be placed in trying situations, but will come out unscathed.

Disease

To dream that you are have a disease denotes a slight attack of illness, or of unpleasant dealings with a relative.

For a young woman to dream that she has a life-threatening disease denotes that she will be likely to lead a life of single blessedness. *See also Illness, Sickness.*

Disgrace

To be worried in your dream over the disgraceful conduct of children or friends warns that unsatisfying hopes, and worries will harass you. To be in disgrace yourself denotes that you will hold morality at a low rate, and you are in danger of lowering your reputation for uprightness. Enemies are also shadowing you.

Dish

To dream of handling dishes denotes good fortune; but if from any cause they should be broken, this warns that fortune will be short-lived for you.

To see shelves of polished dishes denotes success in marriage.

To dream of dishes is prognostic of coming success and gain, and you will be able to fully appreciate your good luck. Soiled dishes represent dissatisfaction and an unpromising future.

Disinherited

To dream that you are disinherited warns you to look well to your business and social standing.

For a young man to dream of losing his inheritance by disobedience warns him that he will find favour in the eyes of his parents by contracting a suitable marriage. For a woman, this dream is a warning to be careful of her conduct, lest she meet with unfavourable fortune.

Dispute

To dream of holding disputes over trifles warns of bad health and unfairness in judging others.

To dream of disputing with learned people shows that you have some latent ability, but are a little sluggish in developing it.

Distaff

To dream of a distaff denotes frugality, with pleasant surroundings. It also signifies that a devotional spirit will be cultivated by you.

Distance

To dream of being a long way from your residence denotes that you will make a journey soon on which you may meet many strangers who will be instrumental in changing life from good to bad.

To dream of friends at a distance denotes slight disappointments.

To dream of distance signifies travel and a long journey. To see men ploughing with oxen at a distance, across broad fields, denotes advancing prosperity and honour. For a man to see strange women in the twilight, at a distance, and throwing kisses to him, foretells that he will enter into an engagement with a new acquaintance, which is likely to result in unhappiness.

Ditch

To dream of falling in a ditch warns of degradation and personal loss; but if you jump over it, you will live down any suspicion of wrongdoing.

Dividend

To dream of dividends augments successful speculations or prosperous harvests. To fail in securing hoped-for dividends proclaims failure in management or love affairs.

Diving

To dream of diving in clear water denotes a favourable termination of some embarrassment. If the water is muddy, you will suffer anxiety at the turn your affairs seem to be taking.

To see others diving indicates pleasant companions. For lovers to dream of diving denotes the consummation of happy dreams and passionate love.

Divining Rods

To see a divining rod in your dreams warns that ill luck will dissatisfy you with unpresent surroundings.

Divorce

To dream of being divorced denotes that you are not satisfied with your companion, and should cultivate a more congenial atmosphere in the home life. It is a dream of warning. Dreams of divorce could also suggest that you are trying to remove yourself from an unfulfilling part of your life, or to cut yourself off from a problem or a person with whom you no longer feel an affinity.

For women to dream of divorce denotes that a single life may be theirs through the infidelity of lovers.

Docks

To dream of being on docks denotes that you are about to make an unpropitious journey. Accidents will threaten you. If you are there, wandering alone, and darkness overtakes you, you will meet enemies, but if the sun is shining, you will escape threatening dangers.

Doctor

A most auspicious dream, denoting good health and general prosperity, is to meet a doctor socially. If you are young and engaged to marry him, then this dream warns you of deceit.

To dream of a doctor professionally signifies discouraging illness and disagreeable differences between members of a family.

To dream that a doctor makes an incision in your flesh, trying to discover blood, but failing in his efforts, denotes that an enemy may try to make you pay out money for his debts. If he finds blood, you are likely to be the loser in some transaction.

For a young woman to dream of a doctor warns that she is wasting her time in frivolous pursuits. If she is ill when she has this dream, she will experience illness and worry but will soon overcome them.

Dogs

Dreams of dogs indicate fidelity at all costs and companionship extending even beyond the grave.

To dream of a vicious dog warns of enemies and misfortune. To dream that a dog fondles you indicates great gain and constant friends.

To dream of owning a dog with fine qualities denotes that you will be possessed of solid wealth.

To dream of small dogs indicates that your thoughts and chief pleasures are of a frivolous order.

To dream of dogs biting you foretells for you a quarrelsome companion either in marriage or business.

Lean, filthy dogs indicate failure in business.

To dream of a dog show is indicative of many and varied favours from fortune.

To hear the barking of dogs foretells news of a depressing nature. Difficulties are more than likely to follow. To see dogs on the chase of foxes, and other large game, denotes an unusual briskness in all affairs.

To see fancy pet dogs signifies a love of show. For a young woman, this dream foretells a fop for a sweetheart.

To hear the growling and snarling of dogs indicates that you are at the mercy of scheming people, and you may be afflicted with unpleasant home surroundings.

To hear the lonely baying of a dog foretells a long separation from friends.

To hear dogs growling and fighting portends that you risk being overcome by your enemies.

To see dogs and cats seemingly on friendly terms, and suddenly turning on each other, showing their teeth and a general fight ensuing, you will meet with disaster in love and worldly pursuits, unless you succeed in quelling the row.

If you dream of a friendly white dog approaching you, it portends for you a victorious engagement whether in business or love. For a woman, this is an omen of an early marriage.

To dream of a many-headed dog, you are trying to maintain too many branches of business at one time. Success always comes with concentration of energies. Someone who wishes to succeed in anything should be warned by this dream.

To dream of a mad dog, your most strenuous efforts will not bring desired results, and fatal disease may be clutching at your vitals. If a mad dog succeeds in biting you, it is a sign that you or some loved one is suffering from emotional problems or stress.

To dream of travelling alone, with a dog following you, foretells stanch friends and successful undertakings.

To dream of dogs swimming indicates for you an easy stretch to happiness and fortune.

See also **Bloodhound, Bulldog, Hounds, Lap Dog, Mad Dog, Mastiff, Puppy.**

Dolphin

To dream of a dolphin indicates your liability to come under a new government. It is not a very good dream.

See also **Porpoise.**

Dome

To dream that you are in the dome of a building, viewing a strange landscape, signifies a favourable change in your life. You will occupy honourable places among strangers.

To behold a dome from a distance portends that you will never reach the height of your ambition; if you are in love, the object of your desires may scorn your attention.

Dominoes

To dream of playing at dominoes, and losing, you will be affronted by a friend, and much uneasiness for your safety will be entertained by your people, as you will not be discreet in your emotional affairs or other matters that engage your attention.

If you are the winner of the game, it foretells that you will be much courted and admired by certain dissolute characters, bringing you selfish pleasures, but much distress to your relatives.

Donkey

To see a donkey in a dream warns that you will meet many annoyances, and delays will accrue in receiving news or goods.

To see donkeys carrying burdens denotes that, after patience and toil, you will succeed in your undertakings, whether of travel or love.

If a donkey pursues you and you are afraid of it, you risk being the victim of scandal or other displeasing reports.

If you unwillingly ride on a donkey, unnecessary quarrels may follow.

Hearing a donkey bray is significant of unwelcome tidings or intrusions.

To dream of a donkey braying in your face denotes that you are about to be publicly insulted by a lewd and unscrupulous person.

To hear the distant braying filling space with melancholy, you will receive wealth and release from unpleasant bonds by a death.

If you see yourself riding on a donkey, you will visit foreign lands and make many explorations into places difficult of passage.

To see others riding donkeys denotes a meagre inheritance for them and a toiling life.

To drive a donkey signifies that all your energies and pluck will be brought into play against a desperate effort on the part of enemies to overthrow you. If you are in love, evil women may cause you trouble.

If you are kicked by this little animal, it shows that you are carrying on illicit connections, from which you will suffer much anxiety from fear of betrayal.

If you lead one by a halter, you will be master of every situation, and lead women into your way of seeing things by flattery.

To see children riding and driving donkeys signifies health and obedience for them.

To fall or be thrown from one denotes ill luck and disappointment in secular affairs. Lovers are likely to quarrel and separate.

To see one dead denotes satiated appetites, resulting from licentious excesses.

To dream of drinking the milk of a donkey denotes that whimsical desires will be gratified, even to the displacement of important duties.

If you see in your dreams a strange donkey among your stock, or on your premises, you will inherit some valuable effects.

To dream of coming into the possession of a donkey as a present, or purchase, you will attain to enviable heights in the business or social world and, if single, will contract a congenial marriage.

To dream of a white donkey denotes an assured and lasting fortune, which will enable you to pursue the pleasures or studies that lie nearest your heart. For a woman, it signals entrance into that society for which she has long entertained the most ardent desire.

Doomsday

To dream that you are living on, and looking forward to seeing doomsday, is a warning for you to give substantial and material affairs close attention, or you will find that the artful and scheming friends you are entertaining will have possession of what they desire from you, which is your wealth, and not your sentimentality.

To a young woman, this dream encourages her to throw aside the attention of men above her in station and accept the love of an honest and deserving man near her.

Door

To dream of entering a door warns of slander, and enemies from whom you are trying in vain to escape. This is the same of any door, except the door of your childhood home. If it is this door you dream of entering, your days will be filled with plenty and congeniality.

To dream of entering a door at night through the rain denotes, to women, unpardonable escapades; to a man, it is significant of a drawing on his resources by unwarranted vice, and also foretells assignations.

To see others go through a doorway denotes unsuccessful attempts to get your affairs into a paying condition. It also means changes to farmers and the political world. To an author, it foretells that the reading public will reprove his way of stating facts by refusing to read his later works.

To dream that you attempt to close a door, and it falls from its hinges, injuring someone, denotes that evil threatens a friend through your unintentionally wrong advice. If you see another attempt to lock a door, and it falls from its hinges, you will have knowledge of some friend's misfortune and be powerless to aid him.

Doorbell

To dream you hear or ring a doorbell foretells unexpected tidings, or a hasty summons to business, or the bedside of a sick relative.

Doves

Dreaming of doves mating and building their nests indicates peacefulness of the world and joyous homes where children render obedience and mercy is extended to all.

To hear the lonely, mournful voice of a dove portends sorrow and disappointment through the death of one to whom you looked for aid.

To see a dead dove is ominous of a separation of husband and wife.

To see white doves denotes bountiful harvests and the utmost confidence in the loyalty of friends.

To dream of seeing a flock of white doves denotes peaceful, innocent pleasures, and fortunate developments in the future.

If one brings you a letter, tidings of a pleasant nature from absent friends is intimated, also a lovers' reconciliation is denoted.

If the dove seems exhausted, a note of sadness will pervade the reconciliation, or a sad touch may be given the pleasant tidings by mention of an invalid friend; if of business, a slight drop may follow. If the letter bears the message that you are doomed, it foretells that illness, either your own or of a relative, may cause you financial misfortune.

Dowry

To dream that you fail to receive a dowry signifies penury and a cold world to depend on for a living. If you receive it, your expectations for the day will be fulfilled.

Dragon

To dream of a dragon denotes that you allow yourself to be governed by your passions, and that you are likely to place yourself in the power of your enemies through those outbursts of sardonic tendencies. You should be warned by this dream to cultivate self-control.

Drama

To see a drama signifies pleasant reunions with distant friends.

To be bored with the performance of a drama, you will be forced to accept an uncongenial companion at some entertainment or secret affair.

To write one portends that you will be plunged into distress and debt, to be extricated as if by a miracle.

Draughts

To dream of playing draughts, you will be involved in difficulties of a serious character, and strange people will come into your life, working you harm.

To dream that you win the game, you will succeed in some doubtful enterprise.

Dressing

To think you are having trouble in dressing, while dreaming, warns that some evil persons will worry and detain you from places of amusement.

If you can't get dressed in time for a train, you will have many annoyances through the carelessness of others. You should depend on your own efforts as far as possible, after these dreams, if you would secure contentment and full success.

Drinking

To be given to drinking alcohol in your dreams omens ill-natured rivalry and contention for small possessions. To think that you have quit drinking alcohol, or to find that others have done so, shows that you will rise above present adversity and rejoice in prosperity.

For a woman to dream of hilarious drinking denotes that she is engaging in affairs which may work to her discredit, though she may now find much pleasure in the same. If she dreams that she fails to drink clear water, though she uses her best efforts to do so, she will fail to enjoy some pleasure that is insinuatingly offered her.

Drinks Machine

To dream of standing at a drinks machine foretells pleasure and profit after many exasperating experiences.

To buy drinks from a drinks machine for yourself and others, you will be rewarded in your efforts although the outlook appears full of contradictions. Both inharmonious conditions and desired results will be forthcoming.

Driving

To dream of driving a carriage signifies unjust criticism of your seeming extravagance. You may be compelled to do things which appear undignified.

To dream of driving a taxi denotes menial labour, with little chance for advancement. If it is a wagon, you may remain in poverty and unfortunate circumstances for some time. If you are driven in these conveyances by others, you will profit by superior knowledge of the world, and will always find some path through difficulties. If you are a man, you will, in affairs with women, drive your wishes to a speedy consummation. If a woman, you will hold men's hearts at low value after succeeding in getting a hold on them.

Dromedary

To dream of a dromedary denotes that you will be the recipient of unexpected beneficence, and will wear your new honours with dignity; you will dispense charity with a gracious hand. To lovers, this dream foretells congenial dispositions.

*See also **Camels***.

Drought

This is an evil dream, denoting warring disputes between nations and much bloodshed therefrom. Shipwrecks and land disasters are likely to occur, and families may quarrel and separate. Sickness may work damage also. Your affairs are likely to go awry.

Drowning

To dream of drowning warns of loss; but if you are rescued, you will rise from your present position to one of wealth and honour.

To see others drowning, and you go to their relief, signifies that you will aid your friend to high places, and will bring deserved happiness to yourself.

Drowning dreams are common and generally indicate that the dreamer is overwhelmed by mundane problems in waking life.

Drum

To hear the muffled beating of a drum denotes that some absent friend is in distress and calls on you for aid.

To see a drum foretells amiability of character and a great aversion to quarrels and dissensions. It is an omen of prosperity to the sailor, the farmer and the trade alike.

Drunk

This is an unfavourable dream if you are drunk on heavy liquors, indicating profligacy and loss of employment. You may even be disgraced by stooping to forgery or theft. This dream urges caution.

If drunk on wine, you will be fortunate in trade and lovemaking, and will scale exalted heights in literary pursuits. This dream is always the bearer of æsthetic experiences.

To see others in a drunken condition foretells for you, and probably others, unhappy states.

Drunkenness in all forms is unreliable as a good dream. All classes are warned by this dream to shift their thoughts into more salubrious channels.

See also **Intoxication, Tipsy**.

Ducks

To dream of seeing wild ducks on a clear stream of water signifies fortunate journeys, perhaps across the sea. White ducks around a farm indicate thrift and a fine harvest.

To hunt ducks denotes displacement in employment and in the carrying out of plans.

To see them shot warns that enemies are meddling with your private affairs.

To see them flying foretells a brighter future for you. It also denotes marriage, and children in the new home.

Duet

To dream of hearing a duet played denotes a peaceful and even existence for lovers. No quarrels, as is customary in this sort of thing. Businesspeople carry on a mild rivalry. To musical people, this denotes competition and wrangling for superiority.

To hear a duet sung warns unpleasant tidings from an absent person; but this will not last, as some new pleasure will displace the unpleasantness.

Dulcimer

To dream of a dulcimer denotes that the highest wishes in life will be attained by exalted qualities of mind. To women, this is significant of a life free from those petty jealousies which usually make women unhappy.

Dumb

To dream of being dumb indicates your inability to persuade others into your mode of thinking, and using them for your profit by your glibness of tongue. To those who cannot speak it denotes false friends.

Dungeon

To dream of being in a dungeon foretells for you struggles with the vital affairs of life but by wise dealing you will free yourself from obstacles and the designs of enemies. For a woman this is a dark foreboding that by her wilful indiscretion she may lose her position among honourable people.

To see a dungeon lighted up portends that you are threatened with entanglements of which your better judgment warns you.

See also Jail, Prison.

154

Dunghill

To dream of a dunghill, you will see profits coming in through the most unexpected sources. To the farmer this is a lucky dream, indicating fine seasons and abundant products from soil and stock. For a young woman. it denotes that she will unknowingly marry a man of great wealth.

Dusk

This is a dream of sadness; it portends an early decline and unrequited hopes. Dark outlook for trade and pursuits of any nature is prolonged by this dream.

Dust

To dream of dust covering you denotes that you will be slightly injured in business by the failure of others. For a young woman, this denotes that she will be set aside by her lover for a newer flame. If you free yourself of the dust by using judicious measures, you will clear up the loss.

Dustbin

To dream of a dustbin signifies the need for the dreamer to have a clear-out and sweep away the cobwebs, both in waking life and inwardly, to make way for fresh ideas and a change for the better.

Dwarf

This is a very favourable dream. If the dwarf is well-formed and pleasing in appearance, it omens that you will never be dwarfed in mind or stature. Health and good constitution will admit of your engaging in many profitable pursuits both of mind and body.

Ugly and hideous dwarfs forebode distressing states.

Dye

To see the dyeing of cloth or garments in process, your bad or good luck depends on the colour. Blues, reds and gold indicate prosperity; black and white indicate sorrow in all forms.

Dying

To dream of dying warns that you are threatened with evil from a source that has contributed to your former advancement and enjoyment.

To see others dying forebodes general ill luck to you and to your friends.

To dream that you are going to die denotes that unfortunate inattention to your affairs will depreciate their value. Illness threatens to damage you also.

To see animals in the throes of death, denotes escape from evil influences if the animal is wild or savage. It is an unlucky dream to see domestic animals dying.

See also **Death**.

Dynamite

To see dynamite in a dream is a sign of approaching change and the expanding of one's affairs. To be frightened by it indicates that a secret enemy is at work against you, and if you are not careful of your conduct he will disclose himself at an unexpected and helpless moment.

Dynamo

To dream of a dynamo omens successful enterprises if attention is shown to details of business. One out of repair warns that you are nearing enemies who may involve you in trouble.

E

'And he said, hear now my words, if there be a Prophet among you, I the Lord will make myself known unto him in a vision, and will speak unto him in a dream.'

—Numbers xii, 6.

Eagles

To see one soaring above you denotes lofty ambitions which you will struggle fiercely to realize; nevertheless you will gain your desires.

To see one perched on distant heights denotes that you will possess fame, wealth and the highest position attainable in your country.

To see young eagles in their eyrie signifies your association with people of high standing, and that you will profit from wise counsel from them. You will in time come into a rich legacy.

To dream that you kill an eagle portends that no obstacles whatever would be allowed to stand before you and the utmost heights of your ambition. You will overcome your enemies and be possessed of untold wealth.

Eating the flesh of one denotes the possession of a powerful will that would not turn aside in ambitious struggles even for death. You will come immediately into rich possessions.

To see a dead eagle killed by others than yourself warns that high rank and fortune will be wrested from you ruthlessly.

To ride on an eagle's back denotes that you will make a long voyage into almost unexplored countries in your search for knowledge and wealth which you will eventually gain.

To be watched by an eagle signifies that you feel guilty and fear being unmasked.

157

Ear

To dream of seeing ears, an evil and designing person is keeping watch over your conversation to work you harm.

Earrings

To see earrings in dreams omens good news and interesting work before you. To see them broken indicates that gossip of a low order will be directed against you.

Earth

Dreams of earth denote fertility and often indicate a desire for harmony, both with yourself and with nature.

To dream of seeing freshly stirred earth around flowers or trees signifies that thrift and healthy conditions abound for the dreamer.

To dream of arid or barren soil signifies that you will need to open yourself to new ideas and fresh beginnings, lest you become stale.

Touching earth, or lying on it, warns the dreamer to be more realistic.

Earthquake

To see or feel the earthquake in your dream warns of business failure and distress caused from turmoils and wars between nations.

Earwig

To dream that you see an earwig, or have one in your ear, denotes that you will have unpleasant news affecting your business or family relations.

Eating

To dream of eating alone signifies loss and melancholy spirits. To eat with others denotes personal gain, cheerful environments and prosperous undertakings.

If your daughter carries away the platter of meat before you are done eating, it foretells that you will have trouble and vexation from those beneath you or dependent upon you. The same would apply to a waiter or waitress.

See also **Food, Meals.**

Ebony

If you dream of ebony furniture or other articles of ebony, you may have many distressing disputes and quarrels in your home.

Echo

To dream of an echo portends that distressful times are upon you. You may be ill, and friends may desert you in time of need.

Ectipse

To dream of the eclipse of the sun denotes temporary failure in business and other secular affairs, also disturbances in families.

The eclipse of the moon portends disease or death.

Ecstasy

To dream of feeling ecstasy denotes you will enjoy a visit from a long-absent friend. If you experience ecstasy in disturbing dreams you will be subjected to sorrow and disappointment.

Education

To dream that you are anxious to obtain an education shows that whatever your circumstances in life may be there will be a keen desire for knowledge on your part, which will place you on a higher plane than your associates. Fortune will also be more lenient to you.

To dream that you are in places of learning foretells for you many influential friends.

Eel

To dream of an eel is good if you can maintain your grip on him. Otherwise fortune will be fleeting.

To see an eel in clear water denotes, for a woman, new but evanescent pleasures.

To see a dead eel signifies that you will overcome your most maliciously inclined enemies. To lovers, the dream denotes an end to long and hazardous courtship by marriage.

Eggs

To dream of finding a nest of eggs denotes wealth of a substantial character, happiness among the married and many children. This dream signifies many and varied love affairs to women.

To eat eggs denotes that unusual disturbances threaten you in your home.

To see broken eggs and they are fresh, fortune is ready to shower upon you her richest gifts. A lofty spirit and high regard for justice will make you beloved by the world.

To dream of rotten eggs warns of loss of property and degradation.

To see a crate of eggs denotes that you will engage in profitable speculations.

To dream of being spattered with eggs denotes that you will sport riches of doubtful origin.

To see bird eggs signifies legacies from distant relations, or gain from an unexpected rise in staple products.

Eight

To dream of the number eight, or symbols thereof such as a mariner's compass, signifies wisdom, justice and loyalty.

Elbows

To see elbows in a dream signifies that arduous duties may devolve upon you, for which you will receive small reimbursements.

For a young woman, this is a prognostic of favourable opportunities to make a reasonably wealthy marriage. If the elbows are soiled, she will lose a good chance of securing a home by marriage.

Elderberries

To dream of seeing elderberries on bushes with their foliage denotes domestic bliss and an agreeable country home with resources for travel and other pleasures.

Elderberries is generally a good dream.

Election

To dream that you are at an election foretells that you will engage in some controversy which may prove detrimental to your social or financial standing.

Electricity

To dream of electricity denotes that there will be sudden changes about you, which will not afford you either advancement or pleasure. If you are shocked by it you will face danger.

To see live electrical wire warns that enemies will disturb your plans, which have given you much anxiety in forming. To dream that you can send a package or yourself out over a wire with the same rapidity that a message can be sent denotes that you will finally overcome obstacles and be able to use your enemies' plans to advance yourself.

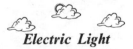

Electric Light

To see an electric light denotes progress and pleasant surroundings. To see one blow, or otherwise fail to work, warns that you are threatened with unseasonable distress.

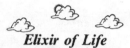

Elephant

To dream of riding an elephant denotes that you will possess wealth of the most solid character, and honours which you will wear with dignity. You will rule absolutely in all lines of your business affairs and your word will be law in the home.

To see many elephants denotes tremendous prosperity. One lone elephant signifies you will live in a small but solid way.

To dream of feeding one denotes that you will elevate yourself in your community by your kindness to those occupying places below you.

Elixir of Life

To dream of the elixir of life denotes that there will come into your environments new pleasures and new possibilities.

Elopement

To dream of eloping is unfavourable. To the married, it denotes that you hold places which you are unworthy to fill, and if your ways are not rectified your reputation will be at stake. To the unmarried, it foretells disappointments in love and the unfaithfulness of men.

To dream that your lover has eloped with someone else warns of his or her unfaithfulness.

To dream of your friend eloping with one whom you do not approve denotes that you will soon hear of them contracting a disagreeable marriage.

Eloquent

If you think you are eloquent of speech in your dreams, there will be pleasant news for you concerning one in whose interest you are working.

To fail in impressing others with your eloquence, there will be much disorder in your affairs.

Embankment

To dream that you drive along an embankment foretells you may be threatened with trouble and unhappiness. If you continue your drive without unpleasant incidents arising, you will succeed in turning these forebodings to useful account in your advancement. To ride on horseback along one denotes that you will fearlessly meet and overcome all obstacles in your way to wealth and happiness. To walk along one, you will have a weary struggle for elevation, but will finally reap a successful reward.

Embarrassment see Difficulty

Embrace

To dream of embracing your husband or wife, as the case may be, in a sorrowing or indifferent way, denotes that you will have dissensions and accusations in your family, also that sickness is threatened.

To embrace relatives warns of unhappiness.

For lovers to dream of embracing foretells quarrels and disagreements arising from infidelity. If these dreams take place under auspicious conditions, the reverse may be expected.

If you embrace a stranger, it signifies that you may have an unwelcome guest.

Embroidery

If a woman dreams of embroidering, she will be admired for her tact and ability to make the best of everything that comes her way. For a married man to see embroidery signifies a new member in his household. For a lover, this denotes a wise and economical wife.

Emerald

To dream of an emerald, you will inherit property concerning which there will be some trouble with others.

163

For a lover to see an emerald or emeralds on the person of his affianced warns him that he is likely to be discarded for some wealthier suitor.

To dream that you buy an emerald warns of unfortunate dealings.

Emperor

To dream of going abroad and meeting the emperor of a nation in your travels denotes that you will make a long journey, which will bring neither pleasure nor much knowledge.

Employee

To see one of your employees denotes disagreements and disturbances if he assumes a disagreeable or offensive attitude. If he is pleasant and has communications of interest, you will find no cause for evil or embarrassing conditions upon waking.

Employment

This is not an auspicious dream. It warns of depression in business circles and loss of employment to wage earners. It may also denote bodily illness.

To dream of being out of work, conversely, denotes that you will have no fear, as you are always sought out for your conscientious fulfilment of contracts, which make you a desired help.

Giving employment to others portends loss for yourself. All dreams of this nature may be interpreted as the above.

Empress

To dream of an empress denotes that you will be exalted to high honours, but you may let pride make you very unpopular.

To dream of an empress and an emperor is not particularly bad, but brings one no substantial good.

Enchantment

To dream of being under the spell of enchantment denotes that if you are not careful you will be exposed to some evil in the form of pleasure. The young should heed the benevolent advice of their elders.

To resist enchantment foretells that you will be much sought after for your wise counsels and your liberality.

To dream of trying to enchant others warns that you risk falling into evil.

Encyclopedia

To dream of seeing or searching through encyclopedias portends that you will secure literary ability to the detriment of prosperity and comfort.

Enemy

To dream that you overcome enemies denotes that you will surmount all difficulties in business, and enjoy the greatest prosperity.

If you are defamed by your enemies, it denotes that you will be threatened with failures in your work. You will be wise to use the utmost caution in proceeding in affairs of any moment.

To overcome your enemies in any form signifies your gain. For them to get the better of you is ominous of adverse fortunes. This dream may be literal.

Engagement

To dream of a business engagement denotes dullness and worries in trade.

For young people to dream that they are engaged denotes that they will not be much admired.

To dream of breaking an engagement denotes a hasty and unwise action in some important matter; take care, or disappointments may follow.

Engine

To dream of an engine denotes that you will encounter grave difficulties and journeys, but you will have substantial friends to uphold you.

Disabled engines stand for misfortune and loss of relatives.

Engineer

To see an engineer forebodes weary journeys but joyful reunions.

English

To dream, if you are not English, of meeting English people denotes that you will have to suffer through the selfish designs of others.

Entertainment

To dream of an entertainment where there is music and dancing, you will have pleasant tidings of the absent, and enjoy health and prosperity. To the young, this is a dream of many and varied pleasures and the high regard of friends.

Envelope

Envelopes seen in a dream omen news of a sorrowful cast.

Envy

To dream that you entertain envy for others denotes that you will make warm friends by your unselfish deference to the wishes of others.

If you dream of being envied by others, it denotes that you will suffer some inconvenience from friends over-anxious to please you.

Epaulette

For a man to dream of wearing epaulettes, if he is a soldier, denotes that he will be in disfavour for a time, but will finally wear honours.

For a woman to dream that she is introduced to a person wearing epaulettes warns her against forming unwise attachments which are likely to result in scandal.

Epidemic

To dream of an epidemic warns of stress and worry brought on by distasteful tasks.

Ermine

To dream that you wear this beautiful and costly raiment denotes exaltation, lofty character and wealth forming a barrier to want and misery.

To see others thus clothed, you will be associated with wealthy people, polished in literature and art.

For a lover to see his sweetheart clothed in ermine is an omen of purity and faithfulness. If the ermine is soiled, the reverse is indicated.

Errands

To go on errands in your dreams means congenial associations and mutual agreement in the home circle. For a young woman to send some person on an errand warns that she may lose her lover by her indifference to meet his wishes.

Escape

To dream of escape from injury or accidents is usually favourable.

If you escape from some place of confinement, it signifies your rise in the world from close application to business.

To escape from any contagion denotes your good health and prosperity. If you try to escape and fail, you may suffer from the design of enemies, who wish to slander and defraud you.

Estate

To dream that you come into the ownership of a vast estate denotes that you will receive a legacy at some distant day, but quite different to your expectations. For a young woman, this dream portends that her inheritance will be of a disappointing nature. She will have to live quite frugally, as her inheritance may well be a poor man and a houseful of children.

Europe

To dream of travelling in Europe foretells that you may soon go on a long journey, which will avail you in the knowledge you gain of the manners and customs of foreign people. You may also be enabled to forward your financial standing. For a young woman to feel that she is disappointed with the sights of Europe omens her inability to appreciate chances for her elevation. She will be likely to disappoint her friends or lover.

Eve

For a young woman to dream that she impersonates Eve, warns her to be careful. She may be wiser than her ancient relative, but the Evil One still has powerful agents in the disguise of a handsome man. Keep your eye on innocent Eve, young man. That apple tree still bears fruit, and you may be persuaded, unwittingly, to share the wealth of its products.

Evening

To dream that evening is about you denotes unrealized hopes; you may make unfortunate ventures.

To see stars shining out clear denotes present distress, but brighter fortune is behind your trouble.

For lovers to walk in the evening warns of coming separation.

Evergreen

This dream denotes boundless resources of wealth, happiness and learning. It is a free presentiment of prosperity to all classes.

Exams

All dreams of exams constitute a form of judgment. These dreams give dreamers an idea of how they see themselves.

Exchange

Exchange denotes profitable dealings in all classes of business. For a young woman to dream that she is exchanging sweethearts with her friend indicates that she will do well to heed this as advice, as she be happier with another.

Execution

To dream of seeing an execution might well signify that you may suffer some misfortune through the carelessness of others.

To dream that you are about to be executed, and that some miraculous intervention occurs, denotes that you will overthrow enemies and succeed in gaining wealth.

Exercise Books

To dream of exercise books indicates that childhood anxieties have not yet evaporated, and that the dreamer is still suffering from childhood fears of being abandoned.

Exile

For a woman to dream that she is exiled, denotes that she may have to make a journey which will interfere with some engagement or pleasure.

Explosion

To dream of explosions portends that disapproving actions of those connected with you will cause you transient displeasure and loss, and that business will also displease you. To think your face, or the face of others, is blackened you will be accused of indiscretion which will be unjust, though circumstances may convict you.

To see the air filled with smoke and débris denotes unusual dissatisfaction in business circles and much social antagonism.

To think you are enveloped in the flames, or are up in the air where you have been blown by an explosion, warns that unworthy friends may infringe on your rights and abuse your confidence. Young women should be careful of associates of the opposite sex after a dream of this character.

Dreams of explosion may also be warning the dreamer of the need to release pent-up inner emotions, before they become a damaging influence or erupt violently to the surface.

Eye

To dream of eyes signifies that you feel under scrutiny in waking life, or desire more privacy.

To dream of seeing an eye warns you that watchful enemies are seeking the slightest chance to work injury to your business. This dream indicates to a lover that a rival will usurp him if he is not careful.

To dream of brown eyes denotes deceit and perfidy. To see blue eyes denotes weakness in carrying out any intention. To see grey eyes denotes a love of flattery for the owner.

To dream of losing an eye, or that the eyes are sore, denotes trouble.

To see a one-eyed man denotes that you may be threatened with loss and trouble.

Eyebrows

Eyebrows denote that you may encounter sinister obstacles in your immediate future.

F

'In Gideon the Lord appeared to Solomon in a dream by night.'
—1st Kings iii, 5.

Fables

To dream of reading or telling fables denotes pleasant tasks and a literary turn of mind. To the young, it signifies romantic attachments.

To hear, or tell, religious fables, denotes that the dreamer will become very devotional.

Face

This dream is favourable if you see happy and bright faces, but significant of trouble if they are disfigured, ugly, or frowning on you.

To a young person, an ugly face foretells lovers' quarrels; or for a lover to see the face of his sweetheart looking old warns of separation and the breaking up of happy associations.

To see a strange and weird-looking face warns that enemies and misfortunes surround you.

To dream of seeing your own face denotes unhappiness; to the married, threats of divorce may be made.

To see your face in a mirror denotes displeasure with yourself for not being able to carry out plans for self-advancement. You may also lose the esteem of friends.

Face Powder

For a woman to dream of powdering her face denotes that she is willing to scheme to obtain admirers.

Factory

To dream of a large factory denotes unusual activity in business circles.

Failure

Dreams of failure are often trying to warn the dreamer of the need to face up to something in waking life.

For a lover, this is sometimes of contrary significance. To dream that he fails in his suit signifies that he only needs more masterfulness and energy in his daring, as he has already the love and esteem of his sweetheart.

(Contrary dreams are those in which the dreamer suffers fear, and not injury.)

For a young woman to dream that her life is going to be a failure denotes that she is not applying her opportunities to good advantage.

For a business man to dream that he has made a failure forebodes loss and bad management, which should be corrected so that failure does not materialize in earnest.

Fainting

To dream of fainting warns of illness in your family and unpleasant news of the absent.

If a young woman dreams of fainting, it denotes that she may fall into ill health and experience disappointment from her careless way of living.

Fair

To dream of being at a fair denotes that you will have a pleasant and profitable business and a congenial companion.

For a young woman, this dream signifies a jovial and even-tempered man for a life partner.

Fairy

To dream of a fairy is a favourable omen to everyone, as it is always a scene with a beautiful face portrayed as a happy child, or woman.

Faithless

To dream that your friends are faithless denotes that they will hold you in worthy esteem. For a lover to dream that his sweetheart is faithless signifies a happy marriage.

Fakir

To dream of a fakir denotes uncommon activity and phenomenal changes in your life. Such dreams may sometimes be of gloomy import.

Falcon

To dream of a falcon denotes that your prosperity may make you an object of envy and malice. For a young woman, this dream denotes that she may be slandered by a rival.

Fall

Dreams of falling are common and often signify that the dreamer has over-achieved in some area, professional or emotional, in waking life. Falling from the top of a building denotes that there is more to be learned before the dreamer feels happy to accept a work promotion or elevated social position.

To dream that you sustain a fall, and are much frightened, denotes that you will undergo some great struggle, but will eventually rise to honour and wealth; but if you are injured in the fall, you may encounter hardships and loss of friends.

Fame

To dream of being famous denotes disappointed aspirations. To dream of famous people portends your rise from obscurity to places of honour.

Family

To dream of one's family as harmonious and happy is significant of health and easy circumstances; but if there is sickness or contentions, it forebodes gloom and disappointment.

Family Tree

To dream of your family tree denotes you will be much burdened with family cares, or will find pleasure in other domains than your own. To see others studying it foretells that you may be forced to yield your rights to others. If any of the branches are missing, you may ignore some of your friends because of their straitened circumstances.

Famine

To dream of a famine is generally bad. If you see your enemies perishing by famine, however, you will be successful in competition.

Famished

To dream that you are famished foretells that you are meeting disheartening failure in some enterprise which you considered a promising success. To see others famished may bring sorrow to others as well as to yourself.

Fan

To see a fan in your dreams denotes that pleasant news and surprises are awaiting you in the near future. For a young woman to dream of fanning herself, or that some one is fanning her, gives promise of a new and pleasing acquaintances; if she loses an old fan, she will find that a warm friend is becoming interested in other women.

Farewell

To dream of bidding farewell is not very favourable, as you are likely to hear unpleasant news of absent friends.

For a young woman to bid her lover farewell portends his indifference to her. If she feels no sadness in this farewell, she will soon find others to comfort her.

*See also **Adieu**.*

Farm

To dream that you are living on a farm denotes that you will be fortunate in all undertakings.

To dream that you are buying a farm denotes abundant crops to the farmer, a profitable deal of some kind to the businessperson, and a safe voyage to travellers and sailors.

If you are visiting a farm, it signifies pleasant associations.

Fat

To dream that you are getting fat denotes that you are about to make a fortunate change in your life.

To see others fat signifies prosperity.

*See also **Obesity**.*

Fate

For a young woman to dream of juggling with fate denotes she will daringly interpose herself between devoted friends or lovers.

Father

To dream of your father signifies that you are about to be involved in a difficulty, and you will need wise counsel if you extricate yourself therefrom.

If you see and talk with your late father, you are about to make some unlucky transaction. Be careful how you enter into contracts, as enemies are about you. Your business is pulling heavily and you will have to use caution in conducting it. Both men and women are warned to look to their reputations after this dream.

For a young woman to dream of her dead father, portends that her lover will, or is, playing her false.

Father-in-law

To dream of your father-in-law denotes contentions with friends or relatives. To see him well and cheerful foretells pleasant family relations.

Fatigue

To feel fatigued in a dream warns of ill health or oppression in business. For a young woman to see others fatigued indicates discouraging progress in health.

Favour

To dream that you ask favours of anyone denotes that you will enjoy abundance and will not especially need anything.

To grant favours warns of a loss.

Fawn

To dream of seeing a fawn denotes that you will have true and upright friends.

To the young, it indicates faithfulness in love.

To dream that a person fawns on you, or cajoles you, is a warning that enemies are about you in the guise of interested friends.

See also **Deer**.

Fears

To dream that you feel fear from any cause denotes that your future engagements may not prove so successful as was expected.

For a young woman, this dream forebodes disappointment and unfortunate love.

Feast

To dream of a feast foretells that pleasant surprises are being planned for you. To see disorder or misconduct at a feast foretells quarrels or unhappiness through the negligence or sickness of some person.

To arrive late at a feast denotes that vexing affairs may occupy you.

Feather

To dream of seeing feathers falling around you denotes that your burdens in life will be light and easily borne.

To see eagle feathers denotes that your aspirations will be realized.

To see chicken feathers denotes small annoyances. To dream of buying or selling goose or duck feathers denotes thrift and fortune.

To dream of black feathers denotes disappointments and unhappy amours.

For a woman to dream of seeing ostrich and other ornamental feathers denotes that she will advance in society, but that her ways of gaining favour will not bear imitating.

February

To dream of February denotes ill health and gloom, generally. If you happen to see a bright sunshiny day in this month, you will be unexpectedly and happily surprised with some good fortune.

Feeble

To dream of being feeble denotes unhealthy occupations and mental worry. Seek to make a change for yourself after this dream.

Feet

To dream of seeing your own feet warns of your being overcome by the will and temper of another. To see others' feet denotes that you will maintain your rights in a pleasant but determined way, and win for yourself a place above the common walks of life.

To dream that you wash your feet denotes that you will let others take advantage of you.

To dream that your feet are hurting you portends troubles of a humiliating character, as they are usually family quarrels.

To see your feet swollen and red, you will make a sudden change in your business by separating from your family. This dream usually foretells scandal and sensation.

Fence

To dream of climbing to the top of a fence denotes that success will crown your efforts.

To fall from a fence warns that if you undertake a project for which you are incapable, you will see your efforts come to naught.

To be seated on a fence with others, and have it fall under you, portends an accident.

To dream that you climb through a fence signifies that you will use means not altogether legitimate to reach your desires.

To throw the fence down and walk into the other side indicates that you will, by enterprise and energy, overcome the stubbornest barriers between you and success.

To see stock jumping a fence, if into your enclosure, you will receive aid from unexpected sources; if out of your lot, loss in trade and other affairs may follow.

To dream of building a fence denotes that you are, by economy and industry, laying a foundation for future wealth. For a young woman, this dream denotes success in love affairs;

or the reverse, if she dreams of the fence falling, or that she falls from it.

Ferns

To see ferns in dreams foretells that pleasant hours will break up gloomy forebodings. To see them withered indicates that illness in your family connections may cause you grave unrest.

Ferry

To wait at a ferry for a boat and see the waters swift and muddy, you will be baffled in your highest wishes and designs by unforeseen circumstances.

To cross a ferry while the water is calm and clear, you will be very lucky in carrying out your plans, and fortune will crown you.

Festival

To dream of being at a festival denotes indifference to the cold realities of life, and a love for those pleasures that make one old before his time. You will never want, but will be largely dependent on others.

Fever

To dream that you are stricken with this malady, signifies that you are worrying over trifling affairs while the best of life is slipping past you, and you should pull yourself into shape and engage in profitable work.

To dream of seeing some of your family sick with fever, denotes temporary illness for some of them.

Field

To dream of dead corn or stubble fields indicates to the dreamer dreary prospects for the future.

To see green fields, or ripe with corn or grain, denotes great abundance and happiness to all classes.

To see newly plouged fields denotes early rise in wealth and fortunate advancement to places of honour.

To see fields freshly harrowed and ready for planting denotes that you are soon to benefit by your endeavour and long struggles for success.

Fiend

To dream that you encounter a fiend forbodes reckless living and loose morals. For a woman, this dream signifies a blackened reputation.

To dream of a fiend warns you of attacks to be made on you by false friends. If you overcome one, you will be able to intercept the evil designs of enemies.

Fife

To dream of hearing a fife denotes that there will be an unexpected call on you to defend your honour, or that of some person near to you.

To dream that you play one yourself indicates that whatever else may be said of you, your reputation will remain intact. If a woman has this dream, she will probably have a soldier husband.

Fight

To dream that you engage in a fight denotes that you will have unpleasant encounters with your business opponents, and lawsuits may threaten you.

To see fighting denotes that you are squandering your time and money. For women, this dream is a warning against slander and gossip.

For a young woman to see her lover fighting is a sign of his unworthiness.

To dream that you are defeated in a fight signifies that you may lose your right to property.

To whip your assailant denotes that you will, by courage and perseverance, win honour and wealth in spite of opposition.

To dream that you see two men fighting with pistols denotes many worries and perplexities, while no real loss is involved in the dream, yet but small profit is predicted and some unpleasantness is denoted.

To dream that you are attacked on your way home, you will be disappointed in your business and much vexed at home.

Figs

Figs warn of ill health if you are eating them, but usually favourable to health and profit if you see them growing.

For a young woman to see figs growing signifies that she will soon wed a wealthy and prominent man.

Figure

To dream of figures indicates stress and wrong. You will be the loser in a big deal if not careful of your actions and conversation.

File

To dream that you see a file signifies that you will transact some business which will prove unsatisfactory in the extreme.

To see files, to store away bills and other important papers, foretells animated discussions over subjects which bear relation to significant affairs, and which will cause you much unrest and disquiet. Unfavourable predictions for the future are also implied in this dream.

Fingers

To dream of seeing your fingers soiled or scratched and bleeding denotes much trouble and suffering. You may despair of making your way through life.

To see beautiful hands, with white fingers, denotes that your love will be requited and that you will become renowned for your benevolence.

Fingernails

To dream of soiled finger-nails forbodes disgrace in your family through the wild escapades of the young.

To see well-kept nails indicates scholarly tastes and some literary attainments; also, thrift.

Fire

Fire is favourable to the dreamer if he does not get burned. It brings continued prosperity to seamen and voyagers, as well as to those on land.

Dreams about fire always signify energy, and may denote impulses towards spirituality and the light of inner truths.

To dream of seeing your home burning denotes a loving companion and obedient children.

For a businessman to dream that his store is burning, and he is looking on, foretells a great rush in business and profitable results.

To dream that you are fighting fire but do not get burned, denotes that you will be much worked and worried as to the conduct of your business. To see the ruins of your business after a fire forebodes ill luck, but some unforeseen good fortune will bear you up again.

If you dream of kindling a fire, you may expect many pleasant surprises. You will have distant friends to visit.

To see a large conflagration denotes to sailors a profitable and safe voyage. To literary people, advancement and honours; to business-people, unlimited success.

See also **Conflagration**.

Firebrand

To dream of a firebrand, denotes favourable fortune, if you are not burned or distressed by it.

Fire Engine

To see a fire engine denotes worry under extraordinary circumstances, but which will result in good fortune. To see one broken down warns of accident or serious loss. For a young woman to ride on one denotes she may engage in some unladylike and obnoxious affair.

Fireman

To see a fireman in your dreams signifies the constancy of your friends.

Firewood

If you dream of seeing dense smoke ascending from a pile of burning firewood, it denotes that enemies may be bearing down on you, but if the wood is burning brightly, you will escape from all unpleasant complications and enjoy great prosperity.

If you walk on burning bundles of wood, you are likely to be injured through the unwise actions of friends. If you succeed in walking on them without being burned, you will have a miraculous rise in prospects.

To dream that you deal in firewood denotes that you will achieve fortune through determined struggle.

Fireworks

To see fireworks indicates enjoyment and good health. For a young woman, this dream signifies entertainments and pleasant visiting to distant places.

Firmament

To dream of the firmament filled with stars denotes many crosses and almost superhuman efforts before you reach the pinnacle of your ambition. Beware of the snare of enemies at work.

To see the firmament illuminated and filled with the heavenly hosts denotes great spiritual research, but a final pulling back on Nature for sustenance and consolation. You will often be disappointed in fortune also.

Fish

To dream that you see fish in clear-water streams denotes that you will be favoured by the rich and powerful.

Dead fish signifies loss of wealth and power.

To dream of dead fish can also signify that you are depressed and living in a dark night of the soul.

For a young woman to dream of seeing fish portends that she will have a handsome and talented lover.

To dream of catching a catfish denotes that you will be embarrassed by evil designs of enemies, but your luck and presence of mind will tide you safely over the trouble.

To wade in water, catching fish, denotes that you will possess wealth acquired by your own ability and enterprise.

To dream of fishing denotes energy and economy; but if you do not succeed in catching any, your efforts to obtain honours and wealth will be futile.

Eating fish denotes warm and lasting attachments.

Fisherman

To dream of a fisherman denotes you are nearing times of greater prosperity than you have yet known.

Fish Hooks

To dream of fish hooks denotes that you have opportunities to make for yourself a fortune and an honourable name if you rightly apply them.

Fishing Net

To dream of a fishing net portends numerous small pleasures and gains. A torn one represents vexatious disappointments.

Fish Market

To visit a fish market in your dream brings competence and pleasure.

To see decayed fish warns that distress will come in the guise of happiness.

Fish Pond

To dream of a fish pond denotes illness through dissipation, if muddy. To see one clear and well-stocked with fish portends profitable enterprises and extensive pleasures. To see one empty proclaims the approach of enemies.

For a young woman to fall into a clear pond omens decided good fortune and reciprocal love. If muddy, the opposite is foretold.

Five

To dream of the number five, or symbols thereof such as a pentagram, signifies personal creativity and magical protection.

Flag

Dreams of flags signify harmony; if at half mast, inner sorrow.

To dream of your national flag portends victory if at war, and if at peace, prosperity.

For a woman to dream of a flag denotes that she may be seduced by a soldier.

To dream of foreign flags denotes ruptures and breach of confidence between nations and friends.

To dream of being signalled by a flag denotes that you should be careful of your health and name, as both are threatened.

Flame

To dream of fighting flames foretells that you will have to put forth your best efforts and energy if you are successful in amassing wealth.

*See also **Fire**.*

185

Flax

To see flax in a dream, prosperous enterprises are denoted. Spinning Flax foretells that you will be given to industrious and thrifty habits.

Fleas

To dream of fleas indicates that you will be provoked to anger and retaliation by the machinations of those close to you.

For a woman to dream that fleas bite her warns that she will be slandered by pretended friends. To see fleas on her lover indicates inconstancy.

Fleet

To see a large fleet moving rapidly in your dreams, denotes a hasty change in the business world. Where dullness oppressed, brisk workings of commercial wheels will go forward. Some rumours of foreign wars will be heard.

Flies

To dream of flies warns of illness. Also that enemies surround you. To a young woman this dream is significant of unhappiness. If she kills or exterminates flies, she will reinstate herself in the love of her intended by her ingenuity.

Flight

To dream of flight warns of disgrace and unpleasant news of the absent.

For a young woman to dream of flight indicates that she has not kept her character above reproach, and that her lover may throw her aside.

To see anything fleeing from you may denotes that you will be victorious in any contention.

Floating

To dream of floating denotes that you will victoriously overcome obstacles which are seemingly overwhelming you. If the water is muddy your victories will not be gratifying.

Floods

To dream of floods destroying vast areas of country and bearing you on with its muddy débris, denotes sickness, loss in business, and the most unhappy and unsettled situation in the marriage state.

See also **Inundation.**

Flour

To dream of flour, denotes a frugal but happy life. For a young woman to dream that she sees flour on herself, denotes that she will be ruled by her husband, and that her life will be full of pleasant cares.

To dream of dealing in flour, denotes hazardous speculations.

Flower

To dream of seeing flowers blooming in gardens signifies pleasure and gain, if bright-hued and fresh; white denotes sadness. Withered and dead flowers signify disappointments and gloomy situations.

To see flowers blooming in barren soil without vestige of foliage foretells that you will have some grievous experience, but your energy and cheerfulness will enable you to climb through these to prominence and happiness.

> 'Held in slumber's soft embrace,
> She enters realms of flowery grace,
> Where tender love and fond caress,
> Bids her awake to happiness.'

See also **Bouquet.**

Flute

To dream of hearing notes from a flute signifies a pleasant meeting with friends from a distance, and profitable engagements.

For a young woman to dream of playing a flute denotes that she will fall in love because of her lover's engaging manners.

Flying

To fly in a dream often signifies an attempt to rise above your conflicts and difficulties. You need to rise higher but, alas, flights in dreams often end unhappily. Dreamers fly because they are anxious about finding themselves on the ground – flying often represents a flight from yourself.

To dream of flying high through a space warns of marital unrest.

To fly low, almost to the ground, indicates sickness and uneasy states from which the dreamer will recover.

To fly over muddy water warns you to keep close with your private affairs, as enemies are watching to entrap you.

To fly over broken places warns of ill luck and gloomy surroundings. If you notice green trees and vegetation below you in flying, you will suffer temporary embarrassment, but will have a flood of prosperity upon you.

To dream of seeing the sun while flying signifies useless worries, as your affairs will succeed despite your fears.

To dream of flying through the firmament passing the moon and other planets warns of troubles of all kinds.

To dream that you fly with black wings portends bitter disappointments. To fall while flying indicates your downfall. If you wake while falling, you will succeed in reinstating yourself.

For a young man to dream that he is flying with white wings above green foliage foretells advancement in business; he will also be successful in love. If he dreams this often it is a sign of increasing prosperity and the fulfilment of desires. If the trees appear barren or dead, there will be obstacles to combat in obtaining desires. He will get along, but his work will bring small results.

For a woman to dream of flying from one city to another, and alighting on church spires, foretells that she will have much to contend against in the way of false persuasions and declarations of love. She will be threatened with ill health.

For a young woman to dream that she is shot at while flying denotes that enemies may endeavour to restrain her advancement into higher spheres of usefulness and prosperity.

Flying Saucer

Flying saucers denote good or bad tidings, depending on whether the dreamer's experience is positive or negative.

Flypaper

To dream of flypaper warns of ill health and disrupted friendships.

Foal

To dream of a foal indicates new undertakings in which you will be rather fortunate.

See also **Horse**.

Fog

Dreams about fog signify a change of direction, literal or spiritual.

To dream of travelling through a dense fog denotes much trouble and business worries. To emerge from it foretells a weary journey, but profitable.

For a young woman to dream of being in a fog denotes that she may be mixed up in a salacious scandal, but if she gets out of the fog she will prove her innocence and regain her social standing.

See also **Mist**.

Food

To dream that you are gorging yourself with food warns of greed and possessiveness.

Offering food to others signifies the dreamer's need to nurture and provide.

Refusing food offered, the dreamer needs to prove his independence.

Sitting around a table enjoying food with friends or family indicates that the dreamer has an outgoing, sociable nature and will enjoy harmonious relationships.

See also **Eating, Meals**.

Ford

To dream of fording a river signifies that the dreamer will undergo inner transformation.

Forest

To dream that you are in a forest signifies that you will seek something within yourself, or will embark on a spiritual quest.

To dream that you find yourself in a dense forest warns of loss in trade, unhappy home influences and quarrels among families. If you are cold and feel hungry, you will be forced to make a long journey to settle some unpleasant affair.

To see a forest of stately trees in foliage denotes prosperity and pleasures. To literary people, this dream foretells fame and much appreciation from the public.

See also **Trees, Woods**.

Forehead

To dream of a fine and smooth forehead denotes that you will be thought well of for your judgment and fair dealings.

An ugly forehead denotes displeasure in your private affairs.

To pass your hand over the forehead of your child indicates sincere praises from friends, because of some talent and goodness displayed by your children.

For a young woman to dream of kissing the forehead of her lover signifies that he may be displeased with her for gaining notice by indiscreet conduct.

Fork

To dream of a fork warns that enemies are working for your displacement. For a woman, this dream denotes unhappy domestic relations.

Form

To see anything ill formed denotes disappointment. To have a beautiful form denotes favourable conditions for health and business.

Forsaking

For a young woman to dream of forsaking her home or friend warns that she may have troubles in love, as her estimate of her lover will decrease with acquaintance and association.

Fort

To dream of defending a fort signifies that your honour and possessions may be attacked, and you will have great worry over the matter.

To dream that you attack a fort and take it denotes victory over your worst enemy, and fortunate engagements.

Fortress

To dream that you are confined in a fortress denotes that enemies will succeed in placing you in an undesirable situation.

To put others in a fortress denotes your ability to rule in business or over others.

Fortune-telling

To dream of telling, or having your fortune told, indicates that you are deliberating over some vexed affair, and you should use much caution in giving consent to its consummation. For a young woman, this portends a choice between two rivals. She will be worried to find out the standing of one in business and social circles. To dream that she is engaged to a fortune-teller denotes that she has gone through the forest and picked the proverbial stick. She should be self-reliant, or poverty may attend her marriage.

Fountain

To dream that you see a clear fountain sparkling in the sunlight denotes vast possessions, ecstatic delights and many pleasant journeys.

A clouded fountain warns of the insincerity of associates and unhappy engagements and love affairs.

A dry and broken fountain warns of death and cessation of pleasures.

For a young woman to see a sparkling fountain in the moonlight signifies ill-advised pleasure which may result in a desertion.

Four

To dream of the number four, or symbols thereof such as a square, signifies fullness, solidity, totality and universality.

Fowl

To dream of seeing fowls denotes temporary worry or illness. For a woman to dream of fowls indicates a short illness or disagreement with her friends.

Fox

To dream of chasing a fox denotes that you are engaging in doubtful speculations and risky love affairs.

If you see a fox slyly coming into your yard, beware of envious friendships; your reputation is being slyly assailed.

To kill a fox denotes that you will win in every engagement.

Fraud

To dream that you are defrauding a person denotes that you may deceive your employer for gain, indulge in degrading pleasures, and fall into disrepute.

If you are defrauded, it signifies the useless attempt of enemies to defame you and cause you loss.

To accuse someone of defrauding you, you will be offered a place of high honour.

Freckles

For a woman to dream that her face is freckled denotes that many displeasing incidents may insinuate themselves into her happiness. If she sees them in a mirror, she will be in danger of losing her lover to a rival.

Freemason

If you dream of seeing a band of the Order of Freemasons in full regalia, it denotes that you will have others beside you to protect and keep you from the evils of life.

Friend

To dream of friends being well and happy denotes pleasant tidings of them, or that you will soon see them or some of their relatives.

To see your friends take the form of animals, warns that enemies will try to separate you from your closest relations.

To see your friend who usually dresses in sombre colours in flaming red foretells that unpleasant things may transpire, causing you anxiety if not loss, and that friends may be implicated.

To dream you see a friend standing like a statue on a hill denotes that you will advance beyond present pursuits, but will retain former impressions of justice and knowledge, seeking these through every change. If the figure below is low, you will ignore your friends of former days in your future advancement. If it is on a plane or level with you, you are likely to fail in your ambition to reach other spheres. If you seem to be going from it, you will force yourself to seek a change in spite of friendly ties or self-admonition.

To dream you see a friend with a white cloth tied over his face denotes that you may be injured by some person who will endeavour to keep up friendly relations with you.

To dream that you are shaking hands with a person who has wronged you, and he is taking his departure and looks sad, foretells you will have differences with a close friend and alienation will perhaps follow.

Frightened

To dream that you are frightened by anything denotes temporary and fleeting worries.

Frogs

To dream of catching frogs denotes carelessness in watching after your health, which may cause no little distress among those of your family.

To see frogs in the grass denotes that you will have a pleasant and even-tempered friend as your confidant and counsellor.

To see a bullfrog denotes, for a woman, marriage with a wealthy widower, but there will be children with him to be cared for.

To see frogs in low marshy places foretells trouble, but you will overcome it by the kindness of others.

To dream of eating frogs signifies fleeting joys and very little gain from associating with some people.

To hear frogs portends that you will go on a visit to friends, but it will in the end prove fruitless of good.

Frost

To dream of seeing frost on a dark gloomy morning signifies exile to a strange country, but your wanderings will end in peace.

To see frost on a small sunlit landscape signifies gilded pleasures from which you will be glad to turn later in life, and by your exemplary conduct will succeed in making your circle forget past escapades.

To dream that you see a friend in a frost denotes a love affair in which your rival will be worsted. For a young woman, this dream signifies the absence of her lover and danger of his affections waning. This dream is bad for everyone in business and love.

Fruit

To dream of seeing fruit ripening among its foliage usually foretells to the dreamer a prosperous future. Green fruit signifies disappointed efforts or hasty action.

For a young woman to dream of eating green fruit indicates her degradation and loss of inheritance. Eating fruit is usually unfavourable.

To buy or sell fruit denotes much business, but not very remunerative.

To see or eat ripe fruit signifies uncertain fortune and pleasure.

Fruit Seller

To dream of a fruit seller denotes you will endeavour to recover your losses too rapidly and will engage in unfortunate speculations.

Funeral

To dream of a funeral, surprisingly, may well be a positive sign that you are putting the past behind you and looking forward to the future. Conversely, it may signify that you are burying feelings which would be better expressed, lest you lock away part of yourself.

Attending the funeral of an unknown person signifies mourning for the dreamer's lost past, or the knowledge that time is passing more quickly than the dreamer would like it to.

Furnace

To dream of a furnace foretells good luck if it is running. If out of repair, you may have trouble with children or hired help. To fall into one warns that some enemy will overpower you in a business struggle.

Furs

To dream of dealing in furs denotes prosperity and an interest in many concerns.

To be dressed in fur signifies your safety from want and poverty.

To see fine fur denotes honour and riches. For a young woman to dream that she is wearing costly furs denotes that she will marry a wise man.

Future

To dream of the future is a prognostic of careful reckoning and avoiding of detrimental extravagance.

G

Gaiter

To dream of gaiters foretells pleasant amusements and rivalries.

Gale

To dream of being caught in a gale warns of business losses and troubles for working people.

Gallows

To dream of seeing a friend threatened by the gallows foretells that desperate emergencies must be met with decision, or a great calamity is likely to befall you.

To dream that you are on a gallows warns that you may suffer from the maliciousness of false friends.

For a young woman to dream that she sees her lover executed by this means warns that she may marry an unscrupulous and designing man.

If you rescue anyone from the gallows, it portends desirable acquisitions.

Gambling

To dream that you are gambling and win signifies low associations

197

and pleasure at the expense of others. If you lose, it foretells that your disgraceful conduct will be the undoing of one near to you.

Game

To dream of game, either shooting or killing or by other means warns of fortunate undertakings, but selfish motions; if you fail to take game on a hunt, it denotes bad management and loss.

Garden

To see a garden in your dreams, filled with evergreen and flowers, denotes great peace of mind and comfort.

To see vegetables warns of misery, or loss of fortune, and slander. To females, this dream foretells that they will be famous, or exceedingly happy in domestic circles.

To dream of walking with one's lover through a garden where flowering shrubs and plants abound, indicates unalloyed happiness and independent means.

Garlic

To dream of passing through a garlic patch denotes a rise from penury to prominence and wealth. To a young woman, this denotes that she will marry from a sense of business, and love will not be considered.

To eat garlic in your dreams denotes that you will take a sensible view of life and leave its ideals to take care of themselves.

Garret

To dream of climbing to a garret denotes your inclination to run after theories while leaving the cold realities of life to others less able to bear them than yourself. To the poor, this dream is an omen of easier circumstances. To a woman, it denotes that her vanity and selfishness should be curbed.

Garter

For a lover to find his lady's garter foretells that he may lose status with her, and encounter rivals.

For a woman to dream that she loses her garter signifies that her lover may be jealous and suspicious of a handsomer person.

For a married man to dream of a garter warns that his wife will hear of his clandestine attachments, and he will have a stormy scene.

For a woman to dream that she is admiring beautiful jewelled garters on her limbs, warns that she may be betrayed in her private movements; if her reputation will hang in the balance of public opinion. If she dreams that her lover fastens them on her, she will hold his affections and faith through all adverse criticisms.

Gas

To dream of gas denotes that you will entertain harmful opinions of others, which will cause you to deal with them unjustly, and you will suffer consequent remorse. To think you are asphyxiated denotes you will have trouble which you will needlessly incur through your own wastefulness and negligence. To try to blow gas out signifies you will entertain enemies unconsciously, who will destroy you if you are not wary.

To extinguish gas denotes you are capable of destroying your own happiness. To light it, you will easily find a way out of oppressive ill fortune.

Gate

To dream of seeing or passing through a gate foretells that distressing tidings may reach you soon of the absent. Business affairs will not be encouraging.

To see a closed gate, inability to overcome present difficulties is predicted. To lock one denotes successful enterprises and well chosen friends. A broken one signifies failure and discordant surroundings. To be troubled to get through one, or open it, denotes that your most engrossing labours will fail to be remunerative or satisfactory. To swing on one foretells that you will engage in idle and dissolute pleasures.

Gauze

To dream of being dressed in gauze denotes uncertain fortune. For a lover to see his sweetheart clothed in filmy material suggests his ability to influence her for good.

Gavel

To dream of a gavel denotes you will be burdened with some unprofitable yet not unpleasant pursuit. To use one denotes that officiousness will be shown by you towards your friends.

Geese

To see geese swimming denotes that your fortune is gradually increasing.

To see them in grassy places denotes assured success. If you see them dead, you may suffer loss and displeasure.

For a lover, geese denote the worthiness of his affianced.

If you are plucking them, you are likely to come into an estate. To eat them denotes that your possessions are disputed.

Gems

To dream of gems foretells a happy fate both in love and business affairs.

Geography

To dream of studying geography denotes that you will travel much and visit places of renown.

Ghost

Dreaming of a ghost warns that you should take great care of all depending on you, as danger may threaten you. Young people should be especially careful in their communications with the opposite sex. Character is likely to be rated at a discount.

To dream of the ghost of either one of your parents warns that you are exposed to danger, and that you should be careful in forming partnerships with strangers.

To see the ghost of a dead friend foretells that you will make a long journey with an unpleasant companion, and suffer disappointments.

For a ghost to speak to you, you may be decoyed into the hands of enemies. For a woman, this is a prognostication of loss and deception.

To see an angel or a ghost appear in the sky portends misfortune.

To see a female ghost on your right in the sky and a male on your left, both of pleasing countenance, signifies a quick rise from obscurity to fame, but only for a short time.

To see a female ghost in long, clinging robes floating calmly through the sky, indicates that you will make progress in scientific studies and acquire wealth almost miraculously, but there will be an undertone of sadness in your life.

To dream that you see the ghost of a living relative or friend denotes that you are in danger of some friend's malice, and you are warned to carefully keep your affairs under personal supervision.

To dream that a ghost is pursuing you portends strange and disturbing experiences.

To see a ghost fleeing from you foretells that troubles will become smaller.

See also **Spirit**.

Giant

To dream of a giant appearing suddenly before you denotes that there will be a great struggle between you and your opponents. If the giant succeeds in stopping your journey, you will be overcome by your enemy. If he runs from you, prosperity and good health will be yours.

For a woman to dream of a giant indicates that there are aspects of her childhood with which she needs to reconcile herself before she can consider herself truly adult.

Gift

To receive gifts in your dreams denotes that you will be unusually fortunate.

To dream that you receive gifts from anyone denotes that you will not be behind in your payments, and will be unusually fortunate in speculations or love matters.

To send a gift signifies that displeasure may be shown you, and ill luck surround your efforts.

For a young woman to dream that her lover sends her rich and beautiful gifts denotes that she will make a wealthy and congenial marriage.

If a gift remains unopened, this denotes that there is a query in the dreamer's life which needs to be answered.

Girdle

To dream of wearing a girdle which is too tight for you denotes that you will be influenced by designing people.

To see others wearing velvet, or jewelled girdles, foretells that you will strive for wealth more than honour.

For a woman to receive one signifies that honours will be conferred upon her.

Girls

To dream of seeing a well, bright-looking girl, foretells pleasing prospects and domestic joys. If she is thin and pale, it denotes unpleasantness.

Glass

To dream that you are looking through glass denotes that bitter disappointments are likely to cloud your brightest hopes.

To break glass dishes, or windows, foretells an unfavourable termination to enterprises.

To receive cut glass denotes that you will be admired for your brilliance and talent.

To make presents of cut glass ornaments signifies that you are likely to fail in your undertakings.

To look clearly through a glass window, you will have employment, but will have to work subordinately. If the glass is clouded, you will be unfortunately situated.

See also **Pane of Glass.**

Glass-blower

To dream that you see glass-blowers at their work denotes you will contemplate change in your business, which will appear for the better, but you will make it at a loss to yourself.

Glasses

To dream of glasses foretells that strangers will cause changes in your affairs. Frauds may be practised on your credulity.

To dream that you see broken glasses warns of estrangement caused by fondness for illegal pleasures.

Gleaning

To see gleaners at work at harvest time denotes prosperous business, and, to the farmer, a bountiful yield of crops. If you are working with the gleaners, you may come into an estate after some trouble in establishing rights. For a woman, this dream foretells marriage with a stranger.

Gloomy

To be surrounded by many gloomy situations in your dream warns you of rapidly approaching unpleasantness and loss.

Gloves

To dream of wearing new gloves denotes that you will be cautious and economical in your dealings with others, but not mercenary. You will have lawsuits, or business troubles, but will settle them satisfactorily to yourself.

If you wear old or ragged gloves, you may be betrayed and suffer loss.

If you dream that you lose your gloves, you will be deserted and earn your own means of livelihood.

To find a pair of gloves denotes a marriage or new love affair.

For a man to fasten a lady's glove, he has, or will have, a woman on his hands who threatens him with exposure.

If you pull your glove off, you are likely to meet with poor success in business or love.

To dream that you sell a pair of soiled, grey cotton gloves to a woman foretells that your opinion of women will place you in hazardous positions. If a woman has this dream, her preference for someone of the male sex will not be appreciated very much by him.

Goat

To dream of goats wandering around a farm is significant of seasonable weather and a fine yield of crops. To see them otherwise denotes cautious dealings and a steady increase of wealth.

If a billy goat butts you, beware that enemies do not get possession of your secrets or business plans.

For a woman to dream of riding a billy goat denotes that she will be held in disrepute because of her coarse and ill-bred conduct.

If a woman dreams that she drinks goat's milk, she will marry for money and will not be disappointed.

Goblet

If you dream that you drink water from a silver goblet, you will meet unfavourable business results in the near future.

To see goblets of ancient design, you will receive favours and benefits from strangers.

For a woman to give a man a glass goblet full of water denotes illicit pleasures.

God

If you dream of seeing God, you may be domineered over by a tyrannical woman masquerading under the cloak of Christianity. No good accrues from this dream.

If God speaks to you, beware that you do not fall into condemnation. Business of all sorts is likely to take an unfavourable turn.

If you dream of worshipping God, you will have cause to repent of an error of your own making. Look well to observing the Ten Commandments after this dream.

To dream that God confers distinct favour upon you, you may become the favourite of a cautious and prominent person who will use his position to advance yours.

To dream that God sends his spirit upon you, great changes in your beliefs will take place. Views concerning dogmatic Christianity should broaden after this dream, or you may be severely chastised for some indiscreet action which has brought shame upon you. God speaks oftener to those who transgress than those who do not. It is the genius of spiritual law or economy to reinstate the prodigal child by signs and visions. Elijah, Jonah, David and Paul were brought to the altar of repentence through the vigilant energy of the hidden forces within.

Goggles

To dream of goggles is a warning of disreputable companions who may wheedle you into lending your money foolishly.

For a young woman to dream of goggles means that she is likely to listen to persuasion which will mar her fortune.

Gold

If you handle gold in your dream, you will be unusually successful in all enterprises. For a woman to dream that she receives presents of gold, either money or ornaments, she will marry a wealthy but mercenary man.

To find gold indicates that your superior abilities will place you easily ahead in the race for honours and wealth.

If you lose gold, you risk missing the grandest opportunity of your life through negligence.

To dream of finding a gold vein denotes that some uneasy honour will be thrust upon you.

If you dream that you contemplate working a gold mine, you will endeavour to usurp the rights of others, and should beware of domestic scandals.

Goldfish

To dream of goldfish is a prognostic of many successful and pleasant adventures. For a young woman, this dream is indicative of a wealthy union with a pleasing man. If the fish are sick or dead, heavy disappointments will fall upon her.

Gold Leaf

To dream of gold leaf signifies a flattering future is before you.

Golf

To be playing golf or watching the game denotes that pleasant and successive wishing will be indulged in by you. To see any unpleasantness connected with golf, you may be humiliated by some thoughtless person.

Gong

To hear the sound of a gong while dreaming denotes that false alarms of illness or loss will vex you excessively.

Gooseberries

To dream of gathering gooseberries is a sign of happiness after trouble, and a favourable indication of brighter prospects in one's business affairs.

If you are eating green gooseberries, you will make a mistake in your course to pleasure, and be precipitated into the vertex of sensationalism. Bad results are sure to follow the tasting of green gooseberries.

To see gooseberries in a dream foretells that you will escape some dreaded work. For a young woman to eat them foretells that she will be slightly disappointed in her expectations.

Gossip

To dream of being interested in common gossip, you may undergo some humiliating trouble caused by over-confidence in transient friendships.

If you are the object of gossip, you may expect some pleasurable surprise.

Gourmet

To dream of sitting at the table with a gourmet denotes that you will enjoy some fine distinction, but you will be surrounded by people of selfish principles.

To dream that you are a gourmet yourself, you will cultivate your mind, body and taste to the highest polish.

For a woman to dream of trying to satisfy a gourmet signifies that she may have a distinguished husband, but to her he will be demanding.

Gout

If you dream of having the gout, you will be sure to be exasperated beyond endurance by the silly conduct of some relative, and suffer small financial loss through the same person.

Grain

Grain is a most fortunate dream, betokening wealth and happiness. For a young woman, it is a dream of fortune. She will meet wealthy and adoring companions.

Grammar

To dream that you are studying grammar denotes that you are soon to make a wise choice in momentous opportunities.

Grandparents

To dream of meeting your grandparents and conversing with them, you will meet with difficulties that will be hard to surmount, but by following good advice you will overcome many barriers.

Grapes

To eat grapes in your dream, you will be hardened with many cares; but if you only see them hanging in profuseness among the leaves, you will soon attain to eminent positions and will be able to impart happiness to others. For a young woman, this dream is one of bright promise. She will have her most ardent wish gratified.

If there arises in your mind a question of the poisonous quality of the fruit you are eating, there will come doubts and fears of success, but they will gradually cease to worry you.

Grass

This is a very propitious dream indeed. It gives promise of a happy and well advanced life to the tradesman, rapid accumulation of wealth and fame to literary and artistic people, and a safe voyage through the turbulent sea of love is promised to all lovers.

To see a rugged mountain beyond the green expanse of grass is momentous of remote trouble.

If, in passing through green grass, you pass withered places, it warns of illness or embarrassments in business.

To be a perfect dream, the grass must be clear of obstruction or blemishes. If you dream of withered grass, the reverse is predicted.

Grasshopper

To dream of seeing grasshoppers on green vegetables denotes that enemies threaten your best interests. If on withered grasses, ill health. Disappointing business may be experienced.

If you see grasshoppers between you and the sun, it denotes that you will have a vexatious problem in your immediate business life to settle, but by using caution it will adjust itself in your favour. To call peoples' attention to the grasshoppers shows that you are not discreet in dispatching your private business.

Grave

To dream that you see a newly made grave, you may have to suffer for the wrongdoings of others.

If you visit a newly made grave, danger of a serious nature is hanging over you. Grave is an unfortunate dream. Ill luck in business transactions may follow, also sickness is threatened.

If you look into an empty grave, it warns of disappointment and loss of friends.

To see your own grave warns that enemies are warily seeking to engulf you in disaster, and that if you fail to be watchful they will succeed.

To dream of digging a grave denotes uneasiness over some undertaking, as enemies will seek to thwart you, but if you finish the grave you will overcome opposition. If the sun is shining, good will come out of seeming embarrassments.

To see a graveyard barren, except on top of the graves, signifies much sorrow and despondency for a time, but greater benefits and pleasure await you if you properly shoulder your burden.

Gravel

To dream of gravel warns of unfruitful schemes and enterprises.

If you see gravel mixed with dirt, it warns you will unfortunately speculate and lose good property.

Gravy

To dream of eating gravy warns of ill health and disappointing business.

Grease

To dream you are in grease is significant of travels being enjoyed with disagreeable but polished strangers.

Greek

To dream of reading Greek denotes that your ideas will be discussed and finally accepted and put in practical use. To fail to read it denotes that technical difficulties are in your way.

Green

To dream of or in green signifies, if the dream is positive, rebirth, regeneration and hope. If the dream is negative, it betokens jealousy, madness and decay.

To see green apparel is a hopeful sign of prosperity and happiness.

Greenhouse

To see a greenhouse foretells you are likely to be injured by listening to flattery. For a young woman to dream that she is living in a greenhouse, her coming trouble and threatened loss of reputation is emphasized.

Greyhound

A greyhound is a fortunate object to see in your dream. If it is following a young girl, you will be surprised with a legacy from unknown people. If a greyhound is owned by you, it signifies friends where enemies were expected.

Grindstone

For a person to dream of turning a grindstone, his dream is prophetic of a life of energy and well-directed efforts bringing handsome competency.

If you are sharpening tools, you will be blessed with a worthy helpmate.

To deal in grindstones is significant of small but honest gain.

Groans

If you hear groans in your dream, decide quickly on your course, for enemies are undermining your business. If you are groaning with fear, you will be pleasantly surprised at the turn for better in your affairs, and you may look for pleasant visiting among friends.

Groceries

To dream of general groceries, if they are fresh and clean, is a sign of ease and comfort.

Grotto

To see a grotto in your dreams is a sign of incomplete and inconstant friendships.

Guardian

To dream of a guardian denotes that you will be treated with consideration by your friends. For a young woman to dream that she is being unkindly dealt with by her guardian, foretells that she may have loss and trouble in the future.

Guitar

To dream that you have a guitar, or are playing one in a dream, signifies a merry gathering and serious lovemaking. For a young

211

woman to think it is unstrung or broken foretells that disappointments in love are likely to overtake her.

Upon hearing the music of a guitar, the dreamer should fortify herself against flattery and soft persuasion, for she is in danger of being tempted by a fascinating evil. If the dreamer be a man, he will be courted, and will be likely to lose his judgment under the wiles of seductive women.

If you play on a guitar, your family affairs will be harmonious.

Gulls

To dream of gulls is a prophecy of peaceful dealings with ungenerous persons. Seeing dead gulls betokens wide separation for friends.

Gun

This is a dream of distress. Hearing the sound of a gun warns of loss of employment, and bad management to proprietors of establishments.

If you shoot a person with a gun, you risk falling into dishonour.

If you are shot, you may be annoyed by evil persons, and perhaps suffer an illness.

For a woman to dream of shooting forecasts for her a quarrelsome and disagreeable reputation connected with sensations. For a married woman, unhappiness through other women.

Gutter

To dream of a gutter is a sign of degradation. You may be the cause of unhappiness to others.

To find articles of value in a gutter, your right to certain property will be questioned.

Gymnast

To dream of a gymnast warns of misfortune in speculation or trade.

Gypsy

If you dream of visiting a gypsy camp, you will have an offer of importance and will investigate the standing of the parties to your disadvantage.

For a woman to have a gypsy tell her fortune is an omen of a speedy and unwise marriage. If she is already married, she may be unduly jealous of her husband.

For a man to hold any conversation with a gypsy, he will be likely to lose valuable property.

To dream of trading with a gypsy, you will lose money in speculation. This dream denotes that material pleasures are the biggest items in your life.

H

'And being warned of God in a dream that they should not return to Herod, they departed into their own country another way.'

—*Matthew* ii, 12.

Haggard

To see a haggard face in your dreams warns of misfortune and defeat in love matters.

To see your own face haggard and distressed denotes trouble over female affairs, which may render you temporarily unable to meet business engagements.

Hail

If you dream of being in a hailstorm, you are likely to meet poor success in an undertaking.

If you watch hailstones fall through sunshine and rain, you will be harassed by cares for a time, but fortune will soon smile upon you. For a young woman, this dream indicates love after many slights.

To hear hail beating the house indicates distressing situations.

Hair

If a woman dreams that she has beautiful hair and combs it, she may be careless in her personal affairs, and will consequently lose advancement by neglecting mental application.

To see yourself covered with hair omens indulgence in vices to such an extent as will debar you from the society of refined people. If a woman, she will resolve herself into a world of her own, claiming the right to act for her own pleasure regardless of moral codes.

If a man dreams that he has black, curling hair, he may deceive people through his pleasing address. He will very likely deceive the women who trust him. If a woman's hair seems black and curly, she may be threatened with seduction.

If you dream of seeing a woman with golden hair, you will prove a fearless lover and be woman's true friend.

To dream that your sweetheart has red hair, you may be denounced by the woman you love for unfaithfulness. Red hair usually suggests changes.

If you see brown hair, you are likely to be unfortunate in choosing a career.

If you see well-kept and neatly combed hair, your fortune will improve.

To dream you cut your hair close to the scalp denotes that you will be generous to the point of lavishness towards a friend. Frugality will be the fruits growing out therefrom.

To see the hair growing out soft and luxuriant signifies happiness and luxury.

For a woman to compare a white hair with a black one, which she takes from her head, foretells that she will be likely to hesitate between two offers of seeming fortune, and unless she uses great care, will choose the one that will afford her loss or distress instead of pleasant fortune.

To see tangled and unkempt hair, life will be a veritable burden, business may fall off, and the marriage yoke be troublesome to carry.

If a woman is unsuccessful in combing her hair, she will lose a worthy man's name by needless show of temper and disdain.

For a young woman to dream of women with grey hair notes that they may come into her life as rivals in the affection of a male relative, or displace the love of her affianced.

To dream of having your hair cut warns of serious disappointments.

For a woman to dream that her hair is falling out, and baldness is apparent, she will have to earn her own livelihood, as fortune has passed her by.

For man or woman to dream that they have hair of snowy whiteness denotes that they will enjoy a pleasing and fortunate journey through life.

For a man to caress the hair of a woman shows he will enjoy the love and confidence of some worthy woman who will trust him despite the world's condemnation.

To see flowers in your hair foretells troubles approaching which, when they come, will give you less fear than when viewed from a distance.

For a woman to dream that her hair turns to white flowers augurs that troubles of a various nature will confront her, and she will do well if she strengthens her soul with patience, and endeavours to bear her trials with fortitude.

To dream that a lock of your hair turns grey and falls out is a sign of trouble and disappointment in your affairs. Sickness may cast gloom over bright expectations.

To see one's hair turn perfectly white in one night, and the face seemingly young, foretells sudden calamity. For a young woman to have this dream, signifies that she should be careful of her associates.

Hairdresser

Should you visit a hairdresser in your dreams, you may be connected with a sensation caused by the indiscretion of a good looking woman. To a woman, this dream means a family disturbance and well-merited censures.

For a woman to dream of having her hair coloured, she will narrowly escape the scorn of society, as enemies will seek to blight her reputation. To have her hair dressed denotes that she will run after frivolous things, and use any means to bend people to her wishes.

Halter

To dream that you put a halter on a young horse shows that you will manage a very prosperous and clean business. Love matters will shape themselves to suit you.

To see other things haltered denotes that fortune will be withheld from you for a while. You will win it, but with much toil.

Ham

To dream of seeing hams signifies you are in danger of being treacherously used. To cut large slices of ham denotes that all opposition will be successfully met by you. To dress a ham signifies that you will be leniently treated by others.

To dream of dealing in hams, prosperity will come to you. Also good health is foreboded.

To eat ham, you will lose something of great value. To smell ham cooking, you will be benefited by the enterprises of others.

Hammer

To dream of seeing a hammer denotes you will have some discouraging obstacles to overcome in order to establish firmly your fortune.

Hand

If you see beautiful hands in your dream, you will enjoy great distinction, and rise rapidly in your calling; but ugly and malformed hands point to disappointments and poverty. To see blood on them denotes estrangement and unjust censure from members of your family.

If you have an injured hand, some person will succeed to what you are striving most to obtain.

To see a detached hand indicates a solitary life, that is, people will fail to understand your views and feelings. To burn your hands, you will overreach the bounds of reason in your struggles for wealth and fame, and lose thereby.

To see your hands covered with hair denotes that you will not become a solid and leading factor in your circle.

This dream also indicates that you may be willing to intrigue against innocent people, and warns that you have alert enemies who are working to forestall your designs.

To see your hands enlarged denotes a quick advancement in your affairs. To see them smaller, the reverse is predicted.

To see your hands soiled denotes that you may be envious and unjust to others.

To wash your hands, you will participate in some joyous festivity.

For a woman to admire her own hands is proof that she will win and hold the sincere regard of the man she prizes above all others.

To admire the hands of others, she may be subjected to the whims of a jealous man. To have a man hold her hands, she may be enticed into illicit engagements. If she lets others kiss her hands, she will have gossips busy with her reputation. To handle fire without burning her hands, she will rise to high rank and commanding positions.

To dream that your hands are tied denotes that you will be involved in difficulties. In loosening them, you will force others to submit to your dictations.

Handbag

To dream of a large, untidy handbag denotes that you need to sort out chaos in your life.

Handbills

To dream of distributing handbills over the country is a sign of contentions and possible lawsuits.

If you dream of printing handbills, you may hear unfavourable news.

Handcuffs

To find yourself handcuffed, you will be annoyed and vexed by enemies. To see others thus, you will subdue those oppressing you and rise above your associates.

To see handcuffs, you may be menaced with sickness and danger.

To dream of handcuffs denotes that formidable enemies are surrounding you with objectionable conditions. To break them is a sign that you will escape toils planned by enemies.

Handkerchiefs

To dream of handkerchiefs denotes flirtations and contingent affairs.

To lose one omens a broken engagement through no fault of yours.

To see torn ones foretells that lovers' quarrels may reach such straits that reconciliation will be improbable if not impossible.

To see them soiled warns that you may be corrupted by indiscriminate associations.

To see pure white ones in large lots foretells that you will resist the insistent flattery of unscrupulous and evil-minded persons, and thus gain entrance into high relations with love and matrimony.

To see them coloured denotes that while your engagements may not be strictly moral, you will manage them with such ingenuity that they will elude opprobrium.

If you see silk handkerchiefs, it denotes that your pleasing and magnetic personality will shed its radiating cheerfulness upon others, making for yourself a fortunate existence.

For a young woman to wave adieu or a recognition with her handkerchief, or see others doing this, denotes that she will soon make a questionable pleasure trip, or may knowingly run the gauntlet of disgrace to secure some fancied pleasure.

Handsome

To see yourself handsome-looking in your dreams, you will prove yourself an ingenious flatterer.

To see others appearing handsome denotes that you will enjoy the confidence of fast people.

Handwriting

To dream that you see and recognize your own handwriting warns that malicious enemies may use your expressed opinion to foil you in advancing to some competed position.

Hanging

To see a large concourse of people gathering at a hanging warns that many enemies will club together to try to demolish your position in their midst.

Harbour

To dream of a harbour generally signifies that you will leave behind part of your life in order to progress. This dream can also signify a need for protection.

Hare

If you see a hare escaping from you in a dream, you will lose something valuable in a mysterious way. If you capture one, you will be the victor in a contest.

If you make pets of them, you will have an orderly but unintelligent companion.

To see hares chased by dogs denotes trouble and contentions among your friends, and you will concern yourself to bring about friendly relations.

If you dream that you shoot a hare, you may be forced to use violent measures to maintain your rightful posessions.

See also **Rabbit.**

Harem

To dream that you maintain a harem denotes that you are wasting your best energies on low pleasures. Life holds fair promises, if your desires are rightly directed.

If a woman dreams that she is an inmate of a harem, she will seek pleasure where pleasure is unlawful. If that she is a favorite of a harem, she will be preferred before others in material pleasures, but the distinction will be fleeting.

Harlequin

To dream of a harlequin cheating you, you will find uphill work to identify certain claims that promise profit to you. If you dream of a harlequin, trouble will beset you.

To be dressed as a harlequin denotes passionate error and unwise attacks on strength and purse. Designing women will lure you to paths of sin.

Harness

To dream of possessing bright new harness, you will soon prepare for a pleasant journey.

Harp

To hear the sad sweet strains of a harp denotes a sad ending to what seems a pleasing and profitable enterprise.

To see a broken harp warns of illness, or broken troth between lovers.

To play a harp yourself signifies that your nature is too trusting, and that you should be more careful in placing your confidence as well as love matters.

Harvest

To dream of harvest time is a forerunner of prosperity and pleasure. If the harvest yields are abundant, the indications are good for country and state, as political machinery will grind to advance all conditions.

A poor harvest is a sign of small profits.

Hassock

To dream of a hassock forebodes the yielding of your power and fortune to another. If a woman dreams of a hassock, she should cultivate spirit and independence.

Hat

To dream of losing your hat, you may expect unsatisfactory business and failure of persons to keep important engagements.

To dream of having your hat knocked off denotes a loss of face.

For a man to dream that he wears a new hat predicts change of place and business, which will be very much to his advantage. For a woman to dream that she wears a fine new hat denotes the attainment of wealth, and that she will be the object of much admiration.

For the wind to blow your hat off denotes sudden changes in affairs, and somewhat for the worse.

See also **Bonnet**.

Hatchet

A hatchet seen in a dream denotes that wanton wastefulness will expose you to the evil designs of envious persons. If it is rusty or broken, you will have grief over wayward people.

See also Axe.

Hate

To dream that you hate a person denotes that if you are not careful you will do the party an inadvertent injury or a spiteful action will bring business loss and worry.

If you are hated for unjust causes, you will find sincere and obliging friends, and your associations will be most pleasant. Otherwise, the dream forebodes ill.

Hawk

To dream of a hawk warns that you may be cheated in some way by intriguing persons. To shoot one foretells you will surmount obstacles after many struggles.

For a young woman to frighten hawks away from her chickens signifies she will obtain her most extravagant desires through diligent attention to her affairs. It also denotes that enemies are near you, and they are ready to take advantage of your slightest mistakes. If you succeed in scaring it away before your fowls are injured, you will be lucky in your business.

To see a dead hawk signifies that your enemies will be vanquished.

To dream of shooting at a hawk, you will have a contest with enemies, and will probably win.

Hay

If you dream of mowing hay, you will find much good in life, and if a farmer your crops will yield abundantly.

To see fields of newly cut hay is a sign of unusual prosperity.

If you are hauling and putting hay into barns, your fortune

is assured, and you will realize great profit from some enterprise.

To see loads of hay passing through the street, you will meet influential strangers who will add much to your pleasure.

To feed hay to stock indicates that you will offer aid to someone who will return the favour with love and advancement to higher states.

Hazelnut

This is a favourable dream, denoting a peaceful and harmonious domestic life and profitable business ventures.

To dream of eating them signifies to the young, delightful associations and many true friends.

Head

To see a person's head in your dream, if it is well-shaped and prominent, you will meet persons of power and vast influence who will lend you aid in enterprises of importance.

If you dream of your own head, you are threatened with nervous trouble.

To see yourself with two or more heads foretells phenomenal and rapid rise in life, but the probabilities are that the rise will not be stable.

To dream that your head aches denotes that you will be oppressed with worry.

To dream of a swollen head, you will have more good than bad in your life.

To dream of a child's head, there will be much pleasure in store for you and signal financial success.

To dream of the head of a beast denotes that the nature of your desires will run on a low plane, and only material pleasures will concern you.

To wash your head, you will be sought after by prominent people for your judgment and good counsel.

Headgear

To dream of seeing rich headgear, you will become famous and successful. To see old and worn headgear, you may have to yield up your possessions to others.

Hearse

To dream of a hearse warns of uncongenial relations in the home, and failure to carry on business in a satisfactory manner.

If a hearse crosses your path, you will have a bitter enemy to overcome.

Heart

To dream of your heart paining and suffocating you warns of trouble in your business. Some mistake of your own will bring loss if not corrected.

Seeing your heart warns of failure of energy.

To see the heart of an animal, you will overcome enemies and merit the respect of all.

To eat the heart of a chicken denotes strange desires will cause you to carry out very difficult projects for your advancement.

Heat

To dream that you are oppressed by heat denotes failure to carry out designs on account of some friend betraying you. Heat is not a very favourable dream.

Heather Bells

To dream of heather bells foretells that joyous occasions will pass you in happy succession.

Heaven

If you ascend to heaven in a dream, you are likely to fail to enjoy the distinction you have laboured to gain, and joy may end in sadness.

If young persons dream of climbing to heaven on a ladder, they will rise from a low estate to one of unusual prominence, but will fail to find contentment or much pleasure.

To dream of being in heaven and meeting Christ and friends, you will meet with many losses, but will reconcile yourself to them through your true understanding of human nature.

To dream of the Heavenly City denotes a contented and spiritual nature, and trouble will do you small harm.

See also **Paradise**.

Hedges

To dream of hedges of evergreens denotes joy and profit.

Bare hedges foretell distress and unwise dealings.

If a young woman dreams of walking beside a green hedge with her lover, it foretells that her marriage will soon be consummated.

If you dream of being entangled in a thorny hedge, you may be hampered in your business by unruly partners or persons working under you. To lovers, this dream is significant of quarrels and jealousies.

Heir

To dream that you fall heir to property or valuables denotes that you are in danger of losing what you already possess, and warns you of coming responsibilities. Pleasant surprises may also follow this dream.

Hell

If you dream of being in hell, you risk falling into temptations, which will almost wreck you financially and morally.

To see your friends in hell warns of distress and burdensome cares. You may hear of the misfortune of some friend.

To dream of crying in hell denotes the powerlessness of friends to extricate you from the snares of enemies.

Helmet

To dream of seeing a helmet denotes that threatened misery and loss can be avoided by wise action.

Hemp

To dream of hemp denotes that you will be successful in all undertakings, especially large engagements. For a young woman to dream that some accident befalls her through cultivating hemp warns of a quarrel and separation from a friend.

Hemp Seed

To see hemp seed in dreams denotes the approach of a deep and continued friendship. To the businessperson will be shown favourable opportunity for money-making.

Hen *see* Chickens

Herbs

To dream of herbs denotes that you will have vexatious cares, though some pleasures will ensue.

To dream of poisonous herbs warns you of enemies.

Balm and other useful herbs denote satisfaction in business and warm friendships.

Hermit

To dream of a hermit denotes sadness and loneliness caused by the unfaithfulness of friends.

If you are a hermit yourself, you will pursue researches into intricate subjects, and will take great interest in the discussions of the hour.

To find yourself in the abode of a hermit denotes unselfishness towards enemies and friends alike.

Herring

To dream of seeing herring indicates a tight squeeze to escape financial embarrassment, but you will have success later.

Hidden

To dream that you have hidden away any object denotes embarrassment in your circumstances.

To find hidden things, you will enjoy unexpected pleasures.

For a young woman to dream of hiding objects, she will be the object of much adverse gossip, but will finally prove her conduct orderly.

Hide

To dream of the hide of an animal denotes profit and permanent employment.

Hieroglyphs

Hieroglyphs seen in a dream foretell that wavering judgment in some vital matter may cause you great distress and money loss. To be able to read them, your success in overcoming some evil is foretold.

Hi-Fi

To dream of listening to a Hi-Fi system foretells the advent of some new and pleasing comrade who will lend himself willingly to advance your enjoyment. If it is broken, some fateful occurrence may thwart and defeat delights that you hold in anticipation.

High Tide

To dream of high tide is indicative of favourable progression in your affairs.

Hills

To dream of climbing hills is good if the top is reached, but if you fall back, you will have much envy and contrariness to fight against.
See also Ascent, Climbing.

Hips

To dream that you admire well-formed hips denotes that you will be upbraided by your wife.

For a woman to admire her hips suggest that she will be disappointed in love matters.

To notice fat hips on animals foretells ease and pleasure.

For a woman to dream that her hips are too narrow warns of sickness and disappointments. If too fat, she is in danger of losing her reputation.

Hissing

To dream of hissing persons is an omen that you will be displeased beyond endurance at the discourteous treatment shown you while among newly made acquaintances. If they hiss you, you may be threatened with the loss of a friend.

History

To dream that you are reading history indicates a long and pleasant recreation.

Hives

To dream that your child is affected with hives denotes that it will enjoy good health and be docile.

To see strange children thus affected, you will be unduly frightened over the condition of some favourite.

Hoe

To dream of seeing a hoe denotes that you will have no time for idle pleasures, as there will be others depending upon your work for subsistence.

To dream of using a hoe, you will enjoy freedom from poverty by directing your energy into safe channels.

For a woman to dream of hoeing, she will be independent of others, as she will be self-supporting. For lovers, this dream is a sign of faithfulness.

To dream of a foe striking at you with a hoe, your interests will be threatened by enemies, but with caution you will keep aloof from real danger.

Holiday

To dream of a holiday foretells that interesting strangers will soon partake of your hospitality. For a young woman to dream that she is displeased with a holiday denotes she may be fearful of her own attractions in winning a friend back from a rival.

Holy Communion

To dream that you are taking part in the Holy Communion warns you that you will resign your independent opinions to gain some frivolous desire.

If you dream that there is neither bread nor wine for the supper, you may find that you have suffered your ideas to be proselytized in vain, as you are no nearer your goal.

If you are refused the right of communion but feel worthy, there is hope for your obtaining some prominent position which has appeared extremely doubtful, as your opponents are popular and powerful. If you feel unworthy, you will meet with much discomfort.

To dream that you are in a body of Baptists who are taking communion, denotes that you will find that your friends are growing uncongenial, and will look to strangers for harmony.

Home

To dream of visiting your old home, you will have good news to rejoice over.

To see your old home in a dilapidated state warns you of the sickness or death of a relative. For a young woman this is a dream of sorrow. She may lose a dear friend.

To go home and find everything cheery and comfortable denotes harmony in the present home life and satisfactory results in business.

See also **Abode**.

Homesick

To dream of being homesick foretells that you may lose fortunate opportunities to enjoy travels of interest and pleasant visits.

Honey

To dream that you see honey, you will be possessed of considerable wealth.

To see strained honey denotes wealth and ease, but there will be an undercurrent in your life of unlawful gratification of material desires.

To dream of eating honey foretells that you will attain wealth and love. To lovers, this indicates a swift rush into marital joys.

Honeysuckle

To see or gather, honeysuckles, denotes that you will be contentedly prosperous and your marriage will be a singularly happy one.

Hood

For a young woman to dream that she is wearing a hood is a sign she will attempt to allure some man from rectitude and bounden duty.

Hook

To dream of a hook foretells that unhappy obligations will be assumed by you.

Hoop

To dream of a hoop foretells that you will form influential friendships. Many will seek counsel of you. To jump through, or see others jumping through hoops, denotes you will have discouraging outlooks, but you will overcome them with decisive victory.

Hops

To dream of hops denotes thrift, energy and the power to grasp and master almost any business proposition. Hops is a favourable dream to everyone.

Horn

To dream that you hear the sound of a horn foretells hasty news of a joyful character.

To see a broken horn warns of death or accident.

To see children playing with horns denotes congeniality in the home.

For a woman to dream of blowing a horn foretells that she is more anxious for marriage than her lover.

Hornet

To dream of a hornet signals disruption to lifelong friendship, and loss of money.

For a young woman to dream that one stings her, or she is in a nest of them, foretells that many envious women may seek to disparage her before her admirers.

Horoscope

To dream of having your horoscope drawn by an astrologist foretells unexpected changes in affairs and a long journey; associations with a stranger will probably happen.

If the dreamer has the stars pointed out to him, as his fate is being read, he will find disappointments where fortune and pleasure seem to await him.

Horse

To dream of a horse warns of the crushing of the personality but also looks forward to its rebirth.

A white horse brings rebirth. If you dream of seeing or riding a white horse, the indications are favourable for prosperity and pleasurable commingling with congenial friends and fair women. If the white horse is soiled and lean, your confidence may be betrayed by a jealous friend or a woman. If the horse is black, you will be successful in your fortune, but you will practice deception, and be guilty of assignations. To a woman, this dream denotes that her husband may be unfaithful.

To dream of dark horses signifies prosperous conditions, but a large amount of discontent. Fleeting pleasures usually follow this dream.

To see yourself riding a fine bay horse denotes a rise in fortune and gratification of passion. For a woman, it foretells a yielding to importunate advances. She will enjoy material things.

To ride or see passing horses denotes ease and comfort.

To ride a runaway horse, your interests may be injured by the folly of a friend or employer.

To see a horse running away with others denotes that you may hear of the illness of friends.

To see fine stallions is a sign of success and high living; undue passion may master you.

To see brood mares warns of congeniality and absence of jealousy between the married and sweethearts.

To ride a horse to ford a stream, you will soon experience some good fortune and will enjoy rich pleasures. If the stream is unsettled or murky, anticipated joys will be somewhat disappointing.

To swim on a horse's back through a clear and beautiful stream of water, your conception of passionate bliss will be swiftly realized. To a businessperson, this dream portends great gain.

To see a wounded horse warns of the trouble of friends.

To dream of a dead horse signifies disappointments of various kinds.

To dream of riding a horse that bucks denotes that your desires will be difficult of consummation. To dream that he throws you, you will have a strong rival, and your business will suffer slightly through competition.

To dream of being menaced by a horse betokens impotence in the face of a crushing, destructive force.

To dream that a horse kicks you, you will be repulsed by one you love. Your fortune will be embarrassed by ill health.

To dream of catching a horse to bridle and saddle, or harnessing it, you will see a great improvement in business of all kinds, and people of all callings will prosper. If you fail to catch it, fortune will play you false.

To see spotted horses foretells that various enterprises will bring you profit.

To dream of having a horse shod, your success is assured. For a woman, this dream omens a good and faithful husband.

To dream that you shoe a horse denotes that you will endeavour to and perhaps succeed is making doubtful property your own.

To dream of racehorses denotes that you will be surfeited with fast living, but to the farmer this dream denotes prosperity.

To dream that you ride a horse in a race you will be prosperous and enjoy life.

To dream of killing a horse, you may injure your friends through selfishness.

To mount a horse bareback, you will gain wealth and ease by hard struggles.

To ride bareback in company with men, you will have honest people to aid you, and your success will be merited. If in company with women, your desires will be loose, and your prosperity will not be so abundant as might be if women did not fill your heart.

To dream of trimming a horse's mane, or tail, denotes that you will be a good financier or farmer. Literary people will be painstaking in their work and others will look after their interest with solicitude.

To dream of horses, you will amass wealth and enjoy life to its fullest extent.

To see horses pulling vehicles denotes wealth with some encumbrance, and love will find obstacles.

If you are riding up a hill and the horse falls but you gain the top, you will win fortune, though you will have to struggle against enemies and jealousy. If both the horse and you get to the top, your rise will be phenomenal, but substantial.

For a young girl to dream that she rides a black horse denotes that she should be dealt with by wise authority. Some wishes will be gratified at an unexpected time. Black, in horses, signifies postponements in anticipations.

To see a horse with a tender foot denotes that some unexpected unpleasantness may insinuate itself into your otherwise propitious state.

If you attempt to fit a broken shoe which is too small for the horse's foot, you may be charged with making fraudulent deals with unsuspecting parties.

To ride a horse downhill, your affairs will undoubtedly disappoint you. For a young woman to dream that a friend rides behind her on a horse denotes that she will be foremost in the favours of many prominent and successful men. If she is frightened, she is likely to stir up jealous sensations. If after she alights from the horse it turns into a pig, she will carelessly pass by honourable offers of marriage, preferring freedom until her chances of a desirable marriage are lost. If afterward she sees the pig sliding gracefully along the telegraph wire, she will by intriguing advance her position.

For a young woman to dream that she is riding a white horse up and down hill, often looking back and seeing some one on a black horse, pursuing her, denotes that she will have a mixed season of success and sorow, but that through it all a relentless enemy is working to overshadow her with gloom and disappointment.

See also **Foal, Mare, Pony, Stallion.**

Horseradish

To dream of horseradish foretells pleasant associations with intellectual and congenial people. Fortune is also expressed in this dream. For a woman, it indicates a rise above her present station.

To eat horseradish, you will be the object of pleasant teasing.

Horseshoe

To dream of a horseshoe indicates advance in business and lucky engagements for women.

To see them broken, ill fortune and sickness is portrayed.

To find a horseshoe hanging on the fence denotes that your interests will advance beyond your most sanguine expectations.

To pick one up in the road, you will receive profit from a source you know not of.

Horse Trader

To dream of a horse trader signifies great profit from perilous ventures.

To dream that you are trading horses, and the trader cheats you, you will lose in trade or love. If you get a better horse than the one you traded, you will better yourself in fortune.

Hospital

If you dream that you are a patient in a hospital, you will escape from an outbreak of illness in your community. If you visit patients there, you may hear distressing news of an absent person.

To dream of hospitals can indicate a desire to be taken into the care of others and to abandon your responsibilities.

To dream that you are leaving a hospital denotes your escape from wily enemies who have caused you much worry.

Hotel

To dream of living in a hotel denotes ease and profit.

To visit women in a hotel suggests that your life will be rather dissolute.

To dream of seeing a fine hotel indicates wealth and travel.

If you dream that you are the proprietor of a hotel, you will earn all the fortune you will ever possess.

To work in a hotel, you could find a more remunerative employment than what you have.

To dream of hunting a hotel, you will be baffled in your search for wealth and happiness.

Hotels can also denote an inner dislocation in the dreamer's life.

Hot Toddy

To dream of taking a hot toddy foretells interesting events will soon change your way of living.

Hounds

To dream of hounds on a hunt denotes coming delights and pleasant changes. For a woman to dream of hounds, she will love a man below her in station. To dream that hounds are following her, she will have many admirers, but there will be no real love felt for her.

See also **Dogs**.

House

To dream of building a house, you will make wise changes in your present affairs.

To dream that you own an elegant house denotes that you will soon leave your home for a better, and fortune will be kind to you.

Old and dilapidated houses warn of failure in business or any effort, and declining health.

To dream of a house in the centre of a series of avenues which radiate out omens very good fortune indeed.

Housekeeper

To dream that you are a housekeeper denotes that you will have labours which will occupy your time, and make pleasure an ennobling thing. To employ one signifies that comparative comfort will be possible for your obtaining.

Hugging

If you dream of hugging you are likely to be disappointed in love affairs and in business.

For a woman to dream of hugging a man, she may accept advances of a doubtful character from men.

For a married woman to hug others than her husband, she will endanger her honour if she accepts attentions from others in her husband's absence.

Humidity

To dream that you are overcome with humidity forewarns that you will combat enemies fiercely but their superior force will submerge you in overwhelming defeat.

Hunchback

To dream of a hunchback warns of unexpected reverses in your prospects.

Hunger

To dream that you are hungry is an unfortunate omen. You will not find comfort and satisfaction in your home. To lovers it betokens an unhappy marriage.

Hunting

If you dream of hunting, you will struggle for the unattainable.

If you dream that you hunt game and find it, you will overcome obstacles and gain your desires.

Hurt

If you hurt a person in your dreams, you will do ugly work, revenging and injuring.

If you are hurt, you will have enemies who will overcome you.

Hurricane

To hear the roar and see a hurricane heading towards you with its frightful force, you will undergo suspense, striving to avert failure in your affairs.

If you are in a house which is being blown to pieces by a hurricane, and you struggle in the awful gloom to extricate someone from the falling timbers, your life will suffer a change. You may move and remove to distant places, yet still find no improvement in domestic or business affairs.

If you dream of looking on debris and havoc wrought by a hurricane, you will come close to trouble, which will be averted by the turn in the affairs of others.

To see dead and wounded caused by a hurricane, you will be distressed over the troubles of others.

See also **Tornado, Whirlwind.**

Husband

To dream that your husband is leaving you, and you do not understand why, there will be bitterness between you, but an unexpected reconciliation will ensue. If he mistreats and upbraids you for unfaithfulness, you will hold his regard and confidence, but other worries will ensue and you are warned to be more discreet in receiving attention from men.

To see him cheerful and handsome, your home will be filled with happiness and bright prospects will be yours. If he is sick, you may be mistreated by him.

To dream that he is in love with another woman warns that he may soon tire of his present surroundings and seek pleasure elsewhere.

To be in love with another woman's husband in your dreams denotes that you are not happily married, or that you are not happy unmarried, but, the chances for happiness are doubtful.

For an unmarried woman to dream that she has a husband denotes that she may be wanting in the graces which men most admire.

To see your husband depart from you, and as he recedes from you he grows larger, inharmonious surroundings will prevent immediate congeniality. If disagreeable conclusions are avoided, harmony will be reinstated.

For a woman to dream of seeing her husband in a compromising position with an unsuspected party denotes she may have trouble through the indiscretion of friends. If he is with another woman and a scandal ensues, she may be in danger of separating from her husband or losing property. Unfavourable conditions tend to follow this dream, though the evil is often exaggerated.

Hut

To dream of a hut denotes indifferent success.

To dream that you are sleeping in a hut warns of ill health and dissatisfaction.

To see a hut in a green pasture denotes prosperity, but fluctuating happiness.

Hyacinth

To dream that you see, or gather, hyacinths, you are about to undergo a painful separation from a friend, which will ultimately result in good for you.

Hyena

If you see a hyena in your dreams, you are likely to meet disappointment and ill luck in your undertakings, and your companions will be very uncongenial. If lovers have this dream, they will often be involved in quarrels.

If one attacks you, your reputation may be set upon by busybodies.

Hymns

To dream of hearing hymns sung denotes contentment in the home and average prospects in business affairs.

Hypocrite

To dream that anyone has acted the hypocrite with you, you may be turned over to your enemies by false friends.

To dream that you are a hypocrite denotes that you are likely to prove yourself a deceiver and be false to friends.

Hypnosis

To dream that you are in a hypnotic state or under the power of others portends disastrous results, for your enemies will enthrall you; but if you hold others under a spell you will assert decided will power in governing your surroundings.

For a young woman to dream that she is under strange influences denotes her immediate exposure to danger; she should beware.

To dream of seeing hypnotic and sleight-of-hand performances signifies worries and perplexities in business and domestic circles, and unhealthy conditions of state.

To dream of seeing a hypnotist trying to hypnotize others, and then turning his attention on you and failing to hypnotize you, indicates that a trouble is hanging over you which friends will not succeed in warning off. You alone can avert the impending danger.

Hyssop

To dream of hyssop warns that you may have grave charges preferred against you; if a woman, your reputation will be endangered.

I

'And it shall come to pass in the last days, saith God, I will pour out my Spirit upon all flesh; and your sons and your daughters prophesy – and you young men shall see visions, and your old men shall dream dreams.'

—Acts ii, 17.

Ice

To dream of ice warns of distress; evil-minded persons may seek to injure you in your best work. Beware if you dream of ice: at the most basic level, it can simply signify that you should attach more importance to feelings and the emotional aspect of life. For creative people, it could denote a block. At an extreme level, it may denote that your soul is frozen, your emotions are in danger of dying and you are drawing close to psychic stagnation.

To see ice floating in a stream of clear water denotes that your happiness may be interrupted by ill-tempered and jealous friends.

To dream that you walk on ice, you risk much solid comfort and respect for evanescent joys.

For a young woman to walk on ice is a warning that only a thin veil hides her from shame.

To dream that you make ice, you risk making a failure of your life through egotism and selfishness.

Eating ice foretells sickness. If you drink ice-water, you will bring ill health from dissipation.

Bathing in ice-water, anticipated pleasures will be interrupted with an unforeseen event.

Ice Cream

To dream that you are eating ice cream foretells that you will have happy success in affairs already undertaken. To see children eating it denotes prosperity and happiness will attend you most favourably.

For a young woman to upset her ice cream in the presence of her lover or friend denotes that she will be flirted with because of her unkindness to others. To see sour ice cream denotes that some unexpected trouble will interfere with your pleasures. If it is melted, your anticipated pleasure will reach stagnation before it is realized.

Icicles

To see icicles falling from trees denotes that some distinctive misfortune, or trouble, will soon vanish.

To see icicles on the eaves of houses warns of misery and want of comfort. Ill health is foreboded.

To see icicles on the fence denotes suffering bodily and mentally.

To see them on evergreens, a bright future may be overcast with the shadow of doubtful honours.

Ideal

For a young woman to dream of meeting her ideal foretells a season of uninterrupted pleasure and contentment. For a bachelor to dream of meeting his ideal denotes that he will soon experience a favourable change in his affairs.

Idiot

Idiots in a dream foretell disagreements and losses.

To dream that you are an idiot, you will feel humiliated and downcast over the miscarriage of plans.

To see idiotic children denotes affliction and unhappy changes in life.

Idle

If you dream of being idle, you will fail to accomplish your designs.

To see your friends in idleness, you may hear of some trouble affecting them.

For a young woman to dream that she is leading an idle existence, she risks falling into bad habits, and is likely to marry a shiftless man.

Idols

Should you dream of worshipping idols, you will make slow progress to wealth or fame, as you will let petty things tyrannize over you.

To break idols signifies a strong mastery over self, and that no work will deter you in your upward rise to positions of honour.

To see others worshipping idols, great differences may rise up between you and warm friends.

To dream that you are denouncing idolatry, great distinction is in store for you through your understanding of the natural inclinations of the human mind.

Illness See Disease, Sickness

Image

If you dream that you see images, you are likely to have poor success in business or love.

To set up an image in your home portends that you will be weak-minded and easily led astray. Women should be careful of their reputation after a dream of this kind. If the images are ugly, you will have trouble in your home.

Imitation

To dream of imitations warns that persons are working to deceive you. For a young woman to dream someone is imitating her lover or herself foretells she may be imposed upon, and may suffer for the faults of others.

Imps

To see imps in your dream signifies trouble from what seems a passing pleasure.

To dream that you are an imp, warns that folly and vice will bring you to poverty.

Inauguration

To dream of inauguration denotes that you will rise to higher position than you have yet enjoyed. For a young woman to be disappointed in attending an inauguration predicts that she will fail to obtain her wishes.

Incantation

To dream you are using incantations warns of unpleasantness between husband and wife, or sweethearts. To hear others repeating them implies dissembling among your friends.

Incoherent

To dream of incoherence usually denotes extreme nervousness and excitement through the oppression of changing events.

Income

To dream of coming into the possession of your income denotes that you may deceive someone and cause trouble to your family and friends.

To dream that some of your family inherits an income predicts success for you.

For a woman to dream of losing her income signifies disappointments in life.

To dream that your income is insufficient to support you denotes trouble to relatives or friends.

To dream of a portion of your income remaining signifies that you will be very successful for a short time, but you may expect more than you receive.

Increase

To dream of an increase in your family may denote failure in some of your plans, and success in others.

To dream of an increase in your business signifies that you will overcome existing troubles.

Independent

To dream that you are very independent denotes that you have a rival who may do you an injustice.

To dream that you gain an independence of wealth, you may not be so successful at that time as you expect, but good results are promised.

Indifference

To dream of indifference signifies pleasant companions for a very short time.

For a young woman to dream that her sweetheart is indifferent to her signifies that he may not prove his affections in the most appropriate way. To dream that she is indifferent to him warns that she may prove untrue to him.

Indigestion

To dream of indigestion indicates unhealthy and gloomy surroundings.

Indigo

To see indigo in a dream denotes that you may deceive friendly persons in order to cheat them out of their belongings. To see indigo water warns that you may be involved in an ugly love affair.

Indistinct

If in your dreams you see objects indistinctly, it portends unfaithfulness in friendships, and uncertain dealings.

Indulgence

For a woman to dream of indulgence denotes that she will not escape unfavourable comment on her conduct.

Industry

To dream that you are industrious denotes that you will be unusually active in planning and working out ideas to further your interests, and that you will be successful in your undertakings.

For a lover to dream of being industriously at work shows he will succeed in business, and that his companion will advance his position.

To see others busy is favourable to the dreamer.

Infidelity

To dream that you are unfaithful to your partner foretells that you may be put on trial for some illegal action. If a married woman has this dream, she is in danger of failing to hold her husband's affections, letting her temper and spite overwhelm her at the slightest provocation. If the infidelity involves her husband's friend, she runs the risk of being unjustly ignored by her husband.

Infirmities

To dream of infirmities denotes misfortune in love and business; enemies are not to be misunderstood; sickness may follow.

To dream that you see others infirm warns that you may have various troubles and disappointments in business.

Influence

If you dream of seeking rank or advancement through the influence of others, your desires will fail to materialize; but if you are in an influential position, your prospects will assume a bright form.

To see friends in high positions, your companions will be congenial, and you will be free from vexations.

Inheritance

To dream that you receive an inheritance foretells that you will be successful in easily obtaining your desires.

Injury

To dream of an injury being done to you signifies that an unfortunate occurrence will soon grieve and vex you.

Ink

To see ink spilled over one's clothing, many small and spiteful meannesses may be wrought you through envy.

If a young woman sees ink, she may be slandered by a rival.

To dream that you have ink on your fingers, you will be jealous and seek to injure someone unless you exercise your better nature. If it is red ink, you may be involved in serious trouble.

To dream that you make ink, you may engage in a low and debasing business, and fall into disreputable associations.

To see bottles of ink in your dreams warns of enemies and unsuccessful interests.

Ink Stand

Empty ink stands denote that you will narrowly escape public denunciation for some supposed injustice.

To see them filled with ink, if you are not cautious, enemies will succeed in slander.

247

Inn

To dream of an inn, denotes prosperity and pleasures, if the inn is commodious and well furnished.

To be at a dilapidated and ill-kept inn denotes poor success, or mournful tasks, or unhappy journeys.

Inquest

To dream of an inquest warns that you will be unfortunate in your friendships.

Inquisition

To dream of an inquisition bespeaks for you an endless round of trouble and great disappointment.

If you are brought before an inquisition on a charge of wilfulness you may be unable to defend yourself from malicious slander.

Insane

See also **Madness**

Inscription

To dream you see an inscription warns that you may shortly receive unpleasant communications.

Insolvent

If you dream that you are insolvent, you will not have to resort to this means to square yourself with the world, as your energy and pride will enable you to transact business in a fair way. But other worries may sorely afflict you.

To dream that others are insolvent, you will meet with honest men in your dealings, but by their frankness they may harm you. For a young woman, it means her sweetheart will be honest and thrifty, but vexatious discords may arise in her affairs.

Intemperance

To dream of being intemperate in the use of your intellectual forces, you will seek after foolish knowledge fail to benefit yourself, and give pain and displeasure to your friends.

If you are intemperate in love, or other passions, you will reap disease or loss of fortune and esteem. For a young woman to dream thus, she may lose a lover and incur the displeasure of close friends.

Intercede

To intercede for some one in your dreams shows you will secure aid when you desire it most.

Interpreter

To dream of an interpreter denotes that you will undertake affairs which will fail in profit.

Interview

To dream of being interviewed denotes that you are uncertain of how to proceed in love or business.

If the dreamer is unable to answer questions at an interview, further information will be needed before following a new direction in waking life.

Intoxication

To dream of intoxication denotes that you are cultivating your desires for illicit pleasures.

See also **Drunk, Tipsy**.

Inundation

To dream of seeing cities, country or people submerged in dark, seething waters denotes great misfortune.

To see a large area inundated with clear water denotes profit and ease after seemingly hopeless struggles with fortune.

See also **Floods**.

Invalid

To dream of invalids is a sign of displeasing companions interfering with your interest. To think you are one portends that you are threatened with displeasing circumstances.

Invective

To dream of using invectives warns you of passionate outbursts of anger, which may estrange you from close companions.

To hear others using them warns that enemies are closing you in to apparent wrong and deceits.

Inventor

To dream of an inventor foretells that you will soon achieve some unique work which will add honour to your name. To dream that you are inventing something, or feel interested in some invention, denotes you will aspire to fortune and will be successful in your designs.

Invite

To dream that you invite persons to visit you denotes that some unpleasant event is near, and may cause worry and excitement in your otherwise pleasant surroundings.

If you are invited to make a visit, you may receive sad news.

For a woman to dream that she is invited to attend a party, she will have pleasant anticipations but ill luck will mar them.

Iron

To dream of iron is a harsh omen of distress.

To feel an iron weight bearing you down signifies mental perplexities and material losses.

To strike with iron denotes selfishness and cruelty to those dependent upon you.

To dream that you manufacture iron denotes that you may use unjust means to accumulate wealth.

To sell iron, you are likely to have doubtful success, and your friends will not be of noble character.

To see old, rusty iron warns of poverty and disappointment.

To dream that the price of iron goes down, you will realize that fortune is a very unsafe factor in your life.

If iron advances, you will see a gleam of hope in a dark prospectus.

To see red-hot iron in your dreams denotes failure for you by misapplied energy.

Ironing

To dream of ironing denotes domestic comforts and orderly business.

If a woman dreams that she burns her hands while ironing, it foretells she may have illness or jealousy to disturb her peace. If she scorches the clothes, she may have a rival who will cause her much displeasure and suspicions. If the irons seem too cold, she may lack affection in her home.

Island

To dream that you are on an island in a clear stream signifies pleasant journeys and fortunate enterprises. To a woman, this omens a happy marriage.

A barren island indicates forfeiture of happiness and money through intemperance.

To see an island denotes comfort and easy circumstances after much striving and worrying to meet honourable obligations.

To see people on an island denotes a struggle to raise yourself higher in prominent circles.

Itch

To see persons with the itch, and you endeavour to escape contact, you will stand in fear of distressing results when your endeavours will bring pleasant success.

If you dream you have the itch yourself, you may be harshly used, and will defend yourself by incriminating others. For a young woman to have this dream omens that she may fall into dissolute companionship.

To dream that you itch has unpleasant overtones.

Ivory

To dream of ivory is favourable to the fortune of the dreamer.

To see huge pieces of ivory being carried denotes financial success and pleasures unalloyed.

Ivy

To dream of seeing ivy growing on trees or houses predicts excellent health and increase of fortune. Innumerable joys will succeed this dream. To a young woman, it augurs many prized distinctions. If she sees ivy clinging to the wall in the moonlight, she will have clandestine meetings with young men.

Withered ivy denotes broken engagements and sadness.

J

'Then thou scarest me with dreams, and terrifiest me through visions.'
—Job vii, 14.

Jackdaw

To see a jackdaw warns of ill health and quarrels. To catch one, you will outwit enemies.

To kill one, you will come into possession of disputed property.

Jail

To dream of a jail denotes that you will have engagements which will, unfortunately, result in your loss. To be an inmate of one foretells discontent at home and business setbacks. To escape from one, you will overcome difficult obstacles.

If you dream of being confined in a jail, you will be prevented from carrying out some profitable work by the intervention of envious people; but if you escape from the jail, you will enjoy a season of favourable business.

To see others in jail, you will be urged to grant privileges to persons whom you believe to be unworthy

For a young woman to dream that her lover is in jail, she will be disappointed in his character, as he is likely to prove a deceiver.

*See also **Dungeon, Prison**.*

Jailer

To see a jailer warns that treachery may embarrass your interests and evil women entrap you.

To see a mob attempting to break open a jail is a forerunner of evil; desperate measures may be used to extort money and bounties from you.

Jam

To dream of eating jam, if pure, denotes pleasant surprises and journeys.

To dream of making jam foretells to a woman a happy home and appreciative friends.

Janitor

To dream of a janitor denotes bad management and disobedient children. Unworthy servants will annoy you.

To look for a janitor and fail to find him, petty annoyances will disturb your otherwise placid existence. If you find him, you will have pleasant associations with strangers, and your affairs will have no hindrances.

January

To dream of this month warns that you may be afflicted with unloved companions or children.

Jar

To dream of empty jars denotes impoverishment and distress.

To see them full, you will be successful.

If you buy jars, your success will be precarious and your burden will be heavy.

To see broken jars, disappointment awaits you.

Jasmine

To dream of jasmine denotes you are approximating some exquisite pleasure, but which will be fleeting

Jasper

To dream of seeing jasper is a happy omen, bringing success and love. For a young woman to lose a jasper is a sign of disagreement with her lover.

Jaundice

To dream that you have jaundice denotes prosperity after temporary embarrassments

To see others with jaundice, you may be worried with unpleasant companions and discouraging prospects.

Javelin

To dream of defending yourself with a javelin, your most private affairs will be searched into to establish claims of dishonesty, and you will prove your innocence after much wrangling.

If you are pierced by a javelin, enemies will succeed in giving you trouble.

To see others carrying javelins, your interests are threatened.

Jaws

To dream of seeing heavy, misshapen jaws denotes disagreements; ill feeling may be shown between friends.

If you dream that you are in the jaws of a wild beast, enemies may work injury to your affairs and happiness. This is a vexatious and perplexing dream.

Jay

To dream of a jay foretells pleasant visits from friends and interesting gossips.

To catch a jay denotes pleasant, though unfruitful, tasks.

To see a dead jay denotes domestic unhappiness and many vicissitudes.

Jealousy

To dream that you are jealous of your wife denotes the influence of enemies and narrow-minded persons. If jealous of your sweetheart, you will seek to displace a rival.

If a woman dreams that she is jealous of her husband, she is likely to find many shocking incidents to vex and make her happiness a travesty.

If a young woman is jealous of her lover, she may find that he is more favourably impressed with the charms of some other woman than herself.

If men and women are jealous over common affairs, they will meet many unpleasant worries in the discharge of everyday business.

Jelly

To dream of eating jelly, many pleasant interruptions will take place.

For a woman to dream of making jelly signifies that she will enjoy pleasant reunions with friends.

Jester

To dream of a jester, foretells you will ignore important things in looking after silly affairs.

Jewellery

To dream of broken jewellery denotes keen disappointment in attaining one's highest desires.

If you inherit jewellery, your prosperity will be unusual, but not entirely satisfactory.

To dream of giving jewellery away warns you that some vital estate is threatening you.

Jewels

Dreams of jewels generally have great significance.

To dream of jewels denotes much pleasure and riches.

To wear them brings rank and satisfied ambitions.

To see others wearing them, distinguished places will be held by you, or by some friend.

To dream of jewelled garments betokens rare good fortune to the dreamer. Inheritance or speculation will raise him to high positions.

For a young woman to dream that she receives jewels indicates much pleasure and a desirable marriage. To dream that she loses jewels, she will meet people who will flatter and deceive her.

To find jewels denotes rapid and brilliant advancement in affairs of interest. To give jewels away, you will unconsciously work detriment to yourself.

To buy them proves that you will be very successful in momentous affairs, especially those pertaining to the heart.

Jew's-harp

To dream of a Jew's-harp foretells you will experience a slight improvement in your affairs. To play one is a sign that you will fall in love with a stranger.

Jig

To dance a jig denotes cheerful occupations and light pleasures.

To see your sweetheart dancing a jig, your companion will be possessed with a merry and hopeful disposition.

To see ballet girls dancing a jig, you will engage in undignified amusements and follow low desires.

Jockey

To dream of a jockey omens that you will appreciate a gift from an unexpected source. For a young woman to dream that she associates with a jockey, or has one for a lover, indicates she will win a husband out of her station. To see one thrown from a horse signifies that you will be called on for aid by strangers.

Jolly

To dream that you feel jolly and are enjoying the merriment of companions, you will realize pleasure from the good behaviour of children and have satisfying results in business. If there comes the least rift in the merriment, worry will intermingle with the success of the future.

Journalist

If in your dreams you unwillingly see them, you will be annoyed with small talk, and perhaps quarrels of a low character.

If you are a journalist in your dreams, there will be a varied course of travel offered you; you may experience unpleasant situations, yet there will be some honour and gain attached.

Journey

To dream that you go on a journey signifies profit or a disappointment, as the travels are pleasing and successful or as accidents and disagreeable events take active part in your journeying.

To see your friends start cheerfully on a journey signifies delightful change and more harmonious companions than you have heretofore known. If you see them depart looking sad, it may be many moons before you see them again. Power and loss are implied.

To make a long-distance journey in a much shorter time than you expected denotes you will accomplish some work in a surprisingly short time, which will be satisfactory in the way of reimbursement.

See also **Travel**.

Joy

To dream that you feel joy over any event denotes harmony among friends.

Jubilee

To dream of a jubilee denotes many pleasureable enterprises in which you will be a participant. For a young woman, this is a favourable dream, pointing to matrimony and increase of temporal blessings.

To dream of a religious jubilee denotes close but comfortable environments.

Judge

To dream of coming before a judge signifies that disputes will be settled by legal proceedings. Business or divorce cases may assume gigantic proportions. To have the case decided in your favour denotes a successful termination to the suit; if decided against you, then you are the aggressor and you should seek to right injustice.

Judgment Day

To dream of the judgment day foretells that you will accomplish some well-planned work, if you appear resigned and hopeful of escaping punishment. Otherwise, your work will prove a failure.

For a young woman to appear before the judgment bar and hear the verdict of 'Guilty,' denotes that she will cause much distress among her friends by her selfish and unbecoming conduct. If she sees the dead rising, and all the earth solemnly and fearfully awaiting the end, there will be much struggling for her, and her friends will refuse her aid. It is also a forerunner of unpleasant gossip, and scandal is threatened.

Jug

If you dream of jugs well filled with transparent liquids, your welfare is being considered by more than yourself. Many true friends will unite to please and profit you. If the jugs are empty, your conduct will estrange you from friends and station.

Broken jugs warn of sickness and failures in employment.

If you drink wine from a jug, you will enjoy robust health and find pleasure in all circles. Optimistic views will possess you.

To take an unpleasant drink from a jug, disappointment and disgust will follow pleasant anticipations.

July

To dream of this month denotes that you will be depressed with gloomy outlooks, but, as suddenly, your spirits will rebound to unimagined pleasure and good fortune.

Jumping

If you dream of jumping over any object, you will succeed in every endeavour; but if you jump and fall back, disagreeable affairs will render life almost intolerable.

For a young woman to dream of jumping over an obstruction denotes that she will gain her desires after much struggle and opposition.

To jump down from a wall denotes reckless speculations and disappointment in love.

Jumping Jack

To dream of a jumping jack denotes that idleness and trivial pastimes will occupy your thoughts to the exclusion of serious and sustaining plans.

June

To dream of June foretells unusual gains in all undertakings.

For a woman to think that vegetation is decaying, or that a drought is devastating the land, she may experience sorrow and loss.

Juniper

To dream of seeing a juniper tree portends happiness and wealth out of sorrow and depressed conditions. For a young woman, this dream omens a bright future after disappointing love affairs. To the sick, this is an augury of speedy recovery.

To eat, or gather, the berries of a juniper tree warns of trouble and sickness.

Jury

To dream that you are on the jury denotes dissatisfaction with your employments, and that you will seek to materially change your position.

If you are cleared from a charge by a jury, your business will be successful and affairs will move your way, but if you should be condemned, enemies will harass you beyond endurance.

Justice

To dream that you demand justice from a person denotes that you are threatened with embarrassments through the false statements of people who are eager for your downfall.

If someone demands the same of you, you will find that your conduct and reputation are being assailed, and it will be extremely difficult for you to refute the charges satisfactorily.

K

'In thoughts from the vision of the night, when deep sleep falleth on men, fear came upon me, and trembling, which made all my bones to shake.'

—Job iv, 13–14.

Kaleidoscope

Kaleidoscopes working before you in a dream portend swift changes with little favourable promise in them.

Kangaroo

To see a kangaroo in your dreams, you will outwit a wily enemy who seeks to place you in an unfavourable position before the public and the person you are striving to win.

If a kangaroo attacks you, your reputation will be in jeopardy.

If you kill one, you will succeed in spite of enemies and obstacles.

To see a kangaroo's hide denotes that you are in a fair way to success.

Katydids

To dream of hearing katydids is a prognostic of misfortune and unusual dependence on others. If any sick person asks you what they are, this foretells that there will be surprising events in your present and future.

For a woman to see them signifies she will have a quarrelsome husband or lover.

Keg

To dream of a keg denotes that you will have a struggle to throw off oppression. Broken ones indicate separation from family or friends.

Kerb

To dream of stepping on a kerbstone denotes your rapid rise in business circles, and that you will be held in high esteem by your friends and the public.

For lovers to dream of stepping together on a kerb denotes an early marriage and consequent fidelity; but if in your dream you step or fall from a kerbstone your fortunes will be reversed.

Kettle

To dream you see a kettle implies sudden news which may distress you. For a woman to pour sparkling, cold water from a kettle, she will have unexpected favour shown her.

To see a kettle of boiling water, your struggles will soon end and a change will come to you.

To see a broken kettle denotes failure after a mighty effort to work out a path to success.

For a young woman to dream of handling dark kettles, foretells disappointment in love and marriage; but a light-coloured kettle brings to her absolute freedom from care, and her husband will be handsome and worthy.

Key

To dream of keys denotes unexpected changes.

If the keys are lost, unpleasant adventures will affect you.

To find keys brings domestic peace and brisk turns to business.

Broken keys portends separation.

For a young woman to dream of losing the key to any personal ornament denotes she will have quarrels with her lover, and suffer much disquiet therefrom. If she dreams of unlocking a door with a key, she will have a new lover and have over-confidence in him. If she locks a door with a key, she will be successful in selecting a husband. If she gives the key away, she may fail to use judgment in conversation and darken her own reputation.

Keyhole

To dream that you spy upon others through a keyhole, you may damage some person by disclosing confidence. If you catch others peeping through a keyhole, you may have false friends delving into your private matters to advance themselves over you.

To dream that you cannot find the keyhole, you may unconsciously injure a friend.

Kid

To dream of a kid denotes that you may not be over-scrupulous in your morals or pleasures. You may bring grief to some loving heart.

Kidneys

To dream about your kidneys, warns of illness, or trouble in marriage relations for you.

If they act too freely, you may be a party to some racy intrigue. If they refuse to perform their work, there may be a sensation, and to your detriment. If you eat kidney stew, some officious person may cause you disgust in some secret love affair.

Killing

To dream of killing a defenceless man prognosticates sorrow and failure in affairs.

If you kill one in defence, or kill a ferocious beast, it denotes victory and a rise in position.

King

To dream of a king, you are struggling with your might, and ambition is your master.

To dream that you are crowned king, you will rise above your comrades and co-workers.

If you are censured by a king, you will be reproved for a neglected duty.

For a young woman to be in the presence of a king, she will marry a man whom she will fear. To receive favours from a king, she will rise to exalted positions and be congenially wedded.

Kiss

To dream that you see children kissing denotes happy reunions in families and satisfactory work.

To dream that you kiss your mother, you will be very successful in your enterprises, and be honoured and beloved by your friends.

To kiss a brother or sister denotes much pleasure and good in your association.

To kiss your sweetheart in the dark denotes dangers and immoral engagements.

To kiss her in the light signifies that honourable intentions always your mind occupy in connection with women.

To kiss a strange woman denotes loose morals and perverted integrity.

To dream of kissing illicitly denotes dangerous pastimes. The indulgence of a low passion may bring a tragedy into well-thought-of homes.

To see your rival kiss your sweetheart, you are in danger of losing her esteem.

For married people to kiss each other denotes that harmony is prized in the home life.

To dream of kissing a person on the neck denotes passionate inclinations and weak mastery of self.

If you dream of kissing an enemy, you will make advance towards reconciliation with an angry friend.

For a young woman to dream that some person sees her kiss her lover, indicates that spiteful envy is entertained for her by a false friend. For her to see her lover kiss another, she may be disappointed in her hopes of marriage.

Kitchen

To dream of a kitchen denotes that you may be forced to meet emergencies which will depress your spirits. For a woman to dream that her kitchen is clean and orderly, foretells she will become the mistress of interesting fortunes.

Kite

To dream of flying a kite denotes a great show of wealth, or business, but with little true soundness to it all.

To see the kite thrown upon the ground warns of disappointment and failure.

To dream of making a kite, you will speculate largely on small means and seek to win the one you love by misrepresentations.

To see children flying kites denotes pleasant and light occupation. If the kite ascends beyond the vision, high hopes and aspirations will probably resolve themselves into disappointments and loss.

Kitten

For a woman to dream of a beautiful fat, white kitten, warns that deception will be practised upon her, but her good sense and judgment will prevail in warding off unfortunate complications. If the kittens are soiled, or coloured and lean, she may be victimized into glaring indiscretions.

To dream of kittens denotes that small troubles and vexations may pursue but if you befriend the kittens, you will overcome these worries.

Knapsack

To see a knapsack while dreaming denotes you will find your greatest pleasure away from the associations of friends. For a woman to see an old dilapidated one warns of poverty and disagreeableness for her.

Knee

To dream that your knees are too large, denotes sudden ill luck for you.

For a woman to dream that she has well-formed and smooth knees predicts she will have many admirers, but none to woo her in wedlock.

To dream of knees is an unfortunate omen.

Knife

To dream of a knife is generally bad for the dreamer, as it portends separation and quarrels, and losses in affairs of a business character. However, dreams of knives can occasionally be positive. Using a knife to cut through bonds restraining you signifies liberation; cutting bruised material out of food signifies purification and cleansing. In both of these cases, the dream is a positive, reassuring one.

To see rusty knives means dissatisfaction, and complaints of those in the home, and separation of lovers.

Sharp knives and highly polished denote worry. Foes are ever surrounding you.

Broken knives denote defeat whether in love or business.

To dream that you are wounded with a knife foretells domestic troubles, in which disobedient children will figure largely. To the unmarried, it denotes that disgrace may follow.

To dream that you stab another with a knife denotes baseness of character; you should strive to cultivate a higher sense of right.

Knife Grinder

To dream of a knife grinder warns that unwarrantable liberties may be taken with your possessions. For a woman, this omens unhappy unions and much drudgery.

Knitting

For a woman to dream of knitting denotes that she will possess a quiet and peaceful home, where a loving companion and dutiful children delight to give pleasure.

For a man to be in a kniting factory indicates thrift and a solid rise in prospects.

For a young woman to dream of knitting is an omen of a hasty but propitious marriage.

For a young woman to dream that she works in a knitting factory denotes that she will have a worthy and loyal lover. To see the mill in which she works dilapidated, she will meet with reverses in fortune and love.

Knocker

To dream of using a knocker foretells that you will be forced to ask aid and counsel of others.

Knocking

To hear knocking in your dreams denotes that tidings of a grave nature will soon be received by you. If you are awakened by the knocking, the news will affect you more seriously.

Knots

To dream of seeing knots denotes much worry over the most trifling affairs. If your sweetheart notices another, you will immediately find cause to censure him.

To tie a knot signifies an independent nature; you will refuse to be nagged by ill-disposed lover or friend.

Krishna

To see Krishna in your dreams denotes that your greatest joy will be in pursuit of spiritual knowledge, you will school yourself to the taunts of friends, and cultivate a philosophical bearing toward life and sorrow.

L

'And he dreamed yet another dream, and told it to his brethren, and said, "Behold, I have dreamed a dream more; and, behold, the sun and the moon and the eleven stars made obeisance to me."'

—Genesis xxxvii, 9.

Label

To dream of a label, foretells that you will let an enemy see the inside of your private affairs, and will suffer from the negligence.

Laboratory

To dream of being in a laboratory denotes great energies wasted in unfruitful enterprises when you might succeed in some more practical business.

If you think yourself an alchemist, and try to discover a process to turn other things into gold, you will entertain far-reaching and interesting projects, but you will fail to reach the apex of your ambition. Wealth will prove a myth, and the woman you love will hold a false position towards you.

Labour

To dream that you watch domestic animals labouring under heavy burdens, denotes that you will be prosperous, but unjust to those employed by you.

To see men toiling signifies profitable work and robust health. To labour yourself denotes favourable outlook for any new enterprise, and bountiful crops if the dreamer is interested in farming.

Labyrinth

If you dream of a labyrinth, you may find yourself entangled in intricate and perplexing business conditions, and your wife is likely to make the home environment intolerable; children and sweethearts may well prove ill-tempered and unattractive.

If you are in a labyrinth of night or darkness, it foretells passing, but agonizing sickness and trouble.

A labyrinth of green vines and timbers denotes unexpected happiness from what was seemingly a cause for loss and despair.

A network, or labyrinth of railways assures you of long and tedious journeys. Interesting people will be met, but no financial success will aid you on these journeys.

To dream that you are helping others to find their way out of a labyrinth denotes that you will have power and control.

Lace

See to it, if you are a lover, that your sweetheart wears lace, as this dream brings fidelity in love and a rise in position.

If a woman dreams of lace, she will be happy in the realization of her most ambitious desires, and lovers will bow to her edict. No questioning or imperiousness on their part.

If you buy lace, you will conduct an expensive establishment, but wealth will be a solid friend.

If you sell laces, your desires will outrun your resources.

For a young girl to dream of making lace forecasts that she will win a handsome, wealthy husband. If she dreams of garnishing her wedding garments with lace, she will be favoured with lovers who will bow to her charms, but the wedding will be far removed from her.

Ladder

To dream of a ladder being raised for you to ascend to some height, your energetic and nervy qualifications will raise you into prominence in business affairs.

To ascend a ladder means prosperity and unstinted happiness.

To fall from one warns of despondency and unsuccessful transactions to the tradesman, and poor crops to the farmer.

To see a broken ladder betokens failure.

To descend a ladder betokens disappointment in business and unrequited desires.

To escape from captivity, or confinement, by means of a ladder, you will be successful, though many perilous paths may intervene.

To grow dizzy as you ascend a ladder, denotes that you will not wear new honours serenely. You are likely to become haughty and domineering in your newly acquired position.

Becoming afraid halfway up a ladder denotes that you are not yet ready to scale the dizzy heights of ambition set before you, and must do more work before seeking promotion.

Ladle

To see a ladle in your dreams denotes that you will be fortunate in the selection of a companion. Children will prove sources of happiness.

If the ladle is broken or unclean, you are likely to have a grievous loss.

Lagoon

To dream of a lagoon, denotes that you will be drawn into a whirlpool of doubt and confusion through misapplication of your intelligence.

Lake

For a young woman to dream that she is alone on a turbulent and muddy lake foretells that many vicissitudes are approaching her, and she may regret former extravagances and disregard of virtuous teaching.

If the water gets into the boat, but by intense struggling she reaches the boathouse safely, it denotes she will be under wrong persuasion, but will eventually overcome it, and rise to honour and distinction.

If she sees a young couple in the same position as herself, who succeed in rescuing themselves, she will find that some friend has committed indiscretions, but will succeed in reinstating himself in her favour.

To dream of sailing on a clear and smooth lake, with happy and congenial companions, you will have much happiness, and wealth will meet your demands.

A muddy lake, surrounded with bleak rocks and bare trees, denotes unhappy terminations to business and affection.

A muddy lake, surrounded by green trees, portends that the moral in your nature will fortify itself against passionate desires, and overcoming the same will direct your energy into a safe and remunerative channel. If the lake is clear and surrounded by barrenness, a profitable existence will be marred by immoral and passionate dissipation.

To see yourself reflected in a clear lake denotes coming joys and many ardent friends.

To see foliaged trees reflected in the lake, you will enjoy to a satiety love's draught of passion and happiness.

To see slimy and uncanny inhabitants of the lake rise up and menace you denotes failure and ill health from squandering time, energy and health on illicit pleasures. You will drain the utmost drop of happiness, and drink deeply of remorse's bitter concoction.

Lamb

To dream of lambs frolicking in green pastures betokens chaste friendships and joys. Bounteous and profitable crops to the farmers, and increase of possessions for others.

To see a dead lamb signifies sadness and desolation.

Blood showing on the white fleece of a lamb denotes that innocent ones suffer from betrayal through the wrongdoing of others.

A lost lamb denotes that wayward people will be under your influence, and you should be careful of your conduct.

To see lamb skins denotes comfort and pleasure usurped from others.

To slaughter a lamb for domestic uses, prosperity will be gained through the sacrifice of pleasure and contentment.

To eat lamb chops warns of illness, and much anxiety over the welfare of children.

To see lambs taking nourishment from their mothers denotes happiness through pleasant and intelligent home companions, and many lovable and beautiful children.

To dream that dogs, or wolves devour lambs, innocent people will suffer at the hands of insinuating and designing villains.

To hear the bleating of lambs, your generosity will be appealed to.

To see them in a winter storm, or rain, denotes disappointment in expected enjoyment and betterment of fortune.

To own lambs in your dreams signifies that your environments will be pleasant and profitable.

If you carry lambs in your arms, you will be encumbered with happy cares upon which you will lavish a wealth of devotion, and no expense will be regretted in responding to appeals from the objects of your affection.

To shear lambs shows that you can be cold and mercenary. You will be honest, but inhumane.

See also **Sheep**.

Lame

For a woman to dream of seeing anyone lame, warns that her pleasures and hopes may be unfruitful and disappointing.

Lament

To dream that you bitterly lament the loss of friends, or property, signifies great struggles and much distress, from which will spring causes for joy and personal gain.

To lament the loss of relatives, denotes sickness or disappointments, which will bring you into closer harmony with companions, and will result in brighter prospects for the future.

Lamp

To see lamps filled with oil denotes the demonstration of business activity from which you will receive gratifying results.

Empty lamps represent depression and despondency.

To see lighted lamps burning brightly indicates merited rise in fortune and domestic bliss. If they give out a dull, misty radiance, you may have jealousy and envy, coupled with suspicion, to combat, in which you will be much pleased to find the right person to attack.

To drop a lighted lamp, your plans and hopes will abruptly turn into failure.

If it explodes, former friends may unite with enemies in damaging your interests.

To light a lamp denotes that you will soon make a change in your affairs, which will lead to profit.

To carry a lamp portends that you will be independent and self-sustaining, preferring your own convictions above others. If the light fails, you will meet with unfortunate conclusions.

If you are very afraid, and throw a bewildering light from your window, enemies may ensnare you with professions of friendship and interest in your achievements.

To ignite your apparel from a lamp, you are likely to sustain humiliation from sources from which you expected encouragement and sympathy, and your business may not be fraught with much good.

Lamp Post

To see a lamp post in your dreams, some stranger will prove your staunchiest friend in time of pressing need.

To fall against a lamp post, you will have deception to overcome, or enemies may ensnare you.

To see a lamp post across your path, you can expect much adversity in your life.

Lance

To dream of a lance denotes formidable enemies and injurious experiments.

To be wounded by a lance, error of judgment will cause you annoyance.

To break a lance denotes that seeming impossibilities will be overcome and your desires will be fulfilled.

Land

To dream of land, when it appears fertile, omens good; but if sterile and rocky, failure and dispondency is prognosticated.

To see land from the ocean denotes that vast avenues of prosperity and happiness will disclose themselves to you.

Lantern

To dream of seeing a lantern going before you in the darkness signifies unexpected affluence. If the lantern is suddenly lost to view, then your success may take an unfavourable turn.

To carry a lantern in your dreams denotes that your benevolence will win you many friends. If it goes out, you may fail to gain the prominence you wish. If you stumble and break it, you will seek to aid others, and in so doing may lose your own station, or be disappointed in some undertaking.

To clean a lantern signifies that great possibilities are open to you.

To lose a lantern portends business depression, and disquiet in the home.

If you buy a lantern, it signifies fortunate deals.

For a young woman to dream that she lights her lover's lantern, foretells for her a worthy man, and a comfortable home. If she blows it out, by her own imprudence she may lose a chance of getting married.

Lap

To dream of sitting on some person's lap denotes pleasant security from vexing engagements. If a young woman dreams that she is holding a person on her lap, she may be exposed to unfavourable criticism.

To see a serpent in her lap foretells that she is threatened with humiliation at the hands of enemies. If she sees a cat in her lap, she may be endangered by a seductive enemy.

Lap Dog

To dream of a lap dog foretells that you will be succoured by friends in some approaching dilemma. If it is thin and ill-looking, there may be distressing occurrences to detract from your prospects.

See also **Dogs**.

Lard

To dream of lard signifies that a rise in fortune will soon gratify you. For a woman to find her hand in melted lard foretells her disappointment in attempting to rise in social circles.

Lark

To see larks flying denotes high aims and purposes through the attainment of which you will throw off selfishness and cultivate kindly graces of mind.

To hear them singing as they fly, you will be very happy in a new change of abode, and business will flourish.

To see them fall to the earth and singing as they fall, despairing gloom will overtake you in pleasure's bewildering delights.

A wounded or dead lark portends sadness or death.

To kill a lark portends injury to innocence through wantonness.

If they fly around and light on you, fortune will turn her promising countenance towards you.

To see them eating denotes a plentiful harvest.

Latch

To dream of a latch denotes that you will meet urgent appeals for aid, to which you may well respond unkindly. To see a broken latch foretells disagreements with your dearest friend. Sickness is also foretold in this dream.

Latin

To dream of studying this language denotes victory and distinction in your efforts to sustain your opinion on subjects of grave interest to the public welfare.

Laughing

To dream that you laugh and feel cheerful means success in your undertakings, and bright companions socially.

Laughing immoderately at some weird object denotes disappointment and lack of harmony in your surroundings.

To hear the happy laughter of children means joy and health to the dreamer.

To laugh at the discomfiture of others denotes that you will wilfully injure your friends to gratify your own selfish desires.

To hear mocking laughter denotes illness and disappointing affairs.

Laundry

To dream of laundering clothes denotes struggles, but a final victory in winning fortune. If the clothes are done satisfactorily, then your endeavours will bring complete happiness. If they come out the reverse, your fortune will fail to procure pleasure.

To see pretty girls at this work, you will seek pleasure out of your rank.

If a laundryman calls at your house, you are in danger of sickness, or of losing something very valuable.

To see laundry wagons portends rivalry and contention.

Laurel

Dreaming of the laurel brings success and fame. You will acquire new possessions in love. Enterprises will be laden with gain.

For a young woman to wreath laurel about her lover's head denotes that she will have a faithful man, and one of fame to woo her.

Law and Lawsuits

To dream of engaging in a lawsuit warns you of enemies who are poisoning public opinion against you. If you know that the suit is dishonest on your part, you will seek to dispossess true owners for your own advancement.

If a young man is studying law, he will make rapid rise in any chosen profession.

For a woman to dream that she engages in a lawsuit means she may be slandered, and find enemies among friends.

Lawns

To dream of walking upon well-kept lawns denotes occasions for joy and great prosperity.

To join a merry party upon a lawn denotes many secular amusements, and business engagements will be successfully carried on.

For a young woman to wait upon a green lawn for the coming of a friend or lover denotes that her most ardent wishes concerning wealth and marriage will be gratified. If the grass is dead and the lawn marshy, quarrels and separation may be expected.

To see serpents crawling in the grass before you, betrayal and cruel insinuations are likely to fill you with despair.

Lawyer

For a young woman to dream that she is connected in any way with a lawyer foretells that she will unwittingly commit indiscretions, which will subject her to unfavourable and mortifying criticism.

Lazy

To dream of feeling lazy, or acting so, denotes that you will make a mistake in the formation of enterprises, and may suffer keen disappointment.

For a young woman to think her lover is lazy foretells that she will have bad luck in securing admiration. Her actions may discourage men who mean marriage.

Lead

To dream of lead foretells poor success in any engagement.

A lead mine indicates that your friends will look with suspicion on your money making. Your sweetheart may surprise you with her deceit and ill temper.

To dream of lead ore foretells distress and accidents. Business will assume a gloomy cast.

To hunt for lead denotes discontentment, and a constant changing of employment.

To melt lead foretells that by impatience you will bring failure upon yourself and others.

Leak

To dream of seeing a leak in anything is usually significant of loss and vexations.

Leaping *see* Jumping

Learning

To dream of learning denotes that you will take great interest in acquiring knowledge and, if you are economical with your time, you will advance far into the literary world.

To enter halls, or places of learning, denotes rise from obscurity, and finance will be a congenial adherent.

To see learned men foretells that your companions will be interesting and prominent.

For a woman to dream that she is associated in any way with learned people, she will be ambitious and excel in her endeavours to rise into prominence.

Leather

To dream of leather denotes successful business and favourable engagements with others. You will go into lucky speculations if you dream that you are dressed in leather.

Ornaments of leather denote faithfulness in love and to the home.

Piles of leather denote fortune and happiness.

To deal in leather signifies that no change in the disposition of your engagements is necessary for successful accumulation of wealth.

Leaves

To dream of leaves denotes happiness and wonderful improvement in your business.

Withered leaves indicate false hopes and gloomy forebodings will harass your spirit into a whirlpool of despondency and loss. If a young woman dreams of withered leaves, she will be left lonely on the road to conjugality.

Dreaming that you are buried up to your neck in dead leaves portends that you will be submerged by feelings of anxiety.

To dream that you are sweeping up dead leaves signifies that you are overcoming longings for the past, or that a series of significant events has come to an end.

For a woman to dream of leaves that are green and fresh, she will come into a legacy and marry a wealthy and prepossessing husband.

Ledger

To dream of keeping a ledger, you may have perplexities and disappointing conditions to combat.

To dream that you make wrong entries on your ledger, you will have small disputes and a slight loss will befall you.

To put a ledger into a safe, you will be able to protect your rights under adverse circumstances.

To get your ledger misplaced, your interests may go awry through neglect of duty.

To dream that your ledger gets destroyed by fire, you may suffer through the carelessness of friends.

To dream that you have a woman to keep your ledger, you may lose money trying to combine pleasure with business.

For a young woman to dream of ledgers denotes she will have a solid businessman to make her a proposal of marriage.

To dream that your ledger has worthless accounts denotes bad management and losses; but if the accounts are good, then your business will assume improved conditions.

Leeches

To dream of leeches warns that enemies may run over your interests.
To see them applied to yourself, warns of illness.

If they should bite you, there is danger for you in unexpected places, and you should heed well this warning.

Leeward

To dream of sailing leeward denotes to the sailor a prosperous and merry voyage. To others, a pleasant journey.

Legislature

To dream that you are a member of a legislature foretells that you will be vain of your possessions and will treat members of your family unkindly. You will have no real advancement.

Legs

If you dream of admiring well-shaped feminine legs, you will lose your judgment, and act very silly over some fair charmer.

To see misshapen legs denotes unprofitable occupations and ill-tempered comrades.

A wounded leg foretells losses.

To dream that you have a wooden leg denotes that you may demean yourself in a false way to your friends.

If ulcers are on your legs, it signifies a drain on your income to aid others.

To dream that you have three, or more, legs, indicates that more enterprises are planned in your imagination than will ever benefit you.

For a young woman to admire her own legs denotes vanity; she may be repulsed by the man she admires. If she has hairy legs, she will dominate her husband.

If your own legs are clean and well shaped, it denotes a happy future and devoted friends.

Lemonade

If you drink lemonade in a dream, you will concur with others in signifying some entertainment as a niggardly device to raise funds for the personal enjoyment of others at your expense.

Lemons

To dream of seeing lemons on their native trees among rich foliage denotes jealousy toward some beloved object, but demonstrations will convince you of the absurdity of the charge.

To eat lemons foretells humiliation and disappointments.

Green lemons denote sickness and contagion.

To see shrivelled lemons denotes separation or divorce.

Lending

To dream that you are lending money warns of difficulties in meeting payments of debts and unpleasant influence in private.

To lend other articles betweens impoverishment through generosity.

To refuse to lend things, you will be awake to your interests and keep the respect of friends.

For others to offer to lend you articles, or money, denotes prosperity and close friendships.

Lentil

If you dream of lentils, it denotes quarrels and unhealthy surroundings. For a young woman, this dream portends dissatisfaction with her lover, but parental advice will cause her to accept the inevitable.

Leopard

To dream of a leopard attacking you denotes that while the future seemingly promises fair, success holds many difficulties through misplaced confidence.

To kill one intimates victory in your affairs.

To see one caged denotes that enemies will surround but fail to injure you.

To see leopards in their native place trying to escape from you denotes that you will be embarrassed in business or love, but by persistent efforts you will overcome difficulties.

To dream of a leopard's skin denotes that your interests will be endangered by a dishonest person who will win your esteem.

Letter

To dream that you see a registered letter foretells that some money matters will disrupt long-established relations.

For a young woman to dream that she receives such a letter intimates that she will be offered an income, but it will not be on strictly legal, or moral, grounds; others may play towards her a dishonourable part.

To the lover, this bears heavy presentments of disagreeable mating. His sweetheart may covet other gifts than his own.

To dream of an anonymous letter may denote that you may receive injury from an unsuspected source.

To write one foretells that you will be jealous of a rival, whom you admit to be your superior.

To dream of getting letters bearing unpleasant news, denotes difficulties or illness. If the news is of a joyous character, you will have many things to be thankful for. If the letter is affectionate, but is written on green, or coloured, paper, you may be slighted in love or business. Blue ink denotes constancy and affection, also bright fortune.

Red colours in a letter imply estrangements through suspicion and jealousy, but this may be overcome by wise manoeuvring of the suspected party.

If a young woman dreams that she receives a letter from her lover and places it near her heart, she will be worried very much by a good-looking rival. Truthfulness is often rewarded with jealousy.

If you fail to read the letter, you may lose something either in a business or social way.

To have your letter intercepted, rival enemies are working to defame you.

To dream of trying to conceal a letter from your sweetheart or wife intimates that you are interested in unworthy occupations.

To receive a letter written on black paper with white ink, denotes gloom and disappointment.

To dream that you write a letter denotes that you may be hasty in condemning some one on suspicion, and that regrets may follow.

A torn letter indicates that hopeless mistakes may ruin your reputation.

To receive a letter by hand denotes that you are acting ungenerously towards your companions or sweetheart, and you also are not upright in your dealings.

To dream often of receiving a letter from a friend, foretells his arrival, or you will hear from him by letter or otherwise.

Dreaming that you refuse to accept a letter signifies failure to grasp an opportunity.

Lettuce

To see lettuce growing green and thrifty denotes that you will enjoy some greatly desired good, after an unimportant embarrassment.

If you eat lettuce, illness may separate you from your lover or companion, or perhaps it may be petty jealousy.

To gather it denotes your superabundant sensitiveness, and that your jealous disposition will cause you unmitigated distress and pain.

To buy lettuce warns that you may court your own downfall.

Liar

To dream of thinking people are liars foretells you may lose faith in some scheme which you had urgently put forward. For someone to call you a liar warns that you may have vexations through deceitful persons.

For a woman to think her sweetheart a liar warns her that her unbecoming conduct is likely to lose her a valued friend.

Library

To dream that you are in a library denotes that you will grow discontented with your environments and associations and seek companionship in study and the exploration of ancient customs.

To find yourself in a library for purposes other than study foretells that your conduct may deceive your friends, and where you would have them believe that you had literary aspirations, you will find illicit assignations.

Searching in vain for a particular book denotes that you will need to develop aspects of yourself before you can progress with your search.

Feeling out of place in a library indicates a lack of confidence in the dreamer's own intellect.

Lice

A dream of lice contains much waking worry and distress. It often implies offensive ailments.

To have lice on your body warns that you may conduct yourself unpleasantly with your acquaintances.

To dream of catching lice foretells sickness.

See also **Louse**.

Licence

To dream of a licence is an omen of disputes and loss. Married women will exasperate your cheerfulness. For a woman to see a marriage licence foretells that she may soon enter unpleasant bonds, which will humiliate her pride.

Lifeboat

To dream of being in a lifeboat denotes escape from threatened evil.

To see a lifeboat sinking, friends will contribute to your distress.

To be lost in a lifeboat, you will be overcome with trouble, in which your friends will be included to some extent. If you are saved, you will escape a great calamity.

Life Insurance

To see life-insurance sellers in a dream means that you are soon to meet a stranger who will contribute to your business interests, and change in your home life is fore-shadowed, as interests will be mutual.

If they appear distorted or unnatural, the dream is more unfortunate than good.

Lift

To dream of ascending in a lift denotes that you will swiftly rise to position and wealth, but if you descend in one your misfortunes may crush and discourage you. If you see one go down and think you are left, you will narrowly escape disappointment in some undertaking. To see one standing foretells threatened danger.

To dream that you are stuck in a lift that has broken down indicates frustration and irritation in your waking life.

Light

If you dream of light, success will attend you. To dream of weird light, or if the light goes out, you will be disagreeably surprised by some undertaking resulting in nothing.

To see a dim light indicates partial success.

To dream of someone bathed in light generally signifies that deep insights will soon be revealed to you.

Lighthouse

If you see a lighthouse through a storm, difficulties and grief will assail you, but they will disperse before prosperity and happiness.

To see a lighthouse from a placid sea denotes calm joys and congenial friends.

Lightning

Lightning in your dreams foreshadows happiness and prosperity of short duration.

A flash of lightning can indicate revelation; you will suddenly have insight into a spiritual problem, or a more practical problem which is troubling your waking life.

If the lightning strikes some object near you, and you feel the shock, you may be damaged by the good fortune of a friend, or you may be worried by gossips and scandalmongers.

To see livid lightning parting black clouds, sorrow and difficulties may follow close on to fortune.

If it strikes you, unexpected sorrows are at hand in business or love.

To see the lightning above your head heralds the advent of joy and gain.

To see lightning in the south, fortune will hide herself from you for awhile. If in the southwest, luck will come your way. In the west, your prospects will be brighter than formerly. In the north, obstacles will have to be removed before your prospects will brighten up. If in the east, you will easily win favours and fortune.

Lightning from dark and ominous-looking clouds, is always a forerunner of threats, of loss and of disappointments. Business people should stay close to business, and women near their husbands or mothers; children and the sick should be looked after closely.

Lightning Conductor

To see a lightning conductor denotes that threatened destruction to some cherished work will confront you. If the lightning strikes one, there may be an accident or sudden news to give you sorrow.

If you are having one put up, it is a warning to beware how you begin a new enterprise, as you may well be overtaken by disappointment.

To have one taken, you will change your plans and thereby further your interests. To see many lightning conductors indicates a variety of misfortunes.

Lily

To dream of a lily warns of illness and death. To see lilies growing with their rich foliage, denotes early marriage to the young and subsequent separation.

For a young woman to dream of admiring, or gathering, lilies, denotes sadness coupled with joy.

To dream that you breathe the fragrance of lilies denotes that sorrow will purify and enhance your mental qualities.

Lime

To dream of lime foretells that disaster will prostrate you for a time, but you will revive to greater and richer prosperity than before.

Lime Kiln

To dream of a lime kiln foretells the immediate future holds no favour for speculations in love or business

Limes

To dream of eating limes warns of sickness and adverse straits.

Limp

To dream that you limp in your walk denotes that a small worry will unexpectedly confront you, detracting much from your enjoyment.

To see others limping signifies that you will be naturally offended at the conduct of a friend. Small failures attend this dream.

Linen

To see linen in your dream augurs prosperity and enjoyment.

If a person appears to you dressed in linen garments, you will shortly be the recipient of joyful tidings in the nature of an inheritance.

If you are clothed in clean, fine linen, your fortune and fullest enjoyment in life is assured. If it is soiled, sorrow and ill luck will be met with occasionally, mingled with the good in your life.

Linseed Oil

To see linseed oil in your dreams denotes that your impetuous extravagance will be checked by the kindly interference of a friend.

Lion

To dream of a lion signifies that a great force is driving you.

If you subdue the lion, you will be victorious in any engagement.

If it overpowers you, then you will be open to the successful attacks of enemies.

To see caged lions denotes that your success depends upon your ability to cope with opposition.

To see a man controlling a lion in its cage, or out, denotes success in business and great mental power. You will be favourably regarded by others.

To see young lions denotes new enterprises, which will bring success if properly attended.

For a young woman to dream of young lions denotes new and fascinating lovers.

For a woman to dream that she sees Daniel in the lions' den signifies that by her intellectual qualifications and personal magnetism she will win fortune and lovers to her highest desire.

To hear the roar of a lion signifies unexpected advancement and preferment with women.

To see a lion's head over you, showing his teeth by snarls, you are threatened with defeat in your upward rise to power.

To see a lion's skin denotes a rise to fortune and happiness.

To ride one denotes courage and persistence in surmounting difficulties.

To dream you are defending your children from a lion with a penknife foretells that enemies may threaten to overpower you, and will well nigh succeed if you allow any artfulness to persuade you for a moment from duty and business obligations.

Lips

To dream of unsightly lips signifies disagreeable encounters, hasty decision, and ill temper in the marriage relationship.

Full, sweet cherry lips indicate harmony and affluence. To a lover, they augur reciprocation in love, and fidelity.

Thin lips signify mastery of the most intricate subjects.

Sore, or swollen lips denote privations and unhealthful desires.

289

Liver

To dream of a disordered liver denotes that a querulous person will most likely be your mate, fault-finding will occupy her time, and disquiet will fill your hours.

To dream of eating liver indicates that some deceitful person has installed himself in the affections of your sweetheart.

Lizard

To dream of lizards warns of attacks upon you by enemies.

If you kill a lizard, you will regain your lost reputation or fortune; but if it should escape, you will meet vexations and crosses in love and business.

For a woman to dream that a lizard crawls up her skirt, or scratches her, she is likely to have misfortune.

Load

To dream that you carry a load signifies a long existence filled with labours of love and charity.

To fall under a load denotes your inability to attain comforts that are necessary to those looking to you for subsistence.

To see others thus engaged denotes trials for them in which you will be interested.

Loaves

To dream of loaves of bread denotes frugality. If they are of cake, the dreamer has cause to rejoice over his good fortune, as love and wealth will wait obsequiously upon you.

Broken loaves bring discontent and bickerings between those who love.

To see loaves multiply phenomenally prognosticates great success. Lovers will be happy in their chosen ones.

See also **Bread**.

Lobster

To dream of seeing lobsters denotes great favours, and that riches will endow you.

If you eat them, you will sustain contamination by associating too freely with pleasure-seeking people.

If the lobsters are made into a salad, success will not change your generous nature, but you will enjoy to the fullest your ideas of pleasure.

To order a lobster, you will hold prominent positions and command many subordinates.

Lock

To dream of a lock denotes bewilderment. If the lock works at your command, or efforts, you may discover that some person is working you injury. If you are in love, you will find means to aid you in overcoming a rival; you will also make a prosperous journey.

If the lock resists your efforts, you may be derided and scorned in love and perilous voyages will bring to you little benefit.

To put a lock upon your fiancée's neck and arm foretells that you are distrustful of her fidelity, but future episodes will disabuse your mind of doubt.

Locket

If a young woman dreams that her lover places a locket around her neck, she will be the recipient of many beautiful offerings, and will soon be wedded, and lovely children will crown her life.

If a lover dreams that his sweetheart returns his locket, he will confront disappointing issues. The woman he loves will worry him and conduct herself in a displeasing way toward him.

If a woman dreams that she breaks a locket, she is likely to have a changeable and unstable husband, who will dislike constancy in any form, be it business or affection.

Locomotive

To dream of a locomotive running with great speed denotes a rapid rise in fortune, and foreign travel. If it is disabled, then many vexations will interfere with business affairs, and anticipated journeys will be laid aside through the want of means.

To see one completely demolished signifies distress and loss of property.

To hear one coming denotes news of a foreign nature. Business will assume changes that will mean success to all classes.

To hear it whistle, you will be pleased and surprised at the appearance of a friend who has been absent, or an unexpected offer, which means preferment to you.

Locust

To dream of locusts foretells that discrepancies may be found in your business, for which you will worry and suffer. For a woman, this dream foretells that she may bestow her affections upon ungenerous people.

Lodestone

To dream of a lodestone denotes that you will make favourable opportunities for your own advancement in a material way. For a young woman to think a lodestone is attracting her, is an omen of happy changes in her family.

Lodger

For a woman to dream that she has lodgers, foretells she will be burdened with unpleasant secrets. If one goes away without paying his bills, she will have unexpected trouble with men. For one to pay his bill, omens favour and accumulation of money.

Looking-glass

For a woman to dream of a looking-glass denotes that she is soon to be confronted with shocking deceitfulness and discrepancies, which may result in tragic scenes or separations.

See also **Mirror**.

Loom

To dream of standing by and seeing a loom operated by a stranger denotes much vexation and useless irritation from the talkativeness of those about you. Some disappointment with happy expectations is coupled with this dream.

To see good-looking women attending the loom denotes unqualified success to those in love. It predicts congenial pursuits to the married. It denotes you are drawing closer together in taste.

For a woman to dream of weaving on a loom signifies that she will have a thrifty husband and beautiful children will fill her life with happy solicitations.

To see an idle loom denotes a sulky and stubborn person, who will cause you much anxious care.

Lord's Prayer

To dream of repeating the Lord's Prayer foretells that you are threatened with secret foes and will need the alliance and the support of friends to tide you over difficulties.

To hear others repeat it denotes danger to some friend.

Lottery

To dream of a lottery, and that you are taking great interest in the draw, you will engage in some worthless enterprise, which will cause you to make an unpropitious journey. If you hold the lucky number, you will gain in a speculation which will perplex and give you much anxiety.

To see others winning in a lottery denotes convivialities and amusements, bringing many friends together.

If you lose in a lottery, you may be the victim of designing persons. Gloomy depressions in your affairs may result.

For a young woman to dream of a lottery in any way, denotes that her careless way of doing things may bring her disappointment, and a husband who will not be altogether reliable or constant.

To dream of a lottery denotes that you will have unfavourable friendships in business. Your love affairs will produce temporary pleasure.

Louse

To dream of a louse foretells that you will have uneasy feelings regarding your health, and that an enemy may give you exasperating vexation.

See also **Lice**.

Love

To dream of loving any object denotes satisfaction with your present environment.

To dream that the love of others fills you with happy forebodings, successful affairs will give you contentment and freedom from the anxious cares of life. If you find that your love fails, or is not reciprocated, you will become despondent over some conflicting question arising in your mind as to whether it is best to change your mode of living or to marry and trust fortune for the future advancement of your state.

For a husband or wife to dream that their companion is loving foretells great happiness in the marriage; bright children will contribute to the sunshine of the home.

To dream of the love of parents foretells uprightness in character and a continual progress toward fortune and elevation.

The love of animals indicates contentment with what you possess, though you may not think so. For a time, fortune will crown you.

Lovely

Dreaming of lovely things brings favour to all persons connected with you.

For a lover to dream that his sweetheart is lovely of person and character foretells for him a speedy and favourable marriage.

If through the vista of dreams you see your own fair loveliness, fate bids you, with a gleaming light, awake to happiness.

Lozenges

To dream of lozenges foretells success in small matters. For a woman to eat or throw them away warns that her life may be harassed by little spites from the envious.

Lucky

To dream of being lucky is highly favourable to the dreamer. Fulfilment of wishes may be expected and pleasant duties will devolve upon you.

To the despondent, this dream forebodes an uplifting and a renewal of prosperity.

Luggage

To dream of luggage denotes unpleasant cares. You will be encumbered with people who will prove distasteful to you.

If you are carrying your own luggage, you will be so full of your own distresses that you may be blinded to the sorrows of others.

To lose your luggage denotes some unfortunate speculation or family dissensions. To the unmarried, it warns of broken engagements.

Lute

To dream of playing on one is auspicious of joyful news from absent friends.

Pleasant occupations follow the dreaming of hearing the music of a lute.

Luxury

To dream that you are surrounded by luxury indicates much wealth, but dissipation and love of self will reduce your income.

For a poor woman to dream that she enjoys much luxury denotes an early change in her circumstances.

Lying

To dream that you are lying to escape punishment denotes that you will act dishonourably towards some innocent person.

Lying to protect a friend from undeserved chastisement denotes that you will have many unjust criticisms passed upon your conduct, but you will rise above them and enjoy prominence.

To hear others lying denotes that they are seeking to entrap you.

Lynx

To dream of seeing a lynx, enemies are undermining your business and disrupting your home affairs. For a woman, this dream indicates that she has a wary woman rivalling her in the affections of her lover. If she kills the lynx, she will overcome her rival.

Lyre

To dream of listening to the music of a lyre foretells chaste pleasures and congenial companionship. Business will run smoothly.

For a young woman to dream of playing on one denotes that she will enjoy the undivided affection of a worthy man

M

'And they dreamed a dream both of them, each man his dream in one night, each man according to his interpretation of his dream, the butler and the baker of the King of Egypt, which were bound in the prison.'

—Genesis x, 5.

Macaroni

To dream of eating macaroni denotes small losses. To see it in large quantities denotes that you will save money by the strictest economy. For a young woman, this dream means that a stranger will enter her life.

Machinery

To dream of machinery, denotes you will undertake some project which will give great anxiety, but which will finally result in good for you.

To see old machinery, foretells enemies will overcome in your strivings to build up your fortune. To become entangled in machinery, foretells loss in your business, and much unhappiness will follow.

Loss from bad deals generally follows this dream.

Mad Dog

To dream of seeing a mad dog denotes that enemies may make scurrilous attacks upon you and your friends; if you succeed in killing the dog, you will overcome adverse opinions and prosper greatly in a financial way.

See also **Dog**.

Madness

To dream of being mad warns of trouble ahead for the dreamer. Sickness, by which you may lose property, is threatened.

To see others insane denotes disagreeable contact with suffering and appeals from the poverty-stricken. You may also suffer from the inconstancy of friends and the gloomy ending of bright expectations. The utmost care should be taken of your health after this dream.

For a young woman to dream of madness foretells disappointment in marriage and wealth.

Magic

To dream of accomplishing any design by magic indicates pleasant surprises.

To see others practising this art denotes profitable changes to all who have this dream.

To dream of seeing a magician denotes much interesting travel to those concerned in the advancement of higher education, and profitable returns to the mercenary.

Magic here should not be confounded with sorcery or spiritism. If the reader so interprets, he may expect the opposite to what is here forecast to follow. True magic is the study of the higher truths of Nature.

Magistrate

To dream of a magistrate warns that you may be harassed with threats of lawsuits and losses in your business.

Magnet

To dream of a magnet warns that evil influences may draw you from the path of honour. A woman is probably luring you to ruin. To a woman, this dream foretells that protection and wealth will be showered upon her.

Magnifying Glass

To look through a magnifying glass in your dreams means failure to accomplish your work in a satisfactory manner. For a woman to think she owns one foretells that she will encourage the attention of persons who will ignore her later.

Magpie

To dream of a magpie denotes much dissatisfaction and quarrels. The dreamer should guard well his conduct and speech after this dream.

Malice

To dream of entertaining malice for any person denotes that you will stand low in the opinion of friends because of a disagreeable temper. Seek to control your passion.

If you dream of persons maliciously using you, an enemy in friendly garb is working you harm.

Mallet

To dream of a mallet denotes that you may meet unkind treatment from friends on account of ill health. Disorder in the home is indicated.

Malt

To dream of malt betokens a pleasant existence and riches that will advance your station.

To dream of taking malted drinks denotes that you will interest yourself in some dangerous affair, but will reap much benefit therefrom.

Man

To dream of a man, if handsome, well-formed and supple, denotes that you will enjoy life vastly and come into rich possessions. If he is misshapen and sour-visaged, you will meet disappointments and many perplexities may involve you.

For a woman to dream of a handsome man, she is likely to have distinction offered her. If he is ugly, she may experience trouble through someone whom she considers a friend.

Manners

To dream of seeing ugly-mannered persons denotes failure to carry out undertakings through the disagreeableness of a person connected with the affair.

If you meet people with affable manners, you will be pleasantly surprised by affairs of importance with you taking a favourable turn.

Man-of-war

To dream of a man-of-war denotes long journeys and separation from country and friends; dissension in political affairs is portended.

If she is crippled, foreign elements may work damage to home interests.

If she is sailing upon rough seas, trouble with foreign powers may endanger private affairs.

Personal affairs may also go awry.

Mansion

To dream that you are in a mansion where there is a haunted chamber denotes sudden misfortune in the midst of contentment.

To dream of being in a mansion indicates for you wealthy possessions.

To see a mansion from distant points foretells future advancement.

Manslaughter

For a woman to dream that she sees, or is in any way connected with, manslaughter, denotes that she will be desperately scared lest her name be coupled with some scandalous sensation.

Mantilla

To dream of seeing a mantilla denotes an unwise enterprise which may bring you into unfavourable notice.

Manure

To dream of seeing manure, is a favourable omen. Much good will follow the dream. Farmers especially will feel a rise in fortune.

Manuscript

To dream of a manuscript in an unfinished state forebodes disappointment. If finished and clearly written, great hopes will be realized.

If you are at work on a manuscript, you will have many fears for some cherished hope, but if you keep your work tidy you will succeed in your undertakings. If it is rejected by the publishers, you will feel hopeless for a time, but eventually your most sanguine desires will become a reality.

If you lose it, you will be subjected to disappointment.

If you see it burn, some work of your own will bring you profit and much elevation.

Map

To dream of a map, or studying one, denotes that a change will be contemplated in your business. Some disappointing things will occur, but much profit also will follow the change.

To dream of looking for one denotes that a sudden discontent with your surroundings will inspire you with new energy, and that thus you will rise into better conditions. For a young woman, this dream denotes that she will rise into higher spheres by sheer ambition.

Using a map to find your way may denote that you are lacking direction in your waking life. If you are using the map confidently, this foretells that you are prepared for a change of direction, either inwardly or in the form of a long journey.

If the map is unreadable, you are warned of the need to reassess your life and determine your goals.

Marble

To dream of a marble quarry denotes that your life will be a financial success, but that your social surroundings will be devoid of affection.

To dream of polishing marble, you will come into a pleasing inheritance.

To see it broken, you will fall into disfavour among your associates by defying all moral codes.

March

To dream of marching to the strains of music indicates that you are ambitious to become a soldier or a public official, but you should consider all things well before making final decision.

For women to dream of seeing men marching foretells their inclination for men in public positions. They should be careful of their reputations, should they be thrown much into the company of men.

To dream of the month of March portends disappointing returns in business, and that a woman may be suspicious of your honesty.

Mare

To dream of seeing mares in pastures denotes success in business and congenial companions. If the pasture is barren, it foretells poverty but warm friends. For a young woman, this omens a happy marriage and beautiful children.

See also **Horse**.

Marigold

To dream of seeing marigolds denotes that contentment with frugality should be your aim.

Mariner

See also **Sailor**.

Market

To dream that you are in a market denotes thrift and much activity in all occupations.

To see an empty market indicates depression and gloom.

To see decayed vegetables or meat denotes losses in business.

For a young woman, a market foretells pleasant changes.

Marmalade

To dream of eating marmalade warns of sickness and much dissatisfaction.

For a young woman to dream of making it denotes unhappy domestic associations.

Marmot

To dream of seeing a marmot denotes that sly enemies are approaching you in the shape of fair women.

For a young woman to dream of a marmot foretells that temptation will beset her in the future.

Marriage

To dream of marriage is always important. On a spiritual level, it often signifies harmony between the dreamer and the wider universe.

For a woman to dream that she marries an old, decrepit man, wrinkled face and grey-headed, denotes that she is likely to have a vast amount of trouble and sickness to encounter. If, while the ceremony is in progress, her lover passes, wearing black and looking at her in a reproachful way, she may be driven to desperation by the coldness and lack of sympathy of a friend.

To dream of seeing a marriage denotes high enjoyment, if the wedding guests attend in pleasing colours and are happy; if they are dressed in black or other sombre hues, there is likely to be mourning and sorrow in store for the dreamer.

If you dream of contracting a marriage, you will have unpleasant news from an absent party.

If you are an attendant at a wedding, you will experience much pleasure from the thoughtfulness of loved ones, and business affairs will be unusually promising.

To dream of any unfortunate occurrence in connection with a marriage foretells distress in your family.

For a young woman to dream that she is a bride, and unhappy or indifferent, foretells disappointments in love, and possibly her own illness. She should be careful of her conduct, as enemies are near her.

See also **Bride, Wedding, Wedlock.**

Mars

To dream of Mars warns that your life may be made miserable by the cruel treatment of friends. Enemies may endeavour to ruin you.

If you feel yourself drawn up toward the planet, you will develop keen judgment and advance beyond your friends in learning and wealth.

Marsh

To dream of walking through marshy places warns of illness resulting from overwork and worry. You may suffer much displeasure from the unwise conduct of a near relative.

Martyr

To dream of martyrs, denotes false friends, domestic unhappiness and losses in affairs which concern you most.

To dream that you are a martyr signifies separation from friends, and that enemies may slander you.

Mask

To dream that you are wearing a mask denotes temporary trouble, as your conduct towards some dear one may be misinterpreted, and your endeavours to aid that one misunderstood, but you will profit by the temporary estrangements.

If you are happier wearing the mask, this indicates that you are hiding your true self; you will need to distinguish between what is real and what is faked in your life. If you are uncomfortable wearing the mask, you desire the truth to emerge.

To see others masking denotes that you will combat falsehood and envy.

To see a mask in your dreams denotes that some person may be unfaithful to you, and your affairs may suffer also. For a young woman to dream that she wears a mask foretells she may endeavour to impose upon some friendly person.

If she unmasks, or sees others doing so, she will fail to gain the admiration sought for. She should behave modestly after this dream.

Mason

To dream that you see a mason plying his trade denotes a rise in your circumstances and that a more congenial social atmosphere will surround you.

See also **Freemason**.

Masquerade

To dream of attending a masquerade denotes that you will indulge in foolish and harmful pleasures to the neglect of business and domestic duties.

For a young woman to dream that she participates in a masquerade denotes that she may be deceived.

Mast

To dream of seeing the masts of ships denotes long and pleasant voyages, the making of many new friends, and the gaining of new possessions.

To see the masts of wrecked ships denotes sudden changes in your circumstances which will necessitate giving over anticipated pleasures.

If a sailor dreams of a mast, he will soon sail on an eventful trip.

Master

To dream that you have a master is a sign of lack of leadership skills on your part; you will do better work under the leadership of some strong-willed person.

If you are a master, and command many people under you, you will excel in judgment in the fine points of life, and will hold high positions and possess much wealth.

Mastiff

To feel much fright on seeing a large mastiff denotes that you will experience inconvenience because of efforts to rise above mediocrity. If a woman dreams this, she will marry a wise and humane man.

See also **Dogs**.

Mat

Keep away from mats in your dreams, as they will usher you into sorrow and perplexities.

Match

To dream of matches denotes prosperity and change when least expected.

To strike a match in the dark, unexpected news and fortune is foreboded.

Matting

To dream of matting foretells pleasant prospects and cheerful news from the absent. If it is old or torn, you will have vexing things come before you.

Mattress

To dream of a mattress denotes that new duties and responsibilities will shortly be assumed.

To sleep on a new mattress signifies contentment with present surroundings.

To dream of a mattress factory denotes that you will be connected in business with thrifty partners and will soon amass wealth.

Mausoleum

To dream of a mausoleum warns of trouble for some prominent friend.

To find yourself inside a mausoleum warns of your own illness.

May

To dream of the month of May denotes prosperous times, and pleasure for the young.

To dream that nature appears freakish denotes sudden sorrow and disappointment clouding pleasure.

May Bugs

To dream of May bugs denotes an ill-tempered companion where a congenial one was expected.

Maze see Labyrinth.

Meadow

To dream of meadows predicts happy reunions under bright promises of future prosperity.

Meals

To dream of meals denotes that you will let trifling matters interfere with momentous affairs and business engagements.
*See also **Eating, Food**.*

Measles

To dream that you have measles denotes that much worry, and anxious care will interfere with your business affairs.

To dream that others have this disease denotes that you will be troubled over the condition of others.

Meat

For a woman to dream of raw meat denotes that she will meet with much discouragement in accomplishing her aims. If she sees cooked meat, it denotes that others will obtain the object for which she will strive.

Mechanic

To dream of a mechanic denotes change in your dwelling place and a more active business. Advancement in wages usually follows after seeing mechanics at work on machinery.

Medal

To dream of medals denotes honours gained by application and industry.

To lose a medal denotes misfortune through the unfaithfulness of others.

Medicine

To dream of medicine, if pleasant to the taste, a trouble will come to you, but in a short time it will work for your good; but if you take disgusting medicine, you are likely suffer illness or sorrow.

To give medicine to others denotes that you may work to injure someone who trusted you.

Melancholy

To dream that you feel melancholy over any event is a sign of disappointment in what was thought to be a favourable undertaking.

To dream that you see others melancholy denotes unpleasant interruption in affairs. To lovers, it brings separation.

Melon

To dream of melons denotes ill health and unfortunate ventures in business.

To eat them signifies that hasty action will cause you anxiety.

To see them growing on green vines denotes that present troubles will result in good fortune for you.

Memorandum

To dream that you are writing memoranda warns that you may engage in an unprofitable business, and much worry may result for you.

To see others writing a memorandum signifies that some person will worry you with appeals for aid.

To lose your memorandum, you will experience a slight loss in trade.

To find a memorandum, you will assume new duties that will cause much pleasure to others.

Memorial

To dream of a memorial signifies there will be occasion for you to show patient kindness, as trouble and sickness threatens a relative.

Menagerie

To dream of visiting a menagerie warns of various troubles.

Mending

To dream of mending soiled garments denotes that you will undertake to right a wrong at an inopportune moment; but if the garment is clean, you will be successful in adding to your fortune.

For a young woman to dream of mending foretells that she will be a systematic help to her husband.

Mercury

To dream of mercury is significant of unhappy changes through the constant oppression of enemies. For a woman to be suffering from mercury poisoning warns of desertion and separation.

Mermaid

To dream of a mermaid indicates that you will need to re-evaluate your relationship with someone in your waking life.

Merry

To dream being merry, or in merry company, denotes that pleasant events will engage you for a time, and affairs will assume profitable shapes.

Meshes

To dream of being entangled in the meshes of a net, or similar constructions, warns that enemies may oppress you in times of seeming prosperity. To a young woman, this dream foretells that her environment may draw her into evil and consequent abandonment. If she succeeds in disengaging herself from the meshes, she will narrowly escape slander.

Message

To dream of receiving a message denotes that changes will take place in your affairs.

To dream of sending a message denotes that you may be placed in unpleasant situations.

Metamorphosis

To dream of seeing anything metamorphose denotes that sudden changes will take place in your life, for good or bad, depending on whether the metamorphosis is pleasant or frightful.

Mice

To dream of mice foretells domestic troubles and the insincerity of friends. Business affairs will assume a discouraging tone.

To kill mice denotes that you will conquer your enemies.

To let them escape you is significant of doubtful struggles.

For a young woman to dream of mice warns her of secret enemies, and that deception is being practised upon her. If she should see a mouse in her clothing, it is a sign of scandal in which she will figure.

See also **Mouse**.

Microscope

To dream of a microscope denotes that you will experience failure or small returns in your enterprises.

Midwife

To see a midwife in your dreams warns of unfortunate sickness.

Milepost

To dream you see or pass a milepost foretells that you will be assailed by doubtful fears in business or love. To see one down portends that accidents are threatening to give disorder to your affairs.

Milk

To dream of drinking milk denotes abundant harvest to the farmer and pleasure in the home; for a traveller, it foretells a fortunate voyage. This is a very propitious dream for women.

To see milk in large quantities signifies riches and health.

To dream of dealing in milk commercially, denotes great increase in fortune.

To give milk away shows that you will be too benevolent for the good of your own fortune.

To spill milk denotes that you will experience a slight loss and suffer temporary unhappiness at the hands of friends.

To dream of impure milk denotes that you will be tormented with petty troubles.

To dream of sour milk denotes that you will be disturbed over the distress of friends.

To dream of trying unsuccessfully to drink milk signifies that you will be in danger of losing something of value or the friendship of a highly esteemed person.

To dream of hot milk foretells a struggle, but the final winning of riches and desires.

To dream of bathing in milk denotes pleasures and companionships of congenital friends.

Milking

To dream of milking, and if flows in great streams from the udder, while the cow is restless and threatening, signifies you will see great opportunities withheld from you, but which will result in final favour for you.

Mill

To dream of a mill indicates thrift and fortunate undertakings.
To see a dilapidated mill warns of sickness and ill fortune.

Miller

To see a miller in your dreams signifies that your surroundings will
grow more hopeful. For a woman to dream of a miller failing in an
attempt to start his mill foretells she will be disappointed in her lover's
wealth, as she will think him in comfortable circumstances.

Mine

To dream of being in a mine warns of failure in affairs.
To own a mine, denotes future wealth.
If you dream of hunting for mines, you will engage in worthless
pursuits.

Mineral

To dream of minerals denotes that your present unpromising outlook will
soon grow brighter. To walk over mineral-bearing land signifies distress,
from which you will escape and be bettered in your surroundings.

Mineral Water

To dream of drinking mineral water foretells that fortune will favour
your efforts, and you will enjoy your opportunities to satisfy your
cravings for certain pleasures.

Mining

To see mining in your dreams denotes that an enemy is seeking your
ruin by bringing up past immoralities in your life. You will be likely to
make unpleasant journeys, if you stand near the mine.

Minister

To dream of seeing a minister denotes unfortunate changes and unpleasant journeys.

To hear a minister exhort warns that some designing person may influence you to evil.

To dream that you are a minister may denote that you may usurp another's rights.

See also **Clergyman, Preacher, Priest, Vicar**.

Mink

To dream of a mink denotes that you will have sly enemies to overcome.

If you kill one, you will win your desires. For a young woman to dream that she is partial to mink furs, she will find protection and love in some person who will be inordinately jealous.

Minuet

To dream of seeing the minuet danced signifies a pleasant existence with congenial companions.

To dance it yourself, good fortune and domestic joys are foretold.

Mire

To dream of going through a mire indicates that your dearest wishes and plans will receive a temporary check by the intervention of unusual changes in your surroundings.

Mirror

To see your image in a mirror warns of unfaithfulness and neglect in a marriage, and fruitless speculations. You are likely to meet with a great deal of discouragement.

To see others in a mirror warns that they may act unfairly towards you in order to promote their own interest.

To see another face with your own in a mirror indicates that you are leading a double life, and may deceive your friends.

For a woman to see her lover in a mirror denotes that she is likely to have cause for disagreement with him.

For a married woman to see her husband in a mirror warns that he may give her cause to feel anxiety for her happiness and honour.

If a woman sees men, other than her husband or lover, in a mirror, she should beware of conducting an indiscreet affair, as she will be discovered; this will be humiliating to her and a source of worry to her relations.

For a man to dream of seeing strange women in a mirror denotes that he risks jeopardizing his health and career by indulging in foolish attachments.

To see animals in a mirror warns of disappointment and loss in fortune.

To break a mirror portends bad luck.

An unclear reflection denotes the dreamer's reluctance to face up to reality.

See also **Looking-glass**.

Miser

To dream of a miser warns that you may be unfortunate in finding true happiness owing to selfishness, and that love may disappoint you.

For a woman to dream that she is befriended by a miser foretells than she will gain love and wealth by her intelligence and tactful conduct.

To dream that you arc miserly denotes that you will be obnoxious to others by your conceited bearing.

To dream that any of your friends are misers foretells that you will be distressed by the importunities of others.

Mist

To dream that you are enveloped in a mist denotes uncertain fortunes and domestic unhappiness. If the mist clears away, your troubles will be of short duration.

To see others in a mist, you will profit by the misfortune of others.

See also **Fog**.

Mistletoe

To dream of mistletoe foretells happiness and great rejoicing.

To the young, it omens many pleasant pastimes.

If seen with unpromising signs, disappointment will displace pleasure or fortune.

Mistress

For a man to dream that he is in company with a mistress warns that he is in danger of public disgrace, striving to keep from the world his true character and state of business.

For a woman to dream that she is a mistress indicates that she will degrade herself by her own improprieties.

For a man to dream that his mistress is untrue denotes that he has old enemies to encounter. Expected reverses will arise.

Mocking-bird

To see or hear a mocking-bird signifies that you will be invited to go on a pleasant visit to friends, and your affairs will move along smoothly and prosperously. For a woman to see a wounded or dead one, her disagreement with a friend or lover is signified.

Models

To dream of a model foretells that your social affairs will deplete your purse, and quarrels and regrets will follow. For a young woman to dream that she is a model or seeking to be one foretells that she will be entangled in a love affair which give her trouble through the selfishness of a friend.

Molasses

To dream of molasses is a sign that some one is going to extend you pleasant hospitality and that, through its acceptance, you will meet agreeable and fortunate surprises. To eat molasses warns that you may be discouraged and disappointed in love. To have it smeared on your clothing denotes that you may have disagreeable offers of marriage, and probably losses in business.

Moles

To dream of moles indicates secret enemies.

To dream of catching a mole, you will overcome any opposition and rise to prominence.

To see moles, or such blemishes, on the person, indicates illness and quarrels.

Money

To dream of finding money denotes small worries, but much happiness. Changes will follow.

To pay out money denotes misfortune.

To receive gold, great prosperity and unalloyed pleasures.

To lose money, you will experience unhappy hours in the home and affairs will appear gloomy.

To count your money and find a deficit, you will be worried about making payments.

To dream that you steal money denotes that you are in danger and should guard your actions.

To save money augurs wealth and comfort.

To dream that you swallow money portends that you are likely to become mercenary.

To look upon a quantity of money denotes that prosperity and happiness are within your reach.

To dream you find a roll of currency, and a young woman claims it, foretells you will lose in some enterprise by the interference of some female friend. The dreamer will find that he is spending his money unwisely and is living beyond his means. It is a dream of caution.

To dream that you lack money, or are in a situation where you are unable to pay for what you have purchased, denotes that you have insufficient knowledge to match your aspirations.

Beware lest the innocent fancies of your brain make a place for your money before payday.

See also **Cash**.

Money Box

To see full money boxes augurs the end of business cares and a pleasant retirement.

Money-lender

To find yourself a money-lender in your dreams foretells that you may be treated with coldness by your associates, and your business may decline.

If others are money-lenders, you will discard a former friend on account of disloyalty.

Monk

To dream of seeing a monk foretells dissensions in the family and unpleasant journeyings. To a young woman, this dream signifies that gossip and deceit may be used against her.

To dream that you are a monk warns of personal loss and illness.

Monkey

To dream of a monkey denotes that deceitful people may flatter you to advance their own interests

To see a dead monkey signifies that your worst enemies will soon be removed.

If a young woman dreams of a monkey, she should insist on an early marriage, as her lover will suspect unfaithfulness.

For a woman to dream of feeding a monkey denotes that she is in danger of betrayed by a flatterer.

Monocle

To dream of seeing or wearing a monocle warns that you may be afflicted with disagreeable friendships, from which you must strive to disengage yourself. For a young woman to see her lover wearing a monocle omens disruption of love affairs.

Monster

To dream of being pursued by a monster denotes that sorrow and misfortune hold prominent places in your immediate future.

To slay a monster denotes that you will successfully cope with enemies and rise to eminent positions.

Moon

To dream of seeing the moon with the aspect of the heavens remaining normal prognosticates success in love and business affairs.

A weird and uncanny moon denotes unpropitious love-making, domestic infelicities and disappointing enterprises of a business character.

The moon in eclipse warns of illness in your community.

To see the new moon denotes an increase in wealth and congenial partners in marriage.

To see the full moon indicates peace and serenity; the dreamer should spend more time in quiet contemplation and avoid rushing into a new project.

For a young woman to dream that she appeals to the moon to know her fate denotes that she will soon be rewarded with marriage to the one of her choice. If she sees two moons, she will lose her lover by being mercenary. If she sees the moon grow dim, she will let the supreme happiness of her life slip for want of womanly tact.

To see a blood-red moon warns of war and strife, and she may see her lover march away in defence of his country.

Morning

To see the morning dawn clear in your dreams prognosticates the approach of fortune and pleasure.

A cloudy morning portends weighty affairs will overwhelm you.

Morocco

To see Morocco in your dreams foretells that you will receive substantial aid from unexpected sources. Your love will be rewarded by faithfulness.

Mortgage

To dream that you take out a mortgage on your property denotes that you are threatened with financial upheavals, which will throw you into embarrassing positions.

To take, or hold one, against others, is ominous of adequate wealth to liquidate your obligations.

To find yourself reading or examining mortgages denotes great possibilities before you of love or gain.

To lose a mortgage, if it cannot be found again, implies loss and worry.

Morose

If you find yourself morose in dreams, you will awake to find the world, as far as you are concerned, going fearfully wrong.

To see others morose portends unpleasant occupations and unpleasant companions.

Mortified

To dream that you feel mortified over any deed committed by yourself is a sign that you will be placed in an unenviable position before those to whom you most wish to appear honourable and just. Financial conditions may fall low.

Moses

To dream that you see Moses means personal gain and a connubial alliance which will be a source of sweet congratulation to yourself.

Mosquito

To see mosquitoes in your dreams, you will strive in vain to remain impregnable to the sly attacks of secret enemies. Your patience and fortune will both suffer from these designing persons.

If you kill mosquitoes, you will eventually overcome obstacles and enjoy fortune and domestic bliss.

Moss

To dream of moss denotes that you will fill dependent positions, unless the moss grows in rich soil, in which case you will be favoured with honours.

Moth

To see a moth in a dream, small worries will lash you into hurried contracts, which will prove unsatisfactory. Quarrels of a domestic nature are prognosticated.

Mother

To see your mother in dreams as she appears in the home signifies pleasing results from any enterprise.

To hold her in conversation, you will soon have good news from interests you are anxious over.

For a woman to dream of her mother signifies pleasant duties and connubial bliss.

To hear your mother call you denotes that you are derelict in your duties, and that you are pursuing the wrong course in business.

To hear her cry as if in pain omens her illness, or that some affliction is menacing you.

To dream of your late mother warns you to control your inclination to cultivate a morbid attitude and ill will towards your fellow creatures.

Mother-in-law

To dream of your mother-in-law denotes that there will be pleasant reconciliations for you after some serious disagreement. For a woman to dispute with her mother-in-law, she will find that quarrelsome and unfeeling people will give her annoyance.

Mountain

For a young woman to dream of crossing a mountain in company with her cousin and dead brother, who is smiling, denotes that she will have a distinctive change in her life for the better, but there are also warnings against allurements and deceitfulness of friends. If she becomes exhausted and refuses to go further, she will be slightly disappointed in not gaining quite so exalted a position as was hoped for by her.

If you ascend a mountain in your dreams, and the way is pleasant and verdant, you will rise swiftly to wealth and prominence. If the mountain is rugged, and you fail to reach the top, you may expect reverses in your life, and should strive to overcome all weakness in your nature. To awaken when you are at a dangerous point in ascending, denotes that you will find affairs taking a flattering turn when they appear gloomy.

To see snow-capped mountains in the distance warns you that it will be exceedingly difficult to turn your longings and ambitions into worthy advancement.

*See also **Ascent, Climbing**.*

Mourning

To dream that you wear mourning omens ill luck and unhappiness.

If others wear it, there may be disturbing influences among your friends causing you unexpected dissatisfaction and loss. To lovers, this dream foretells misunderstanding and possible separation.

Mouse

For a woman to dream of a mouse denotes that she may have an enemy who will annoy her by artfulness and treachery.

See also **Mice**.

Mouse-trap

To see a mouse-trap in dreams signifies your need to be careful of character, as wary persons have designs upon you.

To see it full of mice, you are in danger of falling into the hands of enemies.

To set a trap, you will artfully devise means to overcome your opponents.

See also **Rat-trap**.

Moustache

To dream that you have a moustache denotes that your egotism and effrontery will bring you a poor inheritance in worldly goods, and you will betray women to their sorrow.

If a woman dreams of admiring a moustache, her virtue is in danger, and she should be mindful of her conduct.

If a man dreams that he has his moustache shaved off, he will try to turn from evil companions and pleasures, and seek to reinstate himself in former positions of honour.

Mud

To dream that you walk in mud denotes that you may have cause to lose confidence in friendships, and that there may be losses and disturbances in family circles.

To see others walking in mud, ugly rumours may reach you of some friend or employee. To the farmer, this dream is significant of poor crops and unsatisfactory gains from stock.

To see mud on your clothing, your reputation is being assailed. To scrape it off signifies that you will escape the slander of enemies.

To dream that you are sinking slowly into mud indicates that your life is becoming embroiled in an inextricable mess.

Muff

To dream of wearing a muff denotes that you will be well provided for against the vicissitudes of fortune.

For a lover to see his sweetheart wearing a muff denotes that a worthier man may usurp his place in her affections.

Mugging

To dream of a group of unknown men mugging you for your money or valuables warns you that you will have enemies banded together against you. If you escape uninjured, you will overcome any opposition, either in business or love.

Mulberries

To see mulberries in your dreams warns that sickness may prevent you from obtaining your desires, and you may be called upon often to relieve suffering.

To eat them signifies bitter disappointments.

Mule

If you dream that your are riding on a mule, it denotes that you are engaging in pursuits which will cause you the greatest anxiety, but if you reach your destination without interruption, you will be recompensed with substantial results.

For a young woman to dream of a white mule shows she will marry a wealthy foreigner, or one who, while wealthy, will not be congenial in tastes. If she dreams of mules running loose, she will have beaux and admirers, but no offers of marriage.

To be kicked by a mule foretells disappointment in love and marriage.

To see one dead portends broken engagements and social decline.

Murder

To see murder committed in your dreams foretells much sorrow arising from the misdeeds of others.

If you commit murder, it signifies that you are engaging in some dishonourable adventure, which may leave a stigma upon your name. This dream warns that you may suffer great anguish and humiliation through the indifference of others, and that your aura of gloom may cause perplexing worry to those around you.

On a less worrying level, dreaming that you commit murder can indicate your wish to end a professional or personal relationship.

To dream that you are murdered warns that enemies are secretly working to overthrow you.

Muscle

To dream of seeing your muscles well developed, you will have strange encounters with enemies, but you will succeed in surmounting their evil works, and gain fortune.

If they are shrunken, your inability to succeed in your affairs is portended. For a woman, this dream is prophetic of toil and hardships.

Museum

To dream of a museum denotes that you will pass through many and varied scenes in striving for what appears your rightful position. You will acquire useful knowledge, which will stand you in better light than if you had pursued the usual course to learning. If the museum is distasteful, you will have many causes for vexation.

Music

To dream of hearing harmonious music omens pleasure and prosperity.

Discordant music foretells troubles with unruly children, and unhappiness in the household. The dreamer's artistic potential has become blocked or confused.

Musical Instruments

To see musical instruments denotes anticipated pleasures.

If they are broken, the pleasure will be marred by uncongenial companionship. For a young woman, this dream foretells for her the power to make her life what she will.

Mushroom

To see mushrooms in your dreams denotes unhealthy desires and unwise haste in amassing wealth, as it may vanish in lawsuits and vain pleasures.

To eat them warns of humiliation and disgraceful love.

For a young woman to dream of them foretells her defiance of propriety in her pursuit of foolish pleasures.

Musk

To dream of musk foretells unexpected occasions of joy; lovers will agree and cease to be unfaithful.

Mussels

To dream of mussels denotes small fortune, but contentment and domestic enjoyment.

Mustard

To see mustard growing, and green, foretells success and joy to the farmer, and to the seafaring it prognosticates wealth.

To eat mustard seed and feel the burning in your mouth denotes that you will repent bitterly some hasty action, which has caused you to suffer.

To dream of eating green mustard cooked warns of the lavish waste of fortune, and mental strain.

For a young woman to eat newly grown mustard foretells that she will sacrifice wealth for personal desires.

Myrrh

To see myrrh in a dream signifies that your investments will give satisfaction. For a young woman to dream of myrrh brings a pleasing surprise to her in the way of a new and wealthy acquaintance.

Myrtle

To see myrtle in foliage and bloom in your dream denotes that your desires will be gratified, and pleasures will possess you.

For a young woman to dream of wearing a sprig of myrtle foretells to her an early marriage with a well-to-do and intelligent man.

To see it withered denotes that she will miss happiness through careless conduct.

Mystery

To find yourself bewildered by some mysterious event denotes that strangers will harass you with their troubles and claim your aid. It warns you also of neglected duties, for which you feel much aversion. Business may wind you into unpleasant complications.

To find yourself studying the mysteries of creation denotes that a change will take place in your life, throwing you into a higher atmosphere of research and learning, and thus advancing you nearer the attainment of true pleasure and fortune.

N

'And he slept and dreamed the second time; and, behold, seven ears of corn came up upon one stalk, rank and good.'

—Genesis xli, 5.

Nails

To see nails in your dreams indicates much toil and small recompense.

To deal in nails shows that you will engage in honourable work, even if it be lowly.

To see rusty or broken nails warns of sickness and failure in business.

Naked

To dream that you are naked foretells scandal and unwise engagements.

To dream that you are naked in a public place, and that everyone is laughing at you, signifies that you are ashamed of yourself.

To see others naked foretells that you will be tempted by designing persons to leave the path of duty. Sickness will be no small factor against your success.

To dream that you suddenly discover your nudity, and are trying to conceal it, denotes that you have sought illicit pleasure contrary to your noblest instincts and are desirous of abandoning those desires.

For a young woman to dream that she admires her nudity foretells that she will win, but not hold, honest men's regard. She will win fortune by her charms. If she thinks herself ill-formed, her reputation will be sullied by scandal. If she dreams of swimming in clear water naked, she will enjoy illicit loves. If she sees naked men swimming in clear water, she will have many admirers. If the water is muddy, a jealous admirer may cause ill-natured gossip about her.

Napkin

To dream of a napkin, foretells convivial entertainments in which you will figure prominently. For a woman to dream of soiled napkins foretells that humiliating affairs will thrust themselves upon her.

Navy

To dream of the navy, denotes victorious struggles with unsightly obstacles, and the promise of voyages and tours of recreation. If in your dream you seem frightened or disconcerted, you will have strange obstacles to overcome before you reach fortune. A dilapidated navy is an indication of unfortunate friendships in business or love.

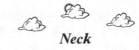

Neck

To dream that you see your own neck foretells that vexatious family relations will interfere with your business.

To admire the neck of another signifies that your worldly mindedness may cause broken domestic ties.

For a woman to dream that her neck is thick foretells that she will become querulous and something of a shrew if she fails to control her temper.

Necklace

For a woman to dream of receiving a necklace omens for her a loving husband and a beautiful home.

To lose a necklace portends ill luck and loss.

Need

To dream that you are in need denotes that you may speculate unwisely and distressing news of absent friends may oppress you.

To see others in need foretells that unfortunate affairs may affect yourself and others.

Needle

To use a needle in your dream is a warning of approaching affliction, in which you may suffer keenly the loss of the sympathy which is rightfully yours.

To dream of threading a needle denotes that you will be burdened with the care of others than your own household.

To look for a needle foretells useless worries.

To find a needle foretells that you will have friends who will appreciate you.

To break one warns of loneliness and poverty.

Neighbour

To see your neighbours in your dreams denotes that many profitable hours may be lost in useless strife and gossip. If they appear sad, or angry, it foretells dissensions and quarrels.

Nephew

To dream of your nephew denotes that you are soon to come into a pleasing income, if he is handsome and good-looking; otherwise, there will be disappointment and discomfort for you.

Nest

To dream of seeing birds' nests denotes that you will be interested in an enterprise which will be prosperous. For a young woman, this dream foretells change of abode.

To see an empty birds' nest warns of gloom and a dull outlook for business. An empty nest may also indicate sorrow through the absence of a friend. With eggs in the nest, good results will follow all engagements. If young ones are in the nest, it denotes successful journeys and satisfactory dealings. If they are lonely and deserted, sorrow, and folly on your part will cause anxiety.

Hens' nests foretell that you will be interested in domesticities, and children will be cheerful and obedient.

To dream of a nest filled with broken or bad eggs portends disappointments and failure.

Nets

To dream of ensnaring anything with a net denotes that you will be unscrupulous in your dealings and deportment with others.

To dream of an old or torn net denotes that your property has mortgages, or attachments, which may cause you trouble.

See also **Meshes**.

Nettles

If in your dreams you walk among nettles without being stung, you will be prosperous.

To be stung by them, you will be discontented with yourself and make others unhappy.

For a young woman to dream of passing through nettles foretells that she will be offered marriage by different men, and her decision will fill her with anxious foreboding.

To dream of nettles is portentous of stringent circumstances and disobedience from children or other household members.

News

To hear good news in a dream denotes that you will be fortunate in affairs, and have harmonious companions; but if the news is bad, contrary conditions will exist.

Newspaper

To dream of newspapers warns that frauds may be detected in your dealings, and your reputation may likewise be affected.

To print a newspaper, you will have opportunities of making foreign journeys and friends.

Trying, but failing, to read a newspaper denotes that you will fail in some uncertain enterprise.

New Year

To dream of the New Year signifies prosperity and connubial anticipations. If you contemplate the new year in weariness, engagement
will be entered into in-auspiciously.

Niece

For a woman to dream of her niece foretells that she will have
unexpected trials and much useless worry in the near future.

Night

If you are surrounded by night in your dreams, you may expect
unusual oppression and hardships in business. If the night seems to be
vanishing, conditions which hitherto seemed unfavourable will now
grow bright, and affairs will assume prosperous phases.

Nightdress

For a woman to dream of a nightdress indicates that she may hear
unfavourable gossip about herself.

Nightgown

If you dream that you are in your nightgown, you will be afflicted with
a slight illness. If you see others thus clad, you may have unpleasant
news of absent friends. Business will receive a setback.

If a lover sees his sweetheart in her nightgown, he is likely to be
superseded.

Nightingale

To dream that you are listening to the harmonious notes of the
nightingale foretells a pleasing existence, and prosperous and healthy
surroundings. This is a most favourable dream to lovers, and parents.

To see nightingales silent foretells slight misunderstandings among friends.

Nightmare

To dream of being attacked with this hideous sensation, denotes wrangling and failure in business. For a young woman, this is a dream prophetic of disappointment and unmerited slights. It may also warn the dreamer to be careful of her health, and food.

Nine

To dream of the number nine signifies that you are coming to the end of one cycle of your life and need to embark on the next. New territories will open up to you.

Nobility

To dream of associating with the nobility denotes that your aspirations are not of the right nature, as you prefer show and pleasures to the higher development of the mind.

For a young woman to dream of the nobility foretells that she will choose a lover for his outward appearance, instead of wisely accepting the man of merit for her protector.

Noise

If you hear a strange noise in your dream, unfavourable news is presaged. If the noise awakes you, there will be a sudden change in your affairs.

Noodles

To dream of noodles denotes an abnormal appetite and desires. There is little good in this dream.

Nose

To see your own nose indicates force of character, and consciousness of your ability to accomplish whatever enterprise you may choose to undertake.

If your nose looks smaller than normal, there may be failure in your affairs. Hair growing on your nose indicates extraordinary undertakings, and that they will be carried through by sheer force of character, or will.

A bleeding nose is prophetic of disaster, whatever the calling of the dreamer may be.

Notary

To dream of a notary is a prediction of unsatisfied desires and probable lawsuits. For a woman to associate with a notary foretells that she will rashly risk her reputation, in gratification of foolish pleasure.

November

To dream of November augurs a season of indifferent success in all affairs.

Nuisance

To dream of being worried over a nuisance of any nature foretells that disturbing elements will prevail in your immediate future.

To see others thus worried denotes that you will be annoyed by some displeasing development.

Numbness

To dream that you feel a numbness creeping over you, in your dreams, is a sign of illness, and disquieting conditions.

Numbers

To dream of numbers denotes that unsettled conditions in business may cause you uneasiness and dissatisfaction.

Nuns

For a religiously inclined man to dream of nuns foretells that material joys may interfere with his spirituality. He should exercise self-control.

For a woman to dream that she is a nun, portends her discontentment with her present situation.

To see a dead nun warns of despair over the disloyalty of loved ones, and impoverished fortune.

For a nun to dream that she discards the robes of her order foretells that longing for worldly pleasures will make her unfit for her chosen duties.

Nurse

To dream that a nurse is retained in your home warns of illness, or unlucky visiting among friends.

To see a nurse leaving your house omens good health in the family.

For a young woman to dream that she is a nurse denotes that she will gain the esteem of people, through her self-sacrifice. If she parts from a patient, she may yield to the persuasion of deceit.

Nutmegs

To dream of nutmegs is a sign of prosperity, and pleasant journeyings.

Nuts

To dream of gathering nuts augurs successful enterprises, and much favour in love.

To eat them, prosperity will aid you in grasping any desired pleasure.

For a woman to dream of nuts foretells that her fortune will be on blissful heights.

Nymph

To see nymphs bathing in clear water denotes that passionate desires will find an ecstatic realization. Convivial entertainments will enchant you.

To see them out of their sphere denotes disappointment with the world.

For a young woman to see them bathing denotes that she will have great favour and pleasure, but they will not rest strictly within the moral code. To dream that she impersonates a nymph is a sign that she is using her attractions for selfish purposes, and thus the undoing of men.

O

'And it shall come to pass afterward, that I will pour out my spirit upon all flesh; and your sons and your daughters shall prophesy, your old men shall dream dreams, your young men shall see visions.'

—Joel ii, 28.

Oak

To dream of seeing a forest of oaks signifies great prosperity in all conditions of life.

To see an oak full of acorns denotes increase and promotion.

If the oak is blasted, it denotes sudden and shocking surprises.

For sweethearts to dream of oaks denotes that they will soon begin life together under favourable circumstances.

Oar

To dream of handling oars portends disappointments for you, inasmuch as you may sacrifice your own pleasure for the comfort of others.

To lose an oar denotes vain efforts to carry out designs satisfactorily.

A broken oar represents interruption in some anticipated pleasure.

Oath

Whenever you take an oath in your dreams, prepare for dissension and altercations on waking.

Oatmeal

To dream of eating oatmeal signifies the enjoyment of worthily earned fortune.

For a young woman to dream of preparing it for the table denotes that she will soon preside over the destiny of others.

Oats

To dream of oats portends a variety of good things. The farmer, especially, will advance in fortune and domestic harmony.

To see decayed oats warns that sorrow may displace bright hopes.

Obedience

To dream that you render obedience to another foretells for you a common place, a pleasant but uneventful period of life.

If others are obedient to you, it shows that you will command fortune and high esteem.

Obelisk

An obelisk looming up stately and cold in your dreams is the forerunner of melancholy tidings.

For lovers to stand at the base of an obelisk denotes serious disagreements.

Obesity

For a person to dream of being obese indicates to the dreamer bountiful increase of wealth and pleasant abiding places.

To see others obese denotes unusual activity and prosperous times.

If a man or woman sees himself or herself looking grossly obese, he or she should look well to their moral nature and impulses. Beware of either concave or convex telescopically or microscopically drawn pictures of yourself or others, as all forbode evil.

See also **Fat**.

338

Obituary

To dream of writing an obituary denotes that unpleasant and discordant duties will devolve upon you.

If you read one, news of a distracting nature will soon reach you.

Obligation

To dream of obligating yourself in any incident denotes that you will be fretted and worried by the thoughtless complaints of others.

If others obligate themselves to you, it portends that you will win the regard of acquaintances and friends.

Observatory

To dream of viewing the heavens and beautiful landscapes from an observatory denotes your swift elevation to prominent positions and places of trust. For a young woman this dream signals the realization of the highest earthly joys. If the heavens are clouded, your highest aims will miss materialization.

Occultist

To dream that you listen to the teachings of an occultist denotes that you will strive to elevate others to a higher plane of justice and forbearance. If you accept his views, you will find honest delight by keeping your mind and person above material frivolities and pleasures.

Ocean

To dream of the ocean when it is calm is propitious. The sailor will have a pleasant and profitable voyage. The business person will enjoy a season of remuneration, and the young man will revel in his sweetheart's charms.

To be far out on the ocean, and hear the waves lash the ship, forebodes disaster in business life, and quarrels and stormy periods in the household.

To be on shore and see the waves of the ocean foaming against each other foretells your narrow escape from injury and the designs of enemies.

To dream of seeing the ocean so shallow as to allow wading, or a view of the bottom, signifies prosperity and pleasure with a mingling of sorrow and hardships.

To sail on the ocean when it is calm is always propitious.

See also **Sea**.

October

To imagine that you are in October is ominous of gratifying success in your undertakings. You will also make new acquaintances which will ripen into lasting friendships.

Odour

To dream of inhaling sweet odours is a sign of a loving partner ministering to your daily life, and financial success.

To smell disgusting odours foretells unpleasant disagreements and unreliable support.

Offence

To dream of being offended denotes that errors may be detected in your conduct, which will cause you inward rage as you attempt to justify yourself.

To give offence predicts many struggles for you before you attain your goals.

For a young woman to give or take offence signifies that she will regret hasty conclusions and disobedience to parents or guardian.

Offering

To bring or make an offering foretells that you will be cringing and hypocritical unless you cultivate higher views of duty.

Office

For a person to dream that he holds office denotes that his aspirations will sometimes make him undertake dangerous paths, but his boldness will be rewarded with success. If he fails by any means to secure a desired office, he will suffer keen disappointment in his affairs.

To dream that you are turned out of office signifies loss of valuables.

Offspring

To see the offspring of domestic animals denotes increase in prosperity.

Oil

To dream of anointing with oil foretells events in which you will be the particular moving power.

Quantities of oil prognosticate excesses in pleasurable enterprises.

For a man to dream that he deals in oil denotes unsuccessful lovemaking, as he will expect unusual concessions.

For a woman to dream that she is anointed with oil indicates that she may be open to indiscreet advances.

Oilcloth

To dream of oilcloth is a warning that you may meet coldness and treachery.

To sell it denotes uncertain speculations.

Ointment

To dream of ointment denotes that you will form friendships which will prove beneficial and pleasing to you. You will prosper under adverse circumstances and convert enemies into friends.

For a young woman to dream that she makes ointment denotes that she will be able to command her own affairs whether they are of a private or public character.

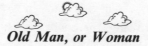

Old Man, or Woman

To dream of seeing an old man, or woman denotes that unhappy cares may oppress you, if they appear otherwise than serene.

Olives

Gathering olives with a merry band of friends foretells favourable results in business and delightful surprises.

If you take them from bottles, it foretells conviviality.

To break a bottle of olives indicates disappointments on the eve of pleasure.

To eat them signifies contentment and faithful friends.

Omelette

To see omelette being served in your dream warns you of flattery and deceit, which is about to be used against you.

To eat it shows that you may be imposed upon by someone seemingly worthy of your confidence.

One

To dream of the number one signifies power. The number itself rarely appears, but there may be symbols thereof, such as a solitary tower, mast or pole.

One-Eyed

To see one-eyed creatures in your dreams is portentous of an overwhelming intimation of secret intriguing against your fortune and happiness.

Onions

Seeing quantities of onions in your dreams represents the amount of spite and envy that you will meet by being successful.

If you eat them, you will overcome all opposition.

If you see them growing, there will be just enough rivalry in your affairs to make things interesting.

Cooked onions denote placidity and small gains in business.

To dream that you are cutting onions and feel the escaping juice in your eyes denotes that you are likely to be defeated by your rivals.

Opal

A woman dreaming of an opal should take care, as it is a stone of bad luck.

Opera

To dream of attending an opera denotes that you will be entertained by congenial friends, and find that your immediate affairs will be favourable.

Opium

To dream of opium signifies that strangers may obstruct your chances of improving your fortune, by sly and seductive means.

Optician

To dream of consulting an optician denotes that you will be dissatisfied with your progress in life, and may resort to artificial means of advancement.

Opulence

For a young woman to dream that she lives in fairy-like opulence warns that she may be deceived, and may live for a time in luxurious ease and splendour, to find only later that she is mated with shame and poverty. When young women dream that they are enjoying solid and real wealth and comforts, they will always wake to find some real pleasure, but when abnormal or fairy-like dreams of luxury and joy seem to encompass them, their waking moments will be filled with disappointments.

See also **Affluence, Riches, Wealth**.

Orange

To dream of or in the colour orange signifies that the dreamer can look forward to a warm welcome.

Seeing a number of orange trees in a healthy condition, bearing ripe fruit, is a sign of health and prosperous surroundings.

To eat oranges is signally bad. Sickness of friends or relatives may be a source of worry to you. Dissatisfaction may pervade the atmosphere in business circles. If they are fine and well-flavoured, there will be a slight abatement of ill luck. A young woman is likely to fall out with her lover if she dreams of eating oranges. If she dreams of seeing a fine one pitched up high, she will be discreet in choosing a husband from many lovers.

To slip on an orange peel warns of a death.

To buy oranges at your wife's solicitation, and she eats them, denotes that unpleasant complications will resolve themselves into profit.

Orang-utang

To dream of an orang-utang, warns that some person is falsely using your influence to further selfish schemes. For a young woman, it portends an unfaithful lover.

Orator

Being under the spell of an orator's eloquence denotes that you will heed the voice of flattery to your own detriment, as you may be persuaded into offering aid to unworthy people.

If a young woman falls in love with an orator, it is proof that in her loves she will be affected by outward show.

Orchard

Dreaming of passing through leaving and blossoming orchards with your sweetheart omens a delightful consummation of a long courtship. If the orchard is filled with ripening fruit, it denotes recompense for faithful service to those under masters, and full fruition of designs for the leaders of enterprises. Happy homes, with loyal husbands and obedient children, for wives.

If you are in an orchard and see pigs eating the fallen fruit, it is a warning that you may lose property in trying to claim what are not really your own belongings.

To gather the ripe fruit is a happy omen of plenty to all classes.

Orchards infested with blight denotes a miserable existence in the midst of joy and wealth.

To be caught in brambles, while passing through an orchard, warns you of a jealous rival, or, if married, a private but large row with your partner.

If you dream of seeing a barren orchard, opportunities to rise to higher stations in life may be ignored.

If you see one robbed of its verdure by seeming winter, it denotes that you have been careless of the future in the enjoyment of the present.

To see a storm-swept orchard brings an unwelcome guest, or duties.

Orchestra

Belonging to an orchestra and playing foretells pleasant entertainments; your sweetheart will be faithful and cultivated.

To hear the music of an orchestra denotes that your knowledge of humanity will at all times prove you to be a much-liked person, and favours will fall unstintedly upon you.

Organ

To hear the pealing forth of an organ in grand anthems signifies lasting friendships and well-grounded fortune.

To see an organ in a church warns of separation.

If you dream of rendering harmonious music on an organ, you will be fortunate on the way to worldly comfort, and much social distinction will be given you.

To hear doleful singing and organ accompaniment denotes that you are nearing a wearisome task, and possible loss of friends or position.

Organist

To see an organist in your dreams warns that a friend may cause you much inconvenience from hasty action. For a young woman to dream that she is an organist foretells that she will be so exacting in her love that she will be threatened with desertion.

Ornament

If you wear ornaments in dreams, you will have a flattering honour conferred upon you.

If you receive them, you will be fortunate in undertakings.

Giving them away denotes recklessness and lavish extravagance.

Losing an ornament brings the loss either of a lover, or a good situation.

Orphan

Condoling with orphans in a dream means that the unhappy cares of others will touch your sympathies and cause you to sacrifice much personal enjoyment.

If the orphans are related to you, new duties may come into your life, causing estrangement from friends and from some person held above mere friendly liking.

Ostrich

To dream of an ostrich denotes that you will secretly amass wealth.

To catch one, your resources will enable you to enjoy travel and extensive knowledge.

Otter

To see otters diving and sporting in limpid streams is certain to bring the dreamer waking happiness and good fortune. You will find ideal enjoyment in an early marriage, if you are single; wives may expect unusual tenderness from their spouses after this dream.

Ottoman

Dreams in which you find yourself luxuriously reposing upon an ottoman, discussing the intricacies of love with your sweetheart, foretell that envious rivals may seek to defame you in the eyes of your affianced, and a hasty marriage may be advisable.

Ouija Board

To dream of working on an ouija board warns of the miscarriage of plans and unlucky partnerships.

To fail to work one is ominous of complications, caused by substituting pleasure for business.

If it writes fluently, you may expect fortunate results from some well-planned enterprise.

If it is stolen, you will meet with trials and vexations past endurance. To recover it foretells that grievances will meet a favourable adjustment.

Oven

For a woman to dream that her oven is red hot denotes that she will be loved by her own family and friends, for her sweet and unselfish nature. If she is baking, temporary disappointments await her. If the oven is broken, she will undergo many vexations from children and elatives.

Overalls

For a woman to dream that she sees a man wearing overalls, she may be deceived as to the real character of her lover. If a wife, she may be deceived in her husband's frequent absence, and the real cause may create suspicions of his fidelity.

Overcoat

To dream of an overcoat warns that you may suffer from contrariness, exhibited by others. To borrow one foretells that you may be unfortunate as a result of mistakes made by strangers. If you see or are wearing a handsome new overcoat, you will be exceedingly fortunate in realizing your wishes.

Owl

To dream of an owl foretells that you will experience an important personal change.

An owl often appears in dreams as a protector and guide. It may also signify wisdom.

To hear the solemn, unearthly cry of an owl may betoken bad tidings.

Ox

To see a well-fed ox signifies that you will become a leading person in your community, and receive much adulation from others.

To see fat oxen in green pastures signifies fortune, and your rise to positions beyond your expectations. If they are lean, your fortune is likely to dwindle, and your friends to fall away from you.

If you see oxen well-matched and yoked, it betokens a happy and wealthy marriage, or that you are already joined to your true mate.

To see a dead ox is a warning of possible bereavement.

If they are drinking from a clear pond, or stream, you will finally come to win something, or someone, that you have desired for a long time.

See also **Cattle**.

Oysters

If you dream that you eat oysters, it warns you against losing all sense of propriety and morality in your pursuit of foolish pleasures.

To deal in oysters denotes that you will not be overmodest in your mode of winning a sweetheart, or a fortune.

To see them denotes easy circumstances; many children are promised to you.

Oyster Shells

To see oyster shells in your dreams denotes that you are likely to be frustrated in your attempt to secure the fortune of another.

P

Pacify

To endeavour to pacify suffering ones denotes that you will be loved for your sweetness of disposition. To a young woman, this dream is one of promise of a devoted husband or friends.

Pacifying the anger of others denotes that you will labour for the advancement of others.

If a lover dreams of soothing the jealous suspicions of his sweetheart, he will find that his love will be unfortunately placed.

Page-boy

To see a page boy warns that you may contract a hasty union with one unsuited to you. You will fail to control your romantic impulses.

If a young woman dreams she acts as a page, it denotes that she is likely to participate in some foolish escapade.

Pagoda

To see a pagoda in your dreams denotes that you will soon go on a long-desired journey.

If a young woman finds herself in a pagoda with her sweetheart, many unforeseen events will transpire before her union is legalized. An empty one warns her of separation from her lover.

Pail

To dream of full pails of milk is a sign of fair prospects and pleasant associations.

An empty pail warns of famine, or bad crops.

For a young woman to be carrying a pail denotes household employment.

Pain

To dream that you are in pain warns of your own unhappiness. This dream foretells useless regrets over some trivial transaction.

To see others in pain warns you that you are making mistakes in your life.

Paint

To paint a room or wall in your dreams signifies your desire to erase the recent past and start again.

To see newly painted houses in dreams foretells that you will succeed with some devised plan.

To have paint on your clothing, you may be made unhappy by the thoughtless criticisms of others.

To dream that you use the brush yourself denotes that you will be well pleased with your present occupation.

Painting

To dream of seeing beautiful paintings, denotes that friends may assume false positions towards you, and you will find that pleasure is illusory.

For a young woman to dream of painting a picture, she is likely to be deceived in her lover, as he may transfer his love to another.

*See also **Pictures, Portrait**.*

Palace

Wandering through a palace and noting its grandeur signifies that your prospects are growing brighter and you will assume new dignity.

To see and hear fine ladies and men dancing and conversing denotes that you will engage in profitable and pleasing associations.

For a young woman of moderate means to dream that she is a participant in the entertainment, and of equal social standing with others, is a sign of her coming social advancement.

Palisade

To dream of palisades denotes that you may alter well-formed plans to please strangers, and by so doing, will impair your own interests.

Pall-bearer

To dream of a pall-bearer warns that some enemy may provoke your ill feeling by constant attacks on your integrity. If you see a pall-bearer, you may antagonize worthy institutions, and make yourself obnoxious to friends.

Pallet

To dream of a pallet denotes that you will suffer temporary uneasiness over your love affairs. For a young woman, it is a sign of a jealous rival.

Palmistry

For a young woman to dream of palmistry foretells that she may be the object of suspicion.

If she has her palm read, she will have many friends of the opposite sex. If she reads others' hands, she will gain distinction by her intelligent bearing. If a minister's hand, she will need friends, even with her elevated status.

Palm Tree

Palm trees seen in your dreams are messages of hopeful situations and happiness of a high order.

For a young woman to pass down an avenue of palms omens a cheerful home and a faithful husband. If the palms are withered, some unexpected sorrowful event will disturb her serenity.

Pancake

Batter, or pancakes, denotes that the affections of the dreamer are well placed and that a home may be bequeathed to him or her.

To dream of eating pancakes denotes that you will have excellent success in all enterprises undertaken at this time.

To cook them denotes that you will be economical and thrifty in your home.

Pane of Glass

To dream that you handle a pane of glass denotes that you are dealing in uncertainties. If you break it, your failure will be accentuated.

To talk to a person through a pane of glass denotes that there are obstacles in your immediate future, and they will cause you no slight inconvenience.

Panorama

To dream of a panorama denotes that you will change your occupation or residence. You should curb your inclinations for change of scene and friends.

Panther

To see a panther and experience fright denotes that contracts in love or business may be cancelled unexpectedly, owing to adverse influences working against your honour. If you kill or overpower it, you will experience joy and be successful in your undertakings. Your surroundings will take on fair prospects.

If one menaces you by its presence, you may have disappointments in business. Other people may well go back on their promises to you.

If you hear the voice of a panther, and experience terror or fright, you will have unfavourable news, coming in the way of reducing profit or gain, and you may have social discord; no fright forebodes less evil.

A panther, generally portends evil to the dreamer, unless he overcomes it.

Pantomime

To dream of seeing pantomimes denotes that your friends may deceive you. If you participate in them, you may have cause for offence. Affairs will not prove satisfactory.

Paper or Parchment

If you have occasion in your dreams to refer to, or handle, any paper or parchment, you will be threatened with losses. They are likely to be in the nature of a law-suit. For a young woman, it means that she will be angry with her lover and that she fears the opinion of acquaintances. Beware, if you are married, of disagreements in the precincts of the home.

Parables

To dream of parables denotes that you will be undecided as to the best course to pursue in dissenting to some business complication. To the lover, or young woman, this is a prophecy of misunderstandings and disloyalty.

Paradise

To dream that you are in Paradise means loyal friends, who are willing to aid you. This dream holds out bright hopes to sailors or those about to make a long voyage. To mothers, this means fair and obedient children. If you are sick and unfortunate, you will have a speedy recovery and your fortune will ripen. To lovers, it is the promise of wealth and faithfulness.

To dream that you start to Paradise and find yourself bewildered and lost, you are likely to undertake enterprises which look exceedingly feasible and full of fortunate returns, but which prove disappointing and vexatious.

See also **Heaven**.

Paralysis

Paralysis is a bad dream warning of financial reverses and disappointment in literary attainment. To lovers, it portends a cessation of affections.

Parasol

To dream of a parasol, denotes, for married people, illicit enjoyments.

If a young woman has this dream, she will engage in many flirtations, some of which may cause her considerable worry, lest her lover find out her inclinations.

Parcel

To dream of a parcel being delivered to you denotes that you will be pleasantly surprised by the return of some absent one, or be cared for in a worldly way.

If you carry a parcel, you will have some unpleasant task to perform.

To let a parcel fall on the way as you go to deliver it, you will see some deal fail to go through.

Parchment see **Paper**

Pardon

To dream that you are endeavouring to gain pardon for an offence which you never committed denotes that you will be troubled, and seemingly with cause, over your affairs, but it will finally appear that it was for your advancement. If offence was committed, you face embarrassment in your affairs.

To receive pardon, you will prosper after a series of misfortunes.

Parents

To see your parents looking cheerful while dreaming denotes harmony and pleasant associates.

If they appear to you after they are dead, it is a warning of approaching trouble, and you should be particular of your dealings.

To see them while they are living, and they seem to be in your home and happy, denotes pleasant changes for you. To a young woman, this usually brings marriage and prosperity. If pale and attired in black, grave disappointments are likely to harass you.

To dream of seeing your parents looking robust and contented denotes that you are under fortunate environments; your business and love interests will flourish. If they appear indisposed or sad, you will find life's favours passing you by without recognition.

Park

To dream of walking through a well-kept park denotes enjoyable leisure. If you walk with your lover, you will be comfortably and happily married. Ill-kept parks, devoid of green grasses and foliage, are ominous of unexpected reverses.

Parrot

Parrots chattering in your dreams signify frivolous employments and idle gossip among your friends.

To see them in repose denotes a peaceful intermission of family broils.

For a young woman to dream that she owns a parrot denotes that her lover will believe her to be quarrelsome.

To teach a parrot, you may have trouble in your private affairs.

A dead parrot warns of the loss of social friends.

Parsley

To dream of parsley denotes hard-earned success; usually the surroundings of the dreamer will be healthy and lively.

To eat parsley is a sign of good health, but the care of a large family will be your destiny.

Parsnips

To see or eat parsnips is a favourable omen of successful business or trade, but love may take on unfavourable and gloomy aspects.

Parting

To dream of parting with friends and companions denotes that many little vexations will come into your daily life.

If you part with enemies, it is a sign of success in love and business.

Partnership

To dream of forming a business partnership with a man denotes uncertain and fluctuating money affairs. If your partner be a woman, you may engage in some enterprise which you endeavour to keep hidden from friends.

To dissolve an unpleasant partnership denotes that things will arrange themselves in accordance with your desires; but if the partnership was pleasant, there may be disquieting news and disagreeable turns in your affairs.

Partridge

Partridges seen in your dreams denote that conditions will be good in your immediate future for the accumulation of property.

To ensnare them signifies that you will be fortunate in expectations.

To kill them foretells that you will be successful, but much of your wealth will be given to others.

To eat them signifies the enjoyment of deserved honours.

To see them flying denotes that a promising future is before you.

Party

To dream of attending a party of any kind for pleasure, you will find that life has much good, unless the party is an inharmonious one.

Passenger

To dream that you see passengers coming in with their luggage denotes improvement in your surroundings. If they are leaving you may lose an opportunity of gaining some desired property. If you are one of the passengers leaving home, you will be dissatisfied with your present living and will seek to change it.

Password

To dream of a password foretells you will have influential aid in some slight trouble soon to attack you. For a woman to dream that she has given away the password signifies that she may endanger her own standing through seeking frivolous or illicit desires.

Pastry

To dream of pastry warns that you may be deceived by some artful person.

To eat it implies heartfelt friendships.

If a young woman dreams that she is cooking it, she will fail to deceive others as to her real intentions.

Patch

To dream that you have patches upon your clothing denotes that you will show no false pride in the discharge of obligations.

To see others wearing patches warns that want and misery are near.

If a young woman discovers a patch on her new dress, it indicates that she will find trouble facing her when she imagines her happiest moments are approaching near. If she tries to hide the patches, she may endeavour to keep some ugly trait in her character from her lover. If she is patching, she will assume duties for which she has no liking.

For a woman to do family patching denotes close and loving bonds in the family, but a scarcity of means is portended.

Patent

To dream of securing a patent denotes that you will be careful and painstaking with any task you set about to accomplish. If you fail to secure your patent, you may suffer failure for the reason that you are engaging in enterprises for which you have no ability.

If you buy one, you will have occasion to make a tiresome and fruitless journey.

To see one, you may suffer unpleasantness from illness.

Patent Medicine

To dream that you resort to patent medicine in your search for health denotes that you will use desperate measures in advancing your fortune, but you will succeed, to the disappointment of the envious.

To see or manufacture patent medicines, you will rise from obscurity to positions above your highest imaginings.

Path

To dream that you are walking along a narrow and rough path, stumbling over rocks and other obstructions, denotes that you will have a rough encounter with adversity, and feverish excitement will weigh heavily upon you.

To dream that you are trying to find your path foretells that you may fail to accomplish some work that you have striven to push to desired ends.

To walk through a pathway bordered with green grass and flowers, denotes your freedom from oppressing loves.

Paunch

To see a large paunch denotes wealth and the total sense of refinement.

Pawnshop

If in your dreams you enter a pawnshop, you are likely to find disappointments and losses in your waking moments.

To pawn articles, you may have unpleasant scenes with your wife or sweetheart, and perhaps disappointments in business.

For a woman to go to a pawnshop indicates that she is guilty of indiscretions, and she is likely to regret the loss of a friend.

To redeem an article denotes that you will regain lost positions.

To dream that you see a pawnshop denotes you are negligent of your trust and are in danger of sacrificing your honourable name in some salacious affair.

Payment

To dream that you receive a demand for payment warns you to look after your affairs and correct all tendency towards neglect of business and love.

Peaches

Dreaming of seeing or eating peaches warns of illness, disappointing returns in business, and failure to make anticipated visits of pleasure; but if you see them on trees with foliage, you will secure some desired position or thing after much striving and risking of health and money.

To see dried peaches warns that enemies may steal from you.

For a young woman to dream of gathering luscious peaches from well-filled trees, she will, by her personal charms and qualifications, win a husband rich in worldly goods and wise in travel. If the peaches prove to be green and knotty, she will meet with unkindness from relatives.

Peacock

For persons dreaming of peacocks, there lies below the brilliant and flashing ebb and flow of the stream of pleasure and riches, the slums of sorrow and failure, which threaten to mix with its clearness at the least disturbing influence.

For a woman to dream that she owns peacocks denotes that she may be deceived in her estimation of man's honour.

To hear their harsh voices while looking upon their proudly spread plumage, denotes that some beautiful and well-appearing person will work you discomfort and uneasiness of mind.

Pearls

To dream of pearls is a forerunner of good business and trade and affairs of social nature.

If a young woman dreams that her lover sends her gifts of pearls, she will indeed be most fortunate, as there will be occasions of festivity and pleasure for her, besides a loving and faithful affianced devoid of the jealous inclinations so ruinous to the peace of lovers. If she loses or breaks her pearls, she will suffer indescribable sadness and sorrow through bereavement or misunderstandings. To find herself admiring them, she will covet and strive for love or possessions with a purity of purpose.

Pears

To dream of eating pears warns of poor success and debilitating health.

To admire the golden fruit upon graceful trees denotes that fortune will wear a more promising aspect than formerly.

To dream of gathering them denotes that pleasant surprises will follow quickly upon disappointment.

To preserve them denotes that you will take reverses philosophically.

Baking them denotes insipid love and friendships.

Peas

Dreaming of eating peas augurs robust health and the accumulation of wealth. Much activity is indicated for farmers and their women folks.

To see them growing denotes fortunate enterprises.

To plant them denotes that your hopes are well grounded and will be realized.

To gather them signifies that your plans will culminate in good and you will enjoy the fruits of your labours.

To dream of canned peas denotes that your brightest hopes will be enthralled in uncertainties for a short season, but they will finally be released by fortune.

To see dried peas denotes that you are overtaxing your health.

To eat dried peas foretells that you will, after much success, suffer a slight decrease in pleasure or wealth.

Pebbles

For a young woman to dream of a pebble-strewn walk, she is likely to be vexed with many rivals and find that there are others with charms that attract besides her own. She who dreams of pebbles should cultivate leniency towards others' faults.

Pecans

To dream of eating this appetizing nut, you will see one of your dearest plans come to full fruition, and seeming failure prove a prosperous source of gain.

To see them growing among leaves signifies a long, peaceful existence. Failure in love or business are indicated if the pecan is decayed; the degree of failure is denoted by the degree of decay.

If they are difficult to crack and the fruit is small, you will succeed after much trouble and expense, but returns will be meagre.

Pelican

To dream of a pelican denotes a mingling of disappointments with success.

To catch one, you will be able to overcome disappointing influences.

To kill one denotes that you will cruelly set aside the rights of others.

To see them flying, you are threatened with changes, which will impress you with ideas of uncertainty as to good.

Pen

To dream of a pen foretells that you are unfortunately being led into serious complications by your love of adventure. If the pen refuses to write, you may be charged with a serious breach of morality.

Penalties

To dream that you have penalties imposed upon you foretells that you will have duties that will rile you and make you rebellious.

To pay a penalty denotes sickness and financial loss. To escape the payment, you will be victor in some contest.

Pencil

To dream of pencils denotes favourable occupations. For a young woman to write with one, foretells she will be fortunate in marriage, if she does not rub out words; in that case, she will be disappointed in her lover.

Penny

To dream of pennies denotes unsatisfactory pursuits. Business may suffer, and lovers and friends complain of a lack of affection.

To lose them signifies lack of deference and failures.

To find them denotes that prospects will advance to your improvement.

To count pennies foretells that you will be businesslike and economical.

Pension

To dream of drawing a pension foretells that you will be aided in your labours by friends.

To fail in your application for a pension warns that you may lose in an undertaking and suffer the loss of friendship.

Pepper

To dream of pepper burning your tongue foretells that you may suffer from your acquaintances through your love of gossip.

To see red pepper growing foretells for you a thrifty and independent marriage partner.

To see piles of red pepper pods signifies that you will aggressively maintain your rights.

To grind black pepper denotes that you may be victimized by the wiles of ingenious men or women. To see it in stands on the table omens sharp reproaches or quarrels.

For a young woman to put it on her food warns that she may be deceived by her friends.

Peppermint

To dream of peppermint denotes pleasant entertainments and interesting affairs.

To see it growing denotes that you will participate in some pleasure in which there will be a dash of romance.

To enjoy drinks in which there is an effusion of peppermint denotes that you will enjoy assignations with some attractive and fascinating person. To a young woman, this dream warns her against seductive pleasures.

Perfume

To dream of inhaling perfume is an augury of happy incidents.

For you to perfume your garments and person denotes that you will seek and obtain adulation.

Being oppressed by it to intoxication denotes that excesses in joy will impair your mental qualities.

To spill perfume denotes that you will lose something which affords you pleasure.

To break a bottle of perfume foretells that your most cherished wishes and desires may end disastrously, even if they promise a happy culmination.

To dream that you are distilling perfume denotes that your employments and associations will be of the pleasantest character.

For a young woman to dream of perfuming her bath foretells ecstatic happenings. If she receives perfume as a gift from a man, she will experience fascinating, but dangerous pleasures.

Petrol

To dream of petrol, denotes that you have an income coming to you from a struggling source.

Petticoat

To dream of seeing new petticoats denotes that pride in your belongings may make you an object of mockery among your acquaintances.

To see your petticoat soiled or torn portends that your reputation will be in great danger.

If a young woman dreams that she wears a silk, or clean, petticoat, it denotes that she will have a doting, but manly husband. If she suddenly perceives that she has left off her petticoat in dressing, it portends ill luck and disappointment. To see her petticoat falling from its place while she is at some gathering, or while walking, she may have trouble in retaining her lover, and other disappointments may follow.

Pewter

To dream of pewter foretells straitened circumstances.

Phantom *see* Ghost

Pheasant

Dreaming of pheasants omens good fellowship among your friends.

To eat one signifies that the jealousy of your wife may cause you to forego friendly relations with your friends.

To shoot them denotes that you will fail to sacrifice one selfish pleasure for the comfort of friends.

Phosphorus

To dream of seeing phosphorus is indicative of fleeting joys.

For a young woman, it foretells a brilliant but brief success with admirers.

Photograph

To dream of a photograph, especially if the subject is a person, indicates that the dreamer has a superficial response to emotional attachments.

If you see photographs in your dreams, it is a sign of approaching deception.

If you receive the photograph of your lover, you are warned that he is not giving you his undivided loyalty, while he tries to so impress you.

For married people to dream of the possession of other persons' photographs warns of unwelcome disclosures.

To dream that you are taking a photograph of someone indicates that in your waking life you are unwilling to experience change.

To dream that you are having your own photograph made foretells that you may unwarily cause yourself and others trouble.

To crumple or burn a photograph denotes that you desire to put some past event behind you.

Piano

To dream of seeing a piano denotes some joyful occasion.

To hear sweet and voluptuous harmony from a piano signals success and health. If discordant music is being played, you will have many exasperating matters to consider. Sad and plaintive music foretells sorrowful tidings.

To find your piano broken and out of tune portends dissatisfaction with your own accomplishments and disappointment in the failure of your friends or children to win honours.

To see an old-fashioned piano denotes that you have, in trying moments, neglected the advice and opportunities of the past; you are warned not to do so again.

For a young woman to dream that she is executing difficult, but entrancing music, she will succeed in winning an indifferent friend to be a most devoted and loyal lover.

Pickaxe

To dream of a pickaxe denotes a relentless enemy is working to overthrow you socially. A broken one warns of disaster to all your interests.

Pickles

To dream of pickles denotes that you will follow worthless pursuits if you fail to call energy and judgment to your aid.

For a young woman to dream of eating pickles foretells an unambitious career.

To dream of pickles denotes vexation in love, but final triumph.

For a young woman to dream that she is eating them, or is hungry for them, foretells she will find many rivals, and may be overcome unless she is careful of her private affairs. Impure pickles indicate disappointing engagements and love quarrels.

Pickpocket

To dream of a pickpocket foretells that an enemy will succeed in harassing and causing you loss. For a young woman to have her pocket picked denotes she may be the object of some person's envy and spite and may lose the regard of a friend through these machinations, unless she keeps her own counsel. If she picks others' pockets, she may incur the displeasure of a companion by her coarse behaviour.

Picnic

To dream of attending a picnic predicts success and real enjoyment.

Dreams of picnics bring undivided happiness to the young.

Storms, or any interfering elements at a picnic, imply the temporary displacement of assured profit and pleasure in love or business.

Pictures

Pictures appearing before you in dreams prognosticate deception and the ill will of contemporaries.

To make a picture denotes that you will engage in some unremunerative enterprise.

To destroy pictures means that you will be pardoned for using strenuous means to establish your rights.

To buy them warns of worthless speculation.

To dream of seeing your likeness in a living tree, appearing and disappearing, denotes that you will be prosperous and seemingly contented, but there will be disappointments in reaching out for companionship and reciprocal understanding of ideas and plans.

To dream of being surrounded with the best efforts of the old and modern masters denotes that you will have insatiable longings and desires for higher attainments, compared to which present success will seem poverty-stricken and miserable.

See also **Painting, Portrait.**

Pier

To stand upon a pier in your dream denotes that you will be brave in your battle for recognition in prosperity's realm, and that you will be admitted to the highest posts of honour.

If you strive to reach a pier and fail, you risk losing the distinction you most covet.

Pies

To dream of eating pies, you will do well to watch your enemies, as they are planning to injure you.

For a young woman to dream of making pies, denotes that she will flirt with men for pastime. She should accept this warning.

Pig

To dream of a fat, healthy pig denotes reasonable success in affairs. If they are wallowing in mire, you will have hurtful associates, and your engagements will be subject to reproach. This dream may bring to a young woman a jealous and greedy companion though the chances are that he will be wealthy.

Lean pigs predict vexatious affairs and trouble with children.

To see a sow and litter of pigs denotes abundant crops to the farmer, and advance in the affairs of others.

To hear pigs squealing denotes unpleasant news from absent friends, and foretells disappointment by failure to realize the amounts you expected in deals of importance.

To dream of feeding your own pigs denotes an increase in your personal belongings.

To dream that you are dealing in hogs, you will accumulate considerable property, but you will have much rough work to perform.

Pigeon

To dream of seeing pigeons and hearing them cooing above their cotes denotes domestic peace and pleasure-giving children. For a young woman, this dream indicates an early and comfortable union.

To see them being used in a shooting match, if you participate, it denotes that cruelty in your nature will show in your dealings; you are warned of low and debasing pleasures.

To see them flying denotes freedom from misunderstanding, and perhaps news from an absent person.

Pilgrim

To dream of pilgrims denotes that you may go on an extended journey, leaving home and its dearest objects in the mistaken idea that it must be thus for their good.

To dream that you are a pilgrim portends struggles with poverty and unsympathetic companions.

For a young woman to dream that a pilgrim approaches her, she may fall an easy dupe to deceit. If he leaves her, she will awaken to her weakness of character and strive to strengthen independent thought.

Pill

To dream that you take pills denotes that you will have responsibilities to look after, but they will bring you no little comfort and enjoyment.

To give them to others signifies that you will be criticised for your disagreeableness.

Pillow

To dream of a pillow denotes luxury and comfort.

For a young woman to dream that she makes a pillow, she will have encouraging prospects of a pleasant future.

Pimple

To dream of your flesh being full of pimples denotes worry over trifles.

To see others with pimples on them warns that you may be troubled with illness and complaints from others.

For a woman to dream that her beauty is marred by pimples, her conduct in home or social circles will be criticised by friends and acquaintances. You may have small annoyances to follow this dream.

Pincers

To dream of feeling pincers on your flesh denotes that you will be burdened with exasperating cares. Any dream of pincers signifies unfortunate incidents.

Pineapple

To dream of pineapples is exceedingly propitious. Success will follow in the near future, if you gather pineapples or eat them.

To dream that you prick your fingers while preparing a pineapple for the table, you will experience considerable vexation over matters which will finally bring pleasure and success.

Pine Tree

To see a pine tree in a dream foretells unvarying success in any undertaking. Dead pine, for a woman, represents cares.

Pins

To dream of pins augurs differences and quarrels in families.

To a young woman, they warn her of unladylike conduct towards her lover.

To dream of swallowing a pin warns that accidents may force you into perilous conditions.

To lose one implies a petty loss or disagreement.

To see a bent or rusty pin signifies that you may lose esteem because of your careless ways.

To stick one into your flesh denotes that some person will irritate you.

Pipe

Pipes, seen in dreams, are representatives of peace and comfort after many struggles.

Sewer, gas, and suchlike pipes denote unusual thought and prosperity in your community.

Old and broken piping signifies ill health and stagnation of business.

To dream that you smoke a pipe denotes that you will enjoy the visit of an old friend, and that peaceful settlements of differences will also take place.

Pirate

To dream of pirates warns that you may be exposed to the evil designs of false friends.

To dream that you are a pirate denotes that you may fall beneath the society of friends and former equals.

For a young woman to dream that her lover is a pirate is a sign of his unworthiness and deceitfulness. If she is captured by pirates, she may be induced to leave her home under false pretences.

Pistol

Seeing a pistol in your dream denotes bad fortune, generally.

If you own one, you will cultivate a low, designing character.

If you hear the report of one, you will be made aware of some scheme to ruin your interests.

To dream of firing your pistol signifies that you will bear some innocent person envy and will go far to revenge the imagined wrong.

Pit

If you are looking into a deep pit in your dream, you will run silly risks in business ventures and will draw uneasiness about your wooing.

To fall into a pit warns of calamity and deep sorrow. To wake as you begin to feel yourself falling into the pit brings you out of distress in fairly good shape.

To dream that you are descending into one signifies that you will knowingly risk health and fortune for greater success.

See also **Abyss, Precipice.**

Pitcher

To dream of a pitcher denotes that you will be of a generous and congenial disposition. Success will attend your efforts.

A broken pitcher denotes loss of friends.

Pitchfork

Pitchforks in dreams denote struggles for betterment of fortune and great labouring, either physically or mentally.

To dream that you are attacked by some person using a pitchfork implies that you have personal enemies who would not scruple to harm you.

Plague

To dream of a plague raging, denotes disappointing returns in business, and a difficult home life.

If you are afflicted with the plague, you will keep your business out of embarrassment with the greatest manoeuvring. If you are trying to escape it, some trouble is pursuing you.

Plain

For a young woman to dream of crossing a plain denotes that she will be fortunately situated, if the grasses are green and luxuriant; if they are arid, or the grass is dead, she will experience discomfort and loneliness.

Plane

To dream that you use a plane denotes that your liberality and successful efforts will be highly commended.

To see carpenters using their planes denotes that you will progress smoothly in your undertakings.

To dream of seeing planes denotes congeniality and even success. A love of the real, and not the false, is portended by this dream.

Planet

To dream of a planet foretells an uncomfortable journey and depressing work.

Plank

For a young woman to dream that she is walking across muddy water on a rotten plank denotes that she will feel keenly the indifference shown her by one she loves, or that other troubles may arise; or her defence of honour may be in danger of collapse.

Walking a good, sound plank, is a good omen, but a person will have to be unusually careful in conduct after such a dream.

Plaster

To dream of seeing walls plainly plastered denotes that success will come, but it will not be stable.

To see plasterers at work denotes that you will have a sufficient income to live above penury.

Plate

For a woman to dream of plates denotes that she will practise economy and win a worthy husband. If already married, she will retain her husband's love and respect by the wise ordering of the household.

Play

For a young woman to dream that she attends a play foretells that she will be courted by a genial friend, and will marry to further her prospects and pleasure seeking. If there is trouble in getting to and from the play, or unpleasant scenes, she may be confronted with many disagreeable surprises.

Pleasure

To dream of pleasure denotes gain and personal enjoyment.

Plough

To dream of a plough signifies unusual success; affairs will reach a pleasing culmination.

To see persons ploughing denotes activity and advancement in knowledge and fortune.

For a young woman to see her lover ploughing indicates that she will have a noble and wealthy husband. Her joys will be deep and lasting.

To plough yourself denotes rapid increase in property and joys.

Plums

Plums, if they are green, unless seen on trees, are signs of personal and relative discomfort.

To see them ripe denotes joyous occasions, which, however, will be of short duration.

To eat them denotes that you will engage in flirtations and other fleeting pleasures.

To gather them, you will obtain your desires, but they will not prove so solid as you had imagined.

If you find yourself gathering them up from the ground, and find rotten ones among the good, you will be forced to admit that your expectations are unrealized, and that there is no life filled with pleasure alone.

Pocket

To dream of your pocket is a portent of evil demonstrations against you.

Poison

To feel that you are poisoned in a dream denotes that some painful influence will immediately reach you.

If you seek to use poison on others, you will be guilty of base thoughts, or the world will go wrong for you.

For a young woman to dream that she endeavours to get rid of a rival in this way, she will be likely to have a deal of trouble in securing a lover.

To throw the poison away denotes that by sheer force you will overcome unsatisfactory conditions.

To handle poison, or see others with it, signifies that unpleasantness will surround you.

To dream that your relatives or children are poisoned, you may receive injury from unsuspected sources.

If an enemy or rival is poisoned, you will overcome obstacles.

To recover from the effects of poison indicates that you will succeed after worry.

To take poisonous medicine under the advice of a physician denotes that you may undertake some affair fraught with danger.

Poker

To dream of seeing a red-hot poker, or fighting with one, signifies that you will meet trouble with combative energy.

To play at poker warns you against evil company; young women, especially, will lose their moral distinctiveness if they find themselves engaged in this game.

Polar Bear

Polar bears in dreams are prognostic of deceit, as misfortune may approach you in a seeming fair aspect. Your bitterest enemies will wear the garb of friendship. Rivals may try to supersede you.

To see the skin of one denotes that you will successfully overcome any opposition.

*See also **Bear**.*

Polecat

To dream of a polecat, signifies salacious scandals.

To inhale the odour of a polecat on your clothes, or otherwise smell one, you will find that your conduct will be considered rude, and your affairs will prove unsatisfactory.

Police

If the police are trying to arrest you for some crime of which you are innocent, it foretells that you will successfully outstrip rivalry.

If the arrest is just, you will have a season of unfortunate incidents.

Polishing

To dream of polishing any article, high attainments will place you in enviable positions.

Politician

To dream of a politician denotes displeasing companionships, and incidents where you will waste time.

If you engage in political wrangling, it portends that misunderstandings and ill feeling will be shown you by friends.

For a young woman to dream of taking interest in politics warns her against designing duplicity.

To dream of talking with the Prime Minister, or the President of the United States, denotes that you are interested in affairs of state and sometimes show a great longing to be a politician.

Polka

To dream of dancing the polka denotes pleasant occupations.

Pomegranate

Pomegranates, when dreamed of, denote that you will wisely use your talents for the enrichment of the mind rather than seeking those pleasures which destroy morality and health.

If your sweetheart gives you one, you will be lured by artful wiles to the verge of distraction but inner forces will hold you safe.

To eat one warns that you will yield yourself a captive to the personal charms of another.

Pond

To see a pond in your dream, denotes that events will bring no emotion, and fortune will retain a placid outlook.

If the pond is muddy, you will have domestic quarrels.

Pony

To dream of a pony signifies vitality and *joie de vivre*.
To see ponies in your dreams, signifies moderate speculations will be rewarded with success.

See also Horse.

Pope

Any dream in which you see the Pope, without speaking to him, warns you of servitude.

To speak to the Pope denotes that certain high honours are in store for you. To see the Pope looking sad or displeased warns you against vice or sorrow of some kind.

If you dream of royal personages speaking to the Pope, you will make the acquaintance of distinguished people.

Poplars

To dream of seeing poplars is an omen of good, if they are in leaf or bloom.

For a young woman to stand by her lover beneath the blossoms and leaves of a poplar, she will realize her most extravagant hopes. Her lover will be handsome and polished. Wealth and friends will be hers. If they are leafless and withered, she will meet with disappointments.

Poppies

Poppies seen in dreams represent a season of seductive pleasures and flattering business, but they all occupy unstable foundations.

If you inhale the odour of one, you will be the victim of artful persuasions and flattery.

Porcelain

To dream of porcelain signifies that you will have favourable opportunities of progressing in your affairs. To see it broken or soiled denotes that mistakes will be made which may cause grave offence.

Porch

To dream of a porch denotes that you will engage in new undertakings, and the future will be full of uncertainties.

If a young woman dreams that she is with her lover on a porch, this implies her doubts about someone's intentions.

To dream that you build a porch, you will assume new duties.

Porcupine

To see a porcupine in your dreams denotes that you will disapprove any new enterprise and repel new friendships with coldness.

For a young woman to dream of a porcupine portends that she may fear her lover.

Pork

If you eat pork in your dreams, you will encounter trouble, but if you only see pork, you will come out of a conflict victoriously.

Porpoise

To see a porpoise in your dreams warns that enemies are thrusting your interest aside, through your own inability to keep people interested in you.

*See also **Dolphin**.*

Port

To dream of visiting a port denotes that you will have opportunities of travelling and acquiring knowledge, but there will be some who will object to your anticipated tours.

Porter

Seeing a porter in a dream warns of bad luck and eventful happenings.

To imagine yourself a porter denotes humble circumstances.

To hire one, you will be able to enjoy whatever success comes to you.

To discharge one warns that disagreeable charges may be preferred against you.

Portfolio

To dream of a portfolio denotes that your employment will not be to your liking, and you will seek a change in your location.

Portrait

To dream of gazing upon the portrait of some beautiful person denotes that, while you enjoy pleasure, you can only feel the disturbing and treacherous nature of such joys. Your general affairs suffer loss after dreaming of portraits.

*See also **Painting, Pictures**.*

Postman

To dream of a postman, denotes that hasty new is most likely to be of a distressing nature than otherwise.

If you dream of the postman coming with your letters, you may soon receive news of an unwelcome nature.

To hear his vehicle denotes the unexpected arrival of a visitor.

If he passes without delivering any post for you, expect disappointment and sadness.

If you give him letters to post, you may suffer injury through envy or jealousy.

To converse with a postman warns that you could be implicated in scandalous proceedings.

Post Office

To dream of a post office warns of unpleasant tiding and ill luck generally.

Pot

To dream of a pot warns that unimportant events may work you vexation. For a young woman to see a boiling pot omens busy employment of pleasant and social duties. To see a broken or rusty one implies that keen disappointment will be experienced by you.

Potatoes

Dreaming of potatoes brings incidents, usually good.

To dream of digging them usually denotes success.

To dream of eating them, you will enjoy substantial gain.

To cook them, congenial employment.

Planting them brings realization of desires.

To see them rotting warns of vanished pleasure and a darkening future.

Potter

To dream of a potter denotes constant employment, with satisfactory results. For a young woman to see a potter foretells that she will enjoy pleasant engagements.

Poultry

To see dressed poultry in a dream foretells that extravagant habits will reduce your security in money matters. For a young woman to dream that she is chasing live poultry foretells she will devote valuable time to frivolous pleasure.

See also **Bantam, Fowl, Chickens.**

Poverty

To dream that you, or any of your friends, appear to be poor is significant of worry and loss.

To dream that you are in poverty warns of unpleasant happenings for you.

To see others in poverty denotes that there will be a call on your generosity.

Powder

To see powder in your dreams denotes that unscrupulous people are dealing with you. You may detect them through watchfulness.

Prairie

To dream of a prairie denotes that you will enjoy ease, and even luxury and unobstructed progress.

An undulating prairie, covered with growing grasses and flowers, signifies joyous happenings.

A barren prairie represents loss and sadness through the absence of friends.

To be lost on one is a sign of sadness and ill luck.

Pram

To dream of a pram or pushchair denotes that you will have a congenial friend who will devise many pleasant surprises for you.

Prayer

To dream of saying prayers, or seeing others doing so, warns that you may be threatened with failure, which will take strenuous efforts to avert.

Preacher

To dream of a preacher, denotes that your ways are not above reproach, and your affairs will not move evenly.

To dream that you are a preacher, foretells for you losses in business, and distasteful amusements will jar upon you.

To hear preaching, implies that you will undergo misfortune.

To argue with a preacher, you will lose in some contest.

To see one walk away from you, denotes that your affairs will move with new energy. If he looks sorrowful, reproaches will fall heavily upon you.

To see a long-haired preacher, denotes that you are shortly to have disputes with overbearing and egotistical people.

See also **Clergyman, Minister, Priest, Vicar**.

Precipice

To dream of standing over a yawning precipice portends the threatenings of misfortunes and calamities.

To fall over a precipice warns of disaster.

See also **Abyss, Pit**.

Pregnancy

To dream that you are expecting a child signifies that an important development will take place in your emotional life.

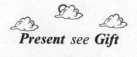

Present *see* Gift

Priest

A priest is an augury of ill, if seen in dreams.

If he is in the pulpit, it warns of sickness and trouble for the dreamer.

If a woman dreams that she is in love with a priest, it warns her of deceptions and an unscrupulous lover. If the priest makes love to her, she may be reproached for her love of gaiety and practical joking.

To confess to a priest warns that you may be subjected to humiliation and sorrow.

These dreams imply that you have done, or will do, something which will bring discomfort to yourself or relatives. The priest or preacher is your spiritual adviser, and any dream of his professional presence is a warning against your own imperfections.

See also **Clergyman, Minister, Preacher, Vicar.**

Primrose

To dream of this little flower starring the grass at your feet is an omen of joys laden with comfort and peace.

Princes and Princesses

Princes and princesses seen in dreams augur well, signifying inner youth, spirituality, reconciliation and the positive changes wrought by love.

Printer

To see a printer in your dreams is a warning of poverty, if you neglect to practice economy and cultivate energy. For a woman to dream that her lover or associate is a printer foretells that she will fail to please her parents in the selection of a close friend.

Printing Office

To be in a printing office in dreams denotes that slander may threaten you.

To run a printing office is indicative of hard luck.

For a young woman to dream that her sweetheart is connected with a printing office denotes that she may have a lover who is unable to lavish money or time upon her, and that she will not be sensible enough to see why he is so stingy.

Prison

To dream of a prison, is the forerunner of misfortune in every instance, if it encircles your friends, or yourself.

To see anyone dismissed from prison, denotes that you will finally overcome misfortune.

See also **Dungeon, Jail.**

Privacy

To dream of intension upon your privacy foretells you will have overbearing people to worry you. For a woman, this dream warns her to look carefully after private affairs. If she intrudes on the privacy of her husband or lover, she may disabuse some one's confidence, if not careful of her conversation.

Prize

To dream of receiving a prize denotes that what you desire lies within your grasp. If someone else is receiving the prize, you feel unworthy to achieve your desires.

Procession

To dream of a procession, denotes that alarming fears will possess you relative to the fulfilment of expectations. If it be a funeral procession, sorrow is fast approaching, and will throw a shadow around pleasures.

To see or participate in a torch-light procession, denotes that you will engage in gaieties which will detract from your real merit.

Profanity

To dream of profanity denotes that you will cultivate those traits which render you coarse and unfeeling toward your fellow man.

To dream that others use profanity is a sign that you will be injured in some way, and probably insulted also.

Profits

To dream of profits brings success in your immediate future.

Promenade

To dream of promenading foretells that you will engage in energetic and profitable pursuits.

To see others promenading signifies that you will have rivals in your pursuits.

Promotion

To dream of being promoted to high positions denotes that study and advancement will bring you the wealth you deserve.

Property

To dream that you own vast property denotes that you will be successful in affairs, and gain friendships.

Publican

To dream of a publican denotes that you may have your sympathies aroused by someone in a desperate condition, and will diminish your own gain for his advancement. To a young woman, this dream brings a worthy lover, but she may trample on his feelings unnecessarily.

Public house

The person who dreams of a public house should be very cautious of his affairs: enemies are watching him.

See also **Bar**.

Publisher

To dream of a publisher foretells long journeys and aspirations to the literary craft.

If a woman dreams that her husband is a publisher, she may be jealous of more than one woman of his acquaintance, and spicy scenes will ensue.

For a publisher to reject your manuscript denotes that you may suffer disappointment at the failure of cherished designs. If he accepts it, you will rejoice in the full fruition of your hopes.

Puddings

To dream of puddings denotes small returns from large investments, if you only see it.

To eat it is proof that your affairs will be disappointing.

For a young woman to cook, or otherwise prepare a pudding, warns that her lover may be sensual and worldly-minded, and that if she marries him, she will see her love and fortune vanish.

Puddle

To find yourself stepping into puddles of clear water in a dream denotes a vexation, but some redeeming good in the future. If the water is muddy, unpleasantness will go a few rounds with you.

To wet your feet by stepping into puddles foretells that your pleasure may work you harm afterwards.

Pulpit

To dream of a pulpit warns of sorrow and vexation.

To dream that you are in a pulpit warns of sickness, and unsatisfactory results in business.

Pulse

To dream of your pulse is a warning to look after your affairs and health with close care.

To dream of feeling the pulse of another may suggest your desire for this person.

Pump

To see a pump in a dream denotes that energy and faithfulness to business will produce desired riches; good health also is usually betokened by this dream.

To see a broken pump warns that the means of advancing in life will be absorbed by family cares.

If you work a pump, your life will be filled with pleasure and profitable undertakings.

Punch

To dream of punch foretells that you will be much pleased with the attention shown you by new acquaintances.

To dream of drinking punch denotes that you will prefer selfish pleasures to honourable distinction and morality.

To dream that you are punching any person with a club or fist denotes quarrels and recriminations.

Puncture

Dreaming that you cannot drive your car because all four tyres are punctured is a warning to take control of your life before it takes control of you.

Puppet

To dream that you are a puppet master signifies that you have a need for power and control. If you are the puppet, you will need to become more assertive and independent in your waking life.

Puppy

To dream of pups denotes that you will entertain the innocent and hapless, and thereby enjoy pleasure. The dream also shows that friendships will grow stronger, and fortune will increase if the pups are healthy and well formed, and *vice versa* if they are lean and filthy.

See also **Dogs**.

Purchases

To dream of purchases usually augurs profit and advancement with pleasure.

Purple

To dream of or in purple denotes temperance.

Purse

To dream of your purse being filled with diamonds and new notes denotes for you associations where 'Good Cheer' is the watchword, and harmony and tender loves will make Earth a beautiful place.

Pursuit

Pursuing someone in your dreams denotes that you are trying to regain a lost opportunity from the past.

If you are being pursued, you will need to reconcile the conflicting demands in your life.

Pushchair see *Pram*

Putty

To dream of working in putty denotes that hazardous chances will be taken with fortune.

If you put in a windowpane with putty, you will seek fortune with poor results.

Pyramid

To dream of pyramids denotes that many changes will come to you.

If you scale them, you will journey a long time before you find the gratification of desires. For the young woman, it prognosticates a husband who is in no sense congenial.

To dream that you are studying the mystery of the ancient pyramids denotes that you will develop a love for the mysteries of nature, and will become learned and polished.

Q

'And he dreamed, and behold a ladder set up on the earth, and the top of it reached to heaven; and behold, the angels of God ascending and descending on it.'

—Genesis xxviii., 12.

Quack Doctor

To see a quack doctor in your dreams denotes that you will be alarmed over some illness and its improper treatment.

Quack Medicine

To dream you take quack medicine shows that you are growing morbid under some trouble, and should overcome it by industrious application to duty. To read an advertisement for it foretells unhappy companions may wrong and distress you.

Quagmire

To dream of being in a quagmire implies your inability to meet obligations. To see others thus situated denotes that the failures of others will be felt by you. Illness is sometimes indicated by this dream.

Quail

To see quails in your dream is a very favourable omen, if they are alive; if dead, you will undergo ill luck.

To shoot quail warns that ill feelings may be shown by you to your best friends.

To eat them, signifies extravagance in your personal living.

Quaker

To dream of a Quaker denotes that you will have faithful friends and fair business. If you are one, you will deport yourself honourably toward an enemy.

For a young woman to attend a Quaker meeting portends that she will by her modest manners win a faithful husband who will provide well for her household.

Quarantine

To dream of being in quarantine denotes that you may be placed in a disagreeable position by the malicious intriguing of enemies.

Quarrel

Quarrels in dreams portend unhappiness and fierce altercations. To a young woman, they are the signal of unpleasantries, and to a married woman they may bring separation or continuous disagreements.

To hear others quarrelling denotes unsatisfactory business and disappointing trade.

Quarry

To dream of being in a quarry and seeing the workmen busy denotes that you will advance by hard labour.

An idle quarry signifies failure and disappointment.

Quartet

To dream of a quartet in which you are playing or singing denotes favourable affairs, jolly companions, and good times.

To see or hear a quartet foretells that you will aspire to something beyond you.

Quay

To dream of a quay denotes that you will contemplate making a long tour in the near future.

To see vessels while standing on the quay denotes the fruition of wishes and designs.

Queen

To dream of a queen foretells succesful ventures. If she looks old or haggard, there may be disappointments connected with your pleasures.

Question

To question the merits of a thing in your dreams denotes that you suspect someone whom you love of unfaithfulness, and will fear for your speculations.

To ask a question foretells that you will earnestly strive for truth and be successful.

If you are questioned, you are likely to be unfairly dealt with.

Quicksand

To find yourself in quicksand while dreaming, you will meet with loss and deceit.

If you are unable to overcome it, you will be involved in overwhelming misfortunes.

For a young woman to be rescued by her lover from quicksand, she will possess a worthy and faithful husband, who will still remain her lover.

Quills

To dream of quills denotes to the literary inclined a season of success.

To dream of them as ornaments signifies a rushing trade, and some remuneration.

For a young woman to be putting a quill in her hat denotes that she will attempt many conquests, and her success will depend upon her charms.

Quilts

To dream of quilts foretells pleasant and comfortable circumstances. For a young woman, this dream foretells that her practical and wise businesslike ways will advance her into the favourable esteem of a man who will seek her for a wife.

If the quilts are clean, but having holes in them, she will win a husband who appreciates her worth, but he will not be the one most desired by her for a companion. If the quilts are soiled, she will bear evidence of carelessness in her dress and manners, and thus fail to secure a very upright husband.

Quinine

To dream of quinine denotes that you will soon be possessed of great happiness, though your prospects for much wealth may be meagre. To take some foretells improvement in health and energy. You will also make new friends, who will lend you commercial aid.

Quoits

To play at quoits in dreams foretells low engagements and loss of good employment. To lose portends distressing conditions.

R

'And the angel of God spake unto me in a dream, saying "Jacob:"
And I said, "Here I am." '

—Genesis xxxi., 11.

Rabbit

To dream of rabbits foretells favourable turns in conditions; you will
be more pleased with your gains than formerly.

To see white rabbits denotes faithfulness in love.

To see rabbits frolicking about denotes that children will contribute
to your joys.

See also **Hare**.

Rabies

To dream that you are afflicted with rabies warns of enemies and
change of business.

To see others thus afflicted, your work will be interrupted.

To dream that an animal with rabies bites you, you may be betrayed
by a friend, and much scandal may be brought to light.

Raccoon

To dream of a raccoon denotes that you are being deceived by the
friendly appearance of enemies.

Race

To dream that you are in a race foretells that others will aspire to the things you are working to possess, but if you win in the race, you will overcome your competitors.

Rack

To dream of a rack denotes the uncertainty of the outcome of some engagement which gives you much anxious thought.

Racket

To dream of a racket warns that you may be foiled in some anticipated pleasure. For a young woman, this dream is ominous of disappointment in not being able to participate in some amusement that has engaged her attention.

Radish

To dream of seeing a bed of radishes growing is an omen of good luck. Your friends will be unusually kind, and your business will prosper.

If you eat them, you may suffer slightly through the thoughtlessness of someone near to you.

To see radishes, or plant them, denotes that your anticipations will be happily realized.

Raffle

If you dream of raffling any article, you risk falling a victim to speculation.

If you are at a church raffle, you may find that disappointment is clouding your future. For a young woman, this dream means empty expectations.

Raft

To dream of a raft denotes that you will go into new locations to engage in enterprises, which will prove successful.

To dream of floating on a raft denotes uncertain journeys. If you reach your destination, you will surely come into good fortune.

If a raft breaks, or any such mishap befalls it, you or friend are at risk from an accident or ill.

Rage

To be in a rage and scolding and tearing up things generally, while dreaming, warns of quarrels, and injury to your friends.

To see others in a rage is a sign of unfavourable conditions for business, and unhappiness in social life.

For a young woman to see her lover in a rage denotes that there will be some discordant note in their love, and misunderstandings will naturally occur.

See also Anger.

Rags

To see yourself in a dream dressed in rags is indicative of a wounded spirit. If you feel at peace, this dream denotes inner wisdom, such as that acquired by hermits and religious ascetics, and points to the insignificance of outward appearances.

Railing

To dream of seeing railings denotes that some person is trying to obstruct your pathway in love or business.

To dream of holding on to a railing foretells that some desperate chance will be taken by you to obtain some object upon which you have set your heart. It may be of love, or of a more material form.

Railway

If you dream of a railway, you will find that your business will need close attention, as enemies are trying to usurp you.

For a young woman to dream of railways, she will make a journey to visit friends, and will enjoy some distinction.

To see an obstruction on a railway line indicates foul play in your affairs.

To walk across the points of a railway signifies a time of worry and laborious work.

To walk the rails, you may expect to obtain much happiness from your skilful manipulation of affairs.

Railway Carriage

To dream of seeing railway carriages denotes journeying and changing in quick succession. To get into one shows that travel which you had been contemplating will take place in different circumstances from those that you envisaged.

To get out of a railway carriage denotes that you will succeed with some interesting schemes which will fill you with self-congratulation.

Rain

To be out in a clear shower of rain denotes that pleasure will be enjoyed with the zest of youth, and prosperity will come to you.

If the rain descends from murky clouds, you will feel alarmed over the gravity of your undertakings.

To see and hear rain approaching, if you escape being wet, you will succeed in your plans, and your designs will mature rapidly.

To be sitting in the house and see through the window a downpour of rain denotes that you will possess fortune, and passionate love will be requited.

To hear the patter of rain on the roof denotes realization of domestic bliss and joy. Fortune will come in a small way.

To dream that your house is leaking during rain, if the water is clear, foretells that illicit pleasure will come to you rather unexpectedly; but if filthy or muddy, you may expect the reverse, and also exposure.

To find yourself regretting some duty unperformed while listening to the rain denotes that you may seek pleasure at the expense of another's sense of propriety and justice.

To see it rain on others, foretells that you will exclude friends from your confidence.

For a young woman to dream of getting her clothes wet and soiled while out in the rain denotes that she may entertain some person indiscreetly, and may suffer the suspicions of friends for yielding unwisely to foolish enjoyments.

To see it raining on livestock foretells disappointment in business, and unpleasantness in social circles.

Stormy rains are always unfortunate.

Rainbow

To see a rainbow in a dream is prognostic of unusual happenings. Affairs will assume a more promising countenance, and crops will give promise of a plentiful yield.

For lovers to see the rainbow is an omen of much happiness from their union.

To see the rainbow hanging low over green trees signifies unconditional success in any undertaking.

Rainbows are relatively rare in dreams, but the rainbow is always an excellent sign when it occurs.

Raisins

To dream of eating raisins warns that discouragements may darken your hopes when they seem about to be realized.

Rake

To dream of using a rake portends that some work which you have left to others will never be accomplished unless you superintend it yourself.

To see a broken rake warns that sickness, or some accident, may bring failure to your plans.

To see others raking foretells that you will rejoice in the fortunate condition of others.

Ram

To dream that a ram pursues you warns that some misfortune threatens you.

To see one quietly grazing denotes that you will have powerful friends, who will use their best efforts for your good.

See also Sheep.

Ramble

To dream that you are rambling through the country denotes that you may be oppressed with sadness, and separation from friends, but your worldly surroundings will be all that one could desire. For a young woman, this dream promises a comfortable home.

Ransom

To dream that a ransom is made for you, you may find that you are deceived and worked for money on all sides. For a young woman, this is prognostic of evil, unless someone pays the ransom and relieves her.

Rapids

To imagine that you are being carried over rapids in a dream warns that you will suffer appalling loss from the neglect of duty and the courting of seductive pleasures.

Raspberry

To see raspberries in a dream warns that you are in danger of entanglements which will prove interesting before you escape from them.

For a woman to eat them warns of distress over circumstantial evidence in some occurrence causing gossip.

Rat

To dream of rats warns that you may be deceived and injured by your neighbours. Quarrels with your companions is also foreboded.

To catch rats means you will scorn the baseness of others, and worthily outstrip your enemies.

To kill one denotes your victory in any contest.

Rattle

To dream of seeing a baby play with its rattle omens peaceful contentment in the home, and that enterprises will be honourable and full of gain. To a young woman, it augurs an early marriage and tender cares of her own.

To give a baby a rattle denotes unfortunate investments.

Rat-trap

To dream of falling into a rat-trap warns that you may be victimized and robbed of some valuable object.

To see an empty one foretells the absence of slander or competition.

A broken one denotes that you will be rid of unpleasant associations.

To set one, you will be made aware of the designs of enemies, but the warning will enable you to outwit them.

See also Mouse-trap.

Red

To dream of or in red evokes fire and energy, and may betoken that the dreamer will be overcome by a consuming passion. A negative dream of or in red warns of hatred and violence.

Red Tape *see* Bureaucracy

Rattan Cane

To dream of rattan cane foretells that you will depend largely upon the judgment of others, and that you should cultivate independence in planning and executing your own affairs.

Raven

To dream of a raven warns of reversal in fortune and inharmonious surroundings. For a young woman, it is implied that her lover will betray her.

Razor

To dream of a razor portends disagreements and contentions over troubles.

To cut yourself with one denotes that you are likely to be unlucky in some deal which you are about to make.

Fighting with a razor warns of disappointing business, and that someone will keep you harassed almost beyond endurance.

A broken or rusty one brings distress.

Reading

To be engaged in reading in your dreams denotes that you will excel in some work which appears difficult.

To see others reading denotes that your friends will be kind, and are well disposed.

To give a reading, or to discuss reading, you will cultivate your literary ability.

Indistinct or incoherent reading implies worries and disappointments.

Reapers

To dream of seeing reapers busy at work at their task denotes prosperity and contentment. If they appear to be going through dried stubble, there will be a lack of good crops, and business will consequently fall off.

To see idle ones denotes that some discouraging event may come in the midst of prosperity.

To see a broken reaping machine warns of loss of employment, or disappointment in trades.

Reception

To dream of attending a reception denotes that you will have pleasant engagements. Confusion at a reception will work you disquietude.

Refrigerator

To see a refrigerator in your dreams portends that your selfishness may offend and injure someone who is endeavouring to gain an honest livelihood.

To put ice in one may bring the dreamer into disfavour.

Register

To dream that someone registers your name at a hotel for you, denotes that you will undertake some work which will be finished by others.

If you register under an assumed name, you will engage in some guilty enterprise which may give you much uneasiness of mind.

Reindeer

To dream of a reindeer signifies faithful discharge of duties, and remaining staunch to friends in their adversity.

To drive them foretells that you will have hours of bitter anguish, but friends will attend you.

Religion

If you dream of discussing religion and feel religiously inclined, you will find much to mar the calmness of your life and business may be disagreeable.

To see religion declining in power denotes that your life will be more in harmony with creation than formerly. Your prejudices will not be so aggressive.

To dream that a minister in a social way tells you that he has given up his work, foretells that you will be the recipient of unexpected tidings of a favourable nature, but if in a professional and warning way, it foretells that you may be overtaken in deceitful intriguing, or other disappointments will follow.

Rent

To dream that you rent a house is a sign that you will enter into new contracts, which will prove profitable.

To fail to rent out property denotes that there will be much inactivity in business.

To pay rent signifies that your financial interest will be satisfactory.

If you can't pay your rent, it is an unlucky sign.

Reprieve

To be under sentence in a dream and receive a reprieve foretells that you will overcome some difficulty which is causing you anxiety.

For a young woman to dream that her lover has been reprieved denotes that she will soon hear of some good luck befalling him, which will be of vital interest to her.

Reptile

If a reptile attacks you in a dream, there is likely to be trouble of a serious nature ahead for you. If you succeed in killing it, you will finally overcome obstacles.

To see a dead reptile come to life denotes that disputes and disagreements, which were thought to be settled, will be renewed and pushed with bitter animosity.

To handle them without harm to yourself foretells that you will be oppressed by the ill humour and bitterness of friends, but you will succeed in restoring pleasant relations.

For a young woman to see various kinds of reptiles, she will have many conflicting troubles. Her lover may develop fancies for others. If she is bitten by any of them, she may be superseded by a rival.

See also Snakes.

Rescue

To dream of being rescued from any danger denotes that you will be threatened with misfortune, and will escape with a slight loss.

To rescue others foretells that you will be esteemed for your good deeds.

Resign

To dream that you resign any position signifies that you will unfortunately embark in new enterprises.

To hear of others resigning warns that you may have unpleaasant tidings.

Resurrection

To dream that you are resurrected from the dead, you will have some great vexation, but will eventually gain your desires. To see others resurrected denotes that unfortunate troubles will be lightened by the thoughtfulness of friends.

Resuscitate

To dream that you are being resuscitated denotes that you will have heavy losses, but will eventually regain more than you lose, and happiness will attend you.

To resuscitate another, you will form new friendships, which will give you prominence and pleasure.

Revelation

To dream of a revelation, if it is of a pleasant nature, you may expect a bright outlook, either in business or love; but if the revelation is gloomy you will have many discouraging features to overcome.

Revenge

To dream of taking revenge is a sign of a weak and uncharitable nature, which if not properly governed, will bring you troubles and loss of friends.

If others revenge themselves on you, there will be much to fear from enemies.

Revival

To dream you attend a religious revival foretells family disturbances and unprofitable engagements.

If you take a part in it, you may incur the displeasure of friends by your contrary ways.

Revolver

For a young woman to dream that she sees her sweetheart with a revolver warns that she may have a serious disagreement with some friend, and even separation from her lover.

Rheumatism

To feel rheumatism attacking you in a dream foretells unexpected delay in the accomplishment of plans.

To see others so afflicted brings disappointments.

Rhinestones

To dream of rhinestones denotes pleasures and favours of short duration. For a young woman to dream that a rhinestone proves to be a diamond foretells that she will be surprised to find that some insignificant act on her part results in good fortune.

Rhinoceros

To dream that you see a rhinoceros foretells that you will have a great loss threatening you, and that you will have secret troubles. To kill one, shows that you will bravely overcome obstacles.

Rhubarb

To dream of rhubarb growing denotes that pleasant entertainments will occupy your time for a while.

To cook it foretells spirited arguments in which you may lose a friend.

To eat it denotes dissatisfaction with present employment.

Rib

To dream of seeing ribs warns of poverty.

Ribbon

Seeing ribbons floating from the costume of any person in your dreams indicates that you will have gay and pleasant companions, and practical cares will not trouble you greatly.

For a young woman to dream of decorating herself with ribbons, she will soon have a desirable offer of marriage, but frivolity may cause her to make a mistake. If she sees other girls wearing ribbons, she may encounter rivalry in her endeavours to secure a husband. If she buys them, she will have a pleasant and easy place in life. If she feels angry or displeased about them, she will find that some other woman is dividing her honours and pleasures with her in her social realm.

Rice

Rice is good to see in dreams, as it foretells success and warm friendships. Prosperity to all trades is promised, and the farmer will be blessed with a bounteous harvest.

To eat it signifies happiness and domestic comfort.

To see it mixed with dirt or otherwise impure denotes sickness and separation from friends.

For a young woman to dream of cooking it shows she will soon assume new duties, which will make her happier, and she will enjoy wealth.

Riches

To dream that you are possessed of riches denotes that you will rise to high places through your constant exertion and attention to your affairs.

See also Affluence, Opulence, Wealth.

Riddles

To dream that you are trying to solve riddles denotes that you will engage in some enterprise which will try your patience and employ your money.

The import of riddles is confusion and dissatisfaction.

Ride

To dream of riding is unlucky for business or pleasure.

If you ride slowly, you are likely to have unsatisfactory results in your undertakings.

Swift riding sometimes means prosperity under hazardous conditions.

Riding School

To attend a riding school, foretells that some friend will act falsely by you, but you will throw off the vexing influence occasioned by it.

Ring

To dream of wearing rings denotes new enterprises in which you will be successful.

For a young woman to receive a ring denotes that worries over her lover's conduct will cease, as he will devote himself to her pleasures and future interest.

To see others with rings denotes increasing prosperity and many new friends.

To see a broken ring warns that order will be displaced by furious and dangerous uprisings, such as jealous contentions often cause. There may well be domestic quarrels and unhappiness.

Ringworm

To dream of having ringworm appear on you, you may have a slight illness and some exasperating difficulty in the near future.

Riot

To dream of riots warns of disappointing affairs.

Rising

If you find yourself rising high into the air, you will come into unexpected riches and pleasures, but you are warned to be careful of your engagements, or you may incur displeasing prominence.

Rival

To dream you have a rival, is a warning not to be slow in asserting your rights, or you will risk losing favour with people of prominence.

For a young woman, this dream is a warning to cherish the love she already holds, as she might unfortunately make a mistake in seeking other bonds.

If you find that a rival has outwitted you, it warns that you will be negligent in your business, and that you love personal ease to your detriment.

If you imagine that you are the successful rival, it is good for your advancement, and you will find congeniality in your choice of a companion.

River

If you see a clear, smooth, flowing river in your dream, you will soon succeed to the enjoyment of delightful pleasures, and prosperity will bear flattering promises.

If the waters are muddy or tumultuous, there will be disagreeable and jealous contentions in your life.

If you are water-bound by the overflowing of a river, there will be temporary embarrassments in your business, or you will suffer unease lest some private escapade reach public notice and cause your reputation harsh criticisms.

To see empty rivers, denotes ill luck.

To bathe in a river signifies purification and spirituality.

Road

To dream that you see or travel on a tarmacked road is significant of pleasant journeys, from which you will derive much benefit. For young people, this dream foretells noble aspirations.

Travelling over a rough, unknown road in a dream signifies new undertakings, which will bring little else than grief and loss of time.

If the road is bordered with trees and flowers, there will be some pleasant and unexpected fortune for you. If friends accompany you, you will be successful in building an ideal home, with happy children and faithful wife, or husband.

To lose the road warns that you may make a mistake in deciding some question of trade, and suffer loss in consequence.

Roast

To see or eat roast in a dream is an omen of domestic infelicity and secret treachery.

Rock

To dream of rocks warns that you will meet reverses, and that there may be discord and general unhappiness.

To climb a steep rock foretells immediate struggles and disappointing surroundings.

See also **Stone**.

Rocket

To see a rocket ascending in your dream foretells sudden and unexpected elevation, successful wooing, and faithful keeping of the marriage vows.

To see them falling, unhappy unions may be expected.

Rocking-chair

Rocking-chairs seen in dreams bring friendly intercourse and contentment with any environment.

To see a mother, wife, or sweetheart in a rocking-chair, is ominous of the sweetest joys that earth affords.

To see vacant rocking-chairs forebodes bereavement or estrangement.

Rogue

To see or think yourself a rogue foretells you are about to commit some indiscretion which will give your friends uneasiness of mind. You are likely to suffer from a passing malady.

For a woman to think her husband or lover is a rogue foretells that she may be painfully distressed over neglect shown her by a friend.

Roman Candle

To see Roman candles while dreaming is a sign of speedy attainment of coveted pleasures and positions.

To imagine that you have a loaded candle and find it empty denotes that you will be disappointed with the possession of some object which you have long striven to obtain.

Roof

To find yourself on a roof in a dream denotes unbounded success. To become frightened and think you are falling, signifies that, while you may advance, you will have no firm hold on your position.

To see a roof falling in, you may be threatened with a sudden calamity.

To repair, or build a roof, you will rapidly increase your fortune.

To sleep on one proclaims your security against enemies and false companions. Your health will be robust.

Rooks

To dream of rooks denotes that while your friends are true, they will not afford you the pleasure and contentment for which you long, as your thoughts and tastes will outstrip their humble conception of life.

A dead rook portends sickness or death.

Room

To find yourself in a beautiful and richly furnished room implies sudden fortune, either through legacies from unknown relatives or through speculation. For a young woman, it denotes that a wealthy stranger will offer her marriage and a fine establishment. If the room is plainly furnished, it denotes that a small income and frugality will be her portion.

Rooster *see* Cockerel

Roots

To dream of seeing roots of plants or trees denotes misfortune, as both business and health may go into decline.

To use them as medicine warns you of approaching illness or sorrow.

Rope

Ropes in dreams signify perplexities and complications in affairs, and uncertain lovemaking.

If you climb one, you will overcome enemies who are working to injure you.

To decend a rope brings disappointment to your most sanguine moments.

If you are tied with them, you are likely to yield to love contrary to your judgment.

To break them signifies your ability to overcome enmity and competition.

To tie ropes, or horses, denotes that you will have power to control others as you may wish.

To catch a rope with your foot denotes that under cheerful conditions you will be benevolent and tender in your administrations.

To dream that you let a rope down from an upper window of a hotel to people below, thinking the proprietors would be adverse to letting them in, denotes that you will engage in some affair which will not look exactly proper to your friends, but the same will afford you pleasure and interest. For a young woman, this dream is indicative of pleasures which do not bear the stamp of propriety.

Rosebush

To see a rosebush in foliage but no blossoms denotes that prosperous circumstances are enclosing you. A wedding will soon take place, and great hopes will be fulfilled. To see a dead rosebush warns of misfortune and sickness for you or relatives.

Rosemary

Rosemary, if seen in dreams, denotes that sadness and indifference may cause unhappiness in homes where there is every appearance of prosperity.

Roses

To dream of seeing roses blooming and fragrant denotes that some joyful occasion is nearing, and you will possess the faithful love of your sweetheart.

For a young woman to dream of gathering roses shows she will soon have an offer of marriage, which will be much to her liking.

For a lover to place a rose in your hair warns that you risk being deceived. If a woman receives a bouquet of roses in springtime, she will have a faithful lover; but if she receives them in winter, she is cherishing false hopes.

Withered roses signify the absence of loved ones.

White roses, if seen without sunshine or dew, denote illness; this may be serious but will not be fatal.

To inhale their fragrance brings unalloyed pleasure.

For a young woman to dream of banks of roses, and that she is gathering and tying them into bouquets, signifies that she will be made very happy by the offering of some person whom she regards very highly.

Rosette

To wear or see rosettes on others while in dreams is significant of frivolous waste of time; though you will experience the thrills of pleasure, they are likely to bring disappointments.

Rouge

To dream of using rouge denotes that you may practise deceit to obtain your wishes.

To see others with it on their faces warns you that you are being artfully used to further the designs of some deceitful persons.

If you see it on your hands, or clothing, you will be detected in some scheme.

If it comes off of your face, you may be humiliated before some rival, and lose your lover by assuming unnatural manners.

Roundabout

To dream of seeing a roundabout warns of unsuccessful struggle to advance in fortune or love.

Rowing Boat

To dream that you are in a rowing boat with others denotes that you will derive much pleasure from the companionship of lively and worldly persons. If the boat is capsized, you may suffer financial losses by engaging in seductive enterprises.

If you find yourself defeated in a rowing race, you are likely to lose favours to your rivals with your sweetheart. If you are the victor, you will easily obtain supremacy with women. Your affairs will move agreeably.

Rubber

To dream of rubber warns of unfavourable changes in your affairs. If you stretch it, you may try to establish a greater level of business than you can support.

To dream of being clothed in rubber garments is a sign that you will have honours conferred upon you because of your steady and unchanging stand of purity and morality. If the garments are ragged or torn, you should be cautious in your conduct, as scandal is ready to attack your reputation.

If you find that your limbs will stretch like rubber, it is a sign that illness is threatening you, and that you are likely to use deceit in your wooing and business.

To dream of rubber goods denotes that your affairs will be conducted on a secret basis, and that your friends may fail to understand your conduct in many instances.

Rubbish

To dream of rubbish denotes that you will manage your affairs badly.

To see heaps of rubbish in your dreams indicates thoughts of social scandal and unfavourable business of every nature. For women, this dream warns of disparagement and desertion by lovers.

To find something worth saving in a pile of rubbish indicates that the dreamer is undervaluing himself and needs to be more positive about his abilities.

Ruby

To dream of a ruby foretells that you will be lucky in speculations of business or love. For a woman to lose one is a warning of the approaching indifference of her lover.

Rudder

To dream of a rudder, you will soom make a pleasant journey to foreign lands, and new friendships will be formed.

A broken rudder augurs disappointment and sickness

Ruins

To dream of ruins often warns of bad luck.

Dreams of ruins can also signify your disappointment with what you have achieved in life.

To dream of ancient ruins foretells that you will travel extensively, but there will be a note of sadness mixed with the pleasure in the realization of a long-cherished hope. You will feel the absence of some friend.

Rum

To dream of drinking rum foretells that you will have wealth, but will lack moral refinement.

Running

To dream of running in company with others, is a sign that you will participate in some festivity, and you will find that your affairs are growing towards fortune. If you stumble or fall, you may lose property and reputation.

Running alone, indicates that you will outstrip your friends in the race for wealth, and will occupy a higher place in social life.

If you run from danger, you will be threatened with losses, and you may despair of adjusting matters agreeably. To see others thus running, you will feel oppressed by the threatened downfall of friends.

To see livestock running warns you to be careful in making new trades or undertaking new tasks.

Rust

To dream of rust on articles, old pieces of tin, or iron warns that sickness, decline in fortune and false friends are filling your sphere.

Rye

To see rye is a dream of good, as prosperity envelopes your future in brightest promises.

To see coffee made of rye denotes that your pleasures will be tempered with sound judgment, and your affairs will be managed without disagreeable friction.

To see livestock entering rye fields denotes that you will be prosperous.

Rye Bread

To see or eat rye bread in your dreams foretells that you will have a cheerful and well-appointed home.

S

'And it came to pass at the end of the two full years, that Pharaoh dreamed; and behold, he stood by the river.'

—Genesis, xli, I.

Saddle

To dream of saddles foretells news of a pleasant nature, also unannounced visitors. You are also, probably, to take a trip which will prove advantageous.

Safe

To dream of seeing a safe denotes security from discouraging affairs of business and love.

To be trying to unlock a safe, you will be worried over the failure of your plans not reaching quick maturity.

To find a safe empty denotes trouble.

Saffron

Saffron seen in a dream warns you that you are entertaining false hopes, as bitter enemies are interfering secretly with your plans for the future.

To drink a tea made from saffron warns that you may have quarrels and alienation within your family.

Sage

To dream of sage foretells that thrift and economy will be practised by your household. For a woman to think she has too much in her food

418

omens that she will regret useless extravagance in love as well as fortune.

Sailing

To dream of sailing on calm waters foretells easy access to blissful joys, and immunity from poverty and whatever brings misery.

To sail on a small vessel denotes that your desires will not excel your power of possessing them.

Sailor

To dream that you are a sailor denotes a long journey to distant countries. Much pleasure will be connected with the trip. If you see your vessel sailing without you, much personal discomfort may be done to you by rivals.

To dream of sailors portends long and exciting journeys. This dream can also signify the dreamer's desire for more adventure in life.

For a young woman to dream of sailors is ominous of a separation from her lover through a frivolous flirtation. If she dreams that she is a sailor, she will indulge in some unmaidenly escapade, and be in danger of losing a faithful lover.

Salad

To dream of eating salad warns of sickness and disagreeable people around you.

For a young woman to dream of making it is a sign that her lover may be changeable and quarrelsome.

Salmon

Dreaming of salmon denotes that much good luck and pleasant duties will employ your time.

For a young woman to eat it foretells that she will marry a cheerful man, with means to keep her comfortable.

Salt

Salt is an omen of discordant surroundings when seen in dreams. You will usually find after dreaming of salt that everything goes awry, and quarrels and dissatisfaction show themselves in the family circle.

To salt meat portends that debts and mortgages may harass you.

For a young woman to eat salt, she risks being deserted by her lover for a more beautiful and attractive girl, thus causing her deep chagrin.

Saltpetre

To dream of saltpetre denotes that change in your way of living may cause loss.

Samples

To dream of receiving samples of merchandise denotes improvement in your business. For a commercial travellor to lose his samples implies that he will find himself embarrassed in business affairs, or in trouble through love engagements. For a woman to dream that she is examining samples sent her denotes that she will have chances to vary her amusements.

Sand

To dream of sand warns of famine and losses.

Sanskrit

To dream of Sanskrit denotes that you may estrange yourself from friends in order to investigate hidden subjects, taking up those occupying the minds of cultured and progressive thinkers.

Sapphire

To dream of sapphire is ominous of fortunate gain, and, to a woman, a wise selection in a lover.

Sardines

To eat sardines in a dream warns that distressing events may come unexpectedly upon you.

For a young woman to dream of putting them on the table denotes that she may be worried by the attentions of a person who is distasteful to her.

Sash

To dream of wearing a sash foretells that you will seek to retain the affections of a flirtatious person.

For a young woman to buy one, she will be faithful to her lover, and win esteem by her frank, womanly ways.

Satan

To dream of Satan foretells that you may have some dangerous adventures, in which you will be forced to use strategy to keep up honourable appearances.

To dream that you kill him foretells that you will desert wicked or immoral companions to live upon a higher plane.

If he comes to you under the guise of literature, it should be heeded as a warning against promiscuous friendships, and especially flatterers.

If he comes in the shape of wealth or power, you may fail to use your influence for harmony, or the elevation of others.

If he takes the form of music, you are likely to go down before his wiles.

If in the form of a fair woman, you may crush your finer feelings.

To feel that you are trying to shield yourself from Satan denotes that you will endeavour to throw off the bondage of selfish pleasure and seek to give others their best desserts.

See also **Devil**.

Sausage

To dream of making sausage denotes that you will be successful in many undertakings.

To eat them, you will have a humble, but pleasant home.

Saw

To dream that you use a handsaw indicates an energetic and busy time, and cheerful home life.

To see big saws in machinery foretells that you will superintend a big enterprise which will yield fair returns. For a woman, this dream denotes that she will be esteemed, and her counsels will be heeded.

To dream of rusty or broken saws warns of failure and accidents.

To lose a saw, you may engage in affairs which culminate in disaster.

To hear the buzz of a saw indicates thrift and prosperity.

To find a rusty saw denotes that you will probably restore your fortune.

To carry a saw on your back foretells that you will carry large, but profitable, responsibilities.

Sawdust

To dream of sawdust signifies that grievous mistakes may cause you distress and quarrelling in your home.

Scabbard

To dream of a scabbard denotes that some misunderstanding will be amicably settled. If you wonder where your scabbard can be, you will have overpowering difficulties to meet.

Scaffold

To dream of a scaffold warns that you will undergo keen disappointment in failing to secure the object of your affection.

To ascend one, you will be misunderstood and censured by your friends for some action, which you never committed.

To descend one, you will be guilty of wrongdoing, and will suffer the penalty.

To fall from one, you will be unexpectedly surprised if engaged in deceiving and working injury to others.

Scalding

To dream of being scalded portends that distressing incidents are likely to blot out pleasurable anticipations.

Scales

To dream of weighing on scales portends that justice will temper your conduct, and you will see your prosperity widening.

For a young woman to weigh her lover, the indications are that she will find him of solid worth, and faithfulness will balance her love.

Scandal

To dream that you are an object of scandal denotes that you are not particular in selecting good and true companions, but rather enjoy having fast men and women contribute to your pleasure. Trade and business of any character is likely to be slow after this dream. This dream can also indicate that you care too much for what others think about you.

Scarcity

To dream of scarcity warns of sorrow in the household.

Scarlet Fever

To dream of scarlet fever warns that you are in danger of sickness, or in the power of an enemy. To dream a relative dies suddenly with it warns of villainous treachery working against you.

Sceptre

To imagine in your dreams that you wield a sceptre, foretells that you will be chosen by friends to positions of trust, and you will not disappoint their estimate of your ability.

To dream that others wield the sceptre over you, denotes that you will seek employment under the supervision of others, rather than exert your energies to act for yourself.

School

To dream of attending school indicates distinction in literary work. If you think you are young and at school as in your youth, you will find that sorrow and reverses will make you sincerely long for the simple trusts and pleasures of days of yore.

If you are unhappy in your dream, you have to learn more before you will be able to achieve your ambitions. You need to resolve childhood insecurities.

To visit your childhood school indicates that discontent and discouraging incidents overshadow the present.

Scissors

To dream of scissors is an unlucky omen; wives are likely to be jealous and distrustful of their husbands, and sweethearts to quarrel and nag each other. Dullness may overshadow business horizons.

To dream that you have your scissors sharpened denotes that you will work to do that which will be repulsive to your feelings.

To break them, there will be quarrels, and probable separations for you.

To lose them, you will seek to escape from unpleasant tasks.

Scorpion

To dream of a scorpion foretells that false friends may seek opportunities to undermine your prosperity. If you fail to kill it, you risk suffering loss from an enemy's attack.

Scrapbook

To dream of a scrapbook denotes that disagreeable acquaintances may shortly be made.

Scratch

To scratch others in your dream denotes that you will be ill-tempered and fault-finding in your dealings with others.

If you are scratched, you may be injured by the enmity of some deceitful person.

To dream that you scratch your head denotes that strangers will annoy you by their flattering attentions, which you will feel are only shown to win favours from you.

Screw

To dream of seeing screws denotes that tedious tasks must be performed, and peevishness in companions must be combated. It also denotes that you must be economical and painstaking.

Sculptor

To dream of a sculptor foretells you will change from your present position to one less lucrative, but more distinguished.

For a woman to dream that her husband or lover is a sculptor foretells that she will enjoy favours from persons in high position.

Scum

To dream of scum signifies that you will experience disappointment over social defeats.

Scythe

To dream of a scythe warns that accidents or sickness may prevent you from attending to your affairs, or making journeys. An old or broken scythe implies separation from friends, or failure in some business enterprise.

Sea

To dream of the sea denotes that you will explore the instinctive and intuitive aspects of your personality.

For a young woman to dream that she glides swiftly over the sea with her lover, there will come to her sweet fruition of maidenly hopes, and joy will stand guard at the door of the consummation of changeless vows.

See also Ocean.

Seal

To dream that you see seals denotes that you are striving for a place that is above your power to maintain.

Dreams of seals usually show that the dreamer has high aspirations and discontent will harass him into struggles to advance his position.

Seamstress

To see a seamstress in a dream portends that you will be deterred from making pleasant visits by unexpected luck.

Sea spray

For a woman to dream of sea spray foretells that pleasure may distract her from the paths of rectitude. If she wears a bridal veil of sea spray, she will be likely to cause sorrow to some of those dear to her, through their inability to gratify her ambition.

Seat

To think, in a dream, that someone has taken your seat, denotes that you will be kept busy by people calling on you for aid. To give a woman your seat implies your yielding to artfulness.

Secondary School

To dream of a secondary school foretells promotion to more elevated positions in love, as well as social and business affairs. For a young woman to be suspended from a secondary school foretells she may have troubles in social circles.

Secret

To dream of being entrusted with an important secret denotes that you will be privileged with knowledge which will enable you to face life with strength.

Secret Order

To dream of any secret order, denotes that you may soon have opportunities for honest pleasures, and desired literary distinctions.

There is a vision of selfish and designing friendships for one who joins a secret order.

Young women should heed the counsel of their guardians, lest they fall into discreditable habits after this dream.

If a young woman meets the head of the order, she should oppose with energy and moral rectitude against allurements that are set brilliantly and prominently before those of her sex. For her to think

427

her mother has joined the order, and she is using her best efforts to have her mother repudiate her vows, denotes that she will be full of love for her parents, yet will wring their hearts with anguish by thoughtless disobedience.

To see or hear that the leader is dead foretells severe strains, and trials which will eventually end in comparative good.

Seduction

For a young woman to dream of being seduced warns that she may be easily influenced by showy persons.

For a man to dream that he has seduced a girl is a warning for him to be on his guard against false accusations. If his sweetheart appears shocked or angry under these proposals, he will find that the woman he loves is above reproach. If she consents, he is possibly being used for her pecuniary pleasures.

Seed

To dream of seed foretells increasing prosperity, even if present indications appear unfavourable.

Sentry

To dream of a sentry denotes that you will have kind protectors, and your life will be smoothly conducted.

Serenade

To hear a serenade in your dream, you will have pleasant news from absent friends, and your anticipations will not fail you.

If you are one of the serenaders, there are many delightful things in your future.

Serpents see **Snakes**

Servant

To dream of a servant is a sign that you will be fortunate, despite gloomy appearances. Anger, however, is likely to precipitate you into useless worries and quarrels.

To discharge one foretells regrets and losses.

To quarrel with one in your dream indicates that you may upon waking, have real cause for censuring someone who is derelict in duty.

To be robbed by one warns that you have someone near you who does not respect the laws of ownership.

Seven

To dream of the number seven, or symbols thereof such as a menorah, signifies accomplishment, perfection, totality and unification.

Sewing

To dream of sewing new garments foretells that domestic peace will crown your wishes.

Shakespeare

To dream of Shakespeare warns of unhappiness, anxiety and loss of passion.

To read Shakespeare's works denotes that you will unalterably attach yourself to literary accomplishments.

Shaking Hands

For a young woman to dream that she shakes hands with some prominent ruler foretells she will be surrounded with pleasures and distinction from strangers. If she avails herself of the opportunity, she will stand in high favour with friends. If she finds she must reach up to shake hands, she will find rivalry and opposition. If she has on gloves, she will overcome these obstacles.

To shake hands with those beneath you denotes that you will be loved and honoured for your kindness and benevolence. If you think that you or they have soiled hands, you may find enemies among seeming friends.

For a young woman to dream of shaking hands with a decrepit old man warns she may find trouble where amusement was sought.

Shampoo

To dream of seeing shampooing going on denotes that you may engage in undignified affairs to please others.

To have your own head shampooed, you will soon make a secret trip, in which you will have much enjoyment, if you succeed in keeping the real purport from your family or friends.

Shanty

To dream of a shanty denotes that you may leave home in the quest of health. This also warns you of decreasing prosperity.

Shark

To dream of sharks denotes formidable enemies.

To see a shark pursuing and attacking you denotes that unavoidable reverses may sink you into despondent foreboding.

To see them sporting in clear water foretells that while you are basking in the sunshine of women and prosperity, jealousy is secretly, but surely, working you disquiet and unhappy fortune.

To see a dead one denotes reconciliation and renewed prosperity.

Shave

To merely contemplate getting a shave, in your dream, denotes you will plan for the successful development of enterprises, but will fail to generate sufficient energy to succeed.

430

To dream that you are being shaved portends that you will let imposters defraud you.

To shave yourself foretells that you will govern your own business and dictate to your household, notwithstanding that the presence of a disagreeable person may cause you quarrels.

If your face appears smooth, you will enjoy quiet, and your conduct will not be questioned by your companions. If old and rough, there will be many squalls on the matrimonial sea.

If your razor is dull and pulls your face, you will give your friends cause to criticize your private life.

If your beard seems grey, you will be absolutely devoid of any sense of justice to those having claims upon you.

Shawl

To dream of a shawl denotes that someone may offer you flattery and favour.

To lose your shawl foretells sorrow and discomfort. A young woman is in danger of being jilted by a good-looking man after this dream.

Shears

To see shears in your dream denotes that you may become miserly and disagreeable in your dealings.

To see them broken, you are likely to lose friends and standing through your eccentric behaviour.

Sheaves

To dream of sheaves of corn denotes joyful occasions. Prosperity holds before you a panorama of delightful events, and fields of enterprise and fortunate gain.

Sheep

To dream of shearing sheep denotes that a season of profitable enterprises will shower down upon you.

To see flocks of sheep, there will be much rejoicing among farmers, and other trades will prosper.

To see them looking scraggy and sick, you are likely to be thrown into despair by the miscarriage of some plan which promised rich returns.

To eat the flesh of sheep denotes that ill-natured persons may outrage your feelings.

See also **Lamb, Ram**.

Shells

Dreaming of shells signifies that you feel a need for protection in your life; alternatively, that you need to express your creative imagination. Interpretation depends on the emotions felt during the dream.

To walk among and gather shells in your dream denotes extravagance. Pleasure will leave you nothing but exasperating regrets and memories.

Shelter

To dream that you are building a shelter signifies that you will escape the evil designs of enemies.

If you are seeking shelter, you will be guilty of cheating, and will try to justify yourself.

Shelves

To see empty shelves in dreams warns of losses and consequent gloom.

Full shelves augur happy contentment through the fulfilment of hope and exertions.

Shepherd

To see shepherds in your dreams watching their flocks, portends bounteous crops and pleasant relations for the farmer, also much enjoyment and profit for others.

To see them in idleness warns of sickness and loss.

Sheriff

To dream of seeing a sheriff denotes that you may suffer great uneasiness over the uncertain changes which loom up before you.

To imagine that you are elected sheriff or feel interested in the office denotes that you may participate in some affair which will afford you neither profit nor honour.

To escape arrest, you will be able to engage further in illicit affairs.

Ship

To dream of ships foretells honour and unexpected elevation to ranks above your mode of life.

To dream of seeing a ship coming in foretells that some pleasant recreation is in store for you. To see one going out, you will probably experience slight losses and disappointments.

To see a ship on her way through a tempestuous storm warns of misfortune in business transactions.

See also *Boat, Vessels*

Shipwreck

To hear of a shipwreck warns of a disastrous turn of events and betrayal by female friends.

To dream of losing your life in a shipwreck warns that you may become involved in an affair from which you will only narrowly salvage your reputation.

To see others shipwrecked indicates that you will attempt in vain to shelter a friend from disgrace and insolvency.

Shirt

To dream of putting on your shirt is a warning that you will estrange yourself from your sweetheart if you indulge in your faithless conduct.

To lose your shirt augurs disgrace in business or love.

A torn shirt represents misfortune and miserable surroundings.

A soiled shirt warns of contagious illness.

Shoemaker

To see a shoemaker in your dream warns you that indications are unfavourable to your advancement. For a woman to dream that her husband or lover is a shoemaker foretells that her wishes will be gratified.

Shoes

To dream of seeing your shoes ragged and soiled denotes that you will make enemies by your unfeeling criticisms.

To have them cleaned in your dreams foretells improvement in your affairs. Some important event will cause you satisfaction.

New shoes augur changes which will prove beneficial. If they pinch your feet, you will be uncomfortably exposed to practical jokes.

To find them untied warns of losses, quarrels and ill health.

To lose them is a warning of separation.

To dream that your shoes have been stolen during the night, but you have two pairs of tights, denotes that you will have a loss, but will gain in some other pursuit.

For a young woman to dream that her shoes are admired while on her feet warns her to be cautious in allowing newly introduced people to approach her in a familiar way.

To remove your shoes in a dream denotes that you are likely to be called upon to perform an act of humility or self-abasement.

Shooting

To dream that you see or hear shooting signifies unhappiness between married couples and sweethearts because of overweaning selfishness, also unsatisfactory business and tasks because of negligence.

Shop

An unhappy dream of a shop denotes that you are likely to be opposed in every attempt you make at self-advancement by scheming and jealous friends.

To dream of a shop filled with merchandise foretells prosperity and advancement. You will be more than capable of dealing with any problems.

An empty shop warns of failure of efforts, and quarrels.

To dream that your shop is burning is a sign of renewed activity in business and pleasure.

To see a shop window full of goods that you cannot afford signifies your feelings of inadequacy in achieving greater things.

To make purchases from a shop denotes the dreamer's positive attitude.

*See also **Department Store***.

Short-sighted

To dream that you are short-sighted signifies embarrassing failure and unexpected visits from unwelcome persons. For a young woman, this dream foretells unexpected rivalry.

To dream that your sweetheart is short-sighted warns that she may disappoint you.

Shot

To dream that you are shot, and are feeling the sensations of dying, denotes that you are to meet unexpected abuse from the ill feelings of friends. If you escape death by waking, you will be fully reconciled with them later on.

To dream that a preacher shoots you signifies that you will be annoyed by some friend advancing views opposed to your own.

Shotgun

To dream of a shotgun warns of domestic troubles and worry with children and other members of the household.

To shoot both barrels of a double-barreled shotgun foretells that you will meet such exasperating and unfeeling attention in your private and public life that good manners give way under the strain and your righteous wrath will be justifiable.

Shoulder

To dream of seeing naked shoulders foretells that happy changes will make you look upon the world in a different light.

To see your own shoulders appearing thin denotes that you will depend upon the caprices of others for entertainment and pleasure.

Shovel

To see a shovel in a dream signifies that laborious but pleasant work will be undertaken. A broken or old one implies frustration of hopes.

Shower

To dream that you are caught in a shower foretells that you will derive exquisite pleasure from the study of creation.

Shrew

To dream of a shrew warns that you will have difficulty in keeping a friend in a cheerful frame of mind, and that you may make yourself unfit for the experiences of everyday existence.

Sickness

To dream of sickness is a sign of trouble and real sickness in your family. Discord is also likely.

To dream of your own sickness is a warning to be unusually cautious of your health. An unforeseen event may well throw you into confusion by causing you to miss some anticipated visit or outing; this is especially likely if you are a woman.

To see any of your family pale and sick warns that some event will break unexpectedly upon your harmonious hearthstone.

See also **Disease, Illness**.

Side

To dream of seeing only the side of any object denotes that some person is going to treat your honest proposals with indifference.

To dream that your side pains you, there will be vexations in your affairs that will gall your endurance.

To dream that you have a fleshy, healthy side, you will be successful in courtship and business.

Sideboard

To see or search through a sideboard denotes that your anticipations are likely to be disappointed. To see one in order indicates pleasant friends and entertainments.

Siege

For a young woman to dream that she is in a siege, and sees cavalry around her, denotes that she will have serious drawbacks to enjoyments, but will surmount them finally, and receive much pleasure and profit from seeming disappointments.

Sieve

To dream of a sieve foretells that some annoying transaction may soon be made by you, which will probably be to your loss. If the meshes are too small, you will have the chance to reverse a decision unfavourable to yourself. If too large, you are eventually likely to lose something that you have recently acquired.

Sigh

To dream that you are sighing over any trouble or sad event denotes that you will have unexpected sadness, but that some redeeming brightness in your season of trouble.

To hear the sighing of others foretells that the misconduct of dear friends is likely to oppress you with a weight of gloom.

Silk

To dream of wearing silk clothes is a sign of high ambitions being gratified. Friendly relations will be established between those who were estranged.

For a young woman to dream of old silk denotes that she will have much pride in her ancestors, and will be wooed by a wealthy, but elderly person. If the silk is soiled or torn, she will drag her ancestral pride into disgrace.

Silkworm

If you dream of a silkworm, you will engage in a very profitable work, which will also place you in a prominent position.

To see them dead, or cutting through their cocoons, is a sign of reverses and trying times.

Silver

To dream of silver is a warning against depending too largely on money for real happiness and contentment.

To find silver money is indicative of shortcomings in others. Hasty conclusions are too frequently drawn by yourself for your own peace of mind.

To dream of silverware denotes worries and unsatisfied desires.

Singing

To hear singing in your dreams betokens a cheerful spirit and happy companions. You are soon to have promising news from someone who is away.

If you are singing while everything around you gives promise of happiness, jealousy may insinuate a sense of insincerity into your joyousness. If there are notes of sadness in the song, you may be unpleasantly surprised at the turn your affairs will take.

Ribald songs signify extravagant waste.

Single

For married persons to dream that they are single foretells that their union will be less than harmonious.

Six

To dream of the number six, or symbols thereof such as a six-pointed star, presages contradictory situations, struggles and trials.

Skate

To dream that you are skating on ice foretells that you are in danger of losing employment, or valuable articles. If you break through the ice, you will have unworthy friends to counsel you.

To see others skating foretells that disagreeable people will connect your name in scandal with some person who admires you.

To see skates denotes discord among your associates.

To see young people skating on roller skates foretells that you will enjoy good health, and feel enthusiastic over the pleasures you are able to contribute to others.

Skeleton

To dream of seeing a skeleton warns of illness, misunderstanding and injury at the hands of others, especially enemies.

To dream that you are a skeleton is a sign that you are suffering under useless worry, and should cultivate a milder disposition.

To dream of a skeleton may also be positive, indicating the resolution of a problem or the termination of an unhappy or unproductive relationship.

Skid

To dream of skidding in a car indicates that you need to exercise more emotional self-control.

Skipping

To dream that you are skipping foretells that you will startle your associates with a thrilling escapade bordering on the sensational.

To skip with children warns you against being selfish and overbearing.

Skull

To dream of skulls grinning at you is a sign of domestic quarrels and jars. Business may feel a shrinkage if you handle them.

To see a friend's skull denotes that you may receive injury from a friend because of your being preferred to him.

To see your own skull denotes that you will feel the servant of remorse.

Sky

To dream of the sky signifies distinguished honours and interesting travel with cultured companions, if the sky is clear. Otherwise, it portends blasted expectations and trouble with the opposite sex.

To see the sky turn red indicates that public disquiet and rioting may be expected.

Slander

To dream that you are slandered denotes that your interests are threatened by evil-minded gossips. This dream is a sign of your untruthful dealings with ignorance. For a young woman, it warns her to be careful of her conduct, as her movements are being critically observed by persons who merely claim to be her friends.

If you slander anyone, you will feel the loss of friends through selfishness.

Sleep

To dream of sleeping on a clean, fresh bed denotes peace and favour from those whom you love.

To sleep in strange resting places warns of sickness and broken promises.

To sleep beside a little child betokens domestic joys and reciprocated love.

To see others sleeping, you will overcome all opposition in your pursuit of love.

To dream of sleeping with a repulsive person or object warns you that your love may wane before that of your sweetheart, and you will suffer for your escapades.

Sleeping Car

To dream of sleeping cars indicates that your struggles to amass wealth are animated by the desire to gratify selfish and lewd principles which should be mastered and controlled.

To find yourself, in a dream, on top of a sleeping car warns that you may make a journey with an unpleasant companion, with whom you will spend time and money that could be used in a more profitable way, and whom you should seek to avoid.

Sleep walking

To imagine while dreaming that you are sleep walking portends that you may unwittingly consent to some agreement of plans which will bring you anxiety or ill fortune

Sleigh

To see a sleigh in your dreams warns that you may fail in some love adventure, and incur the displeasure of a friend. To ride in one foretells that injudicious engagements will be entered into.

For a young woman to dream of sleighing warns her that she is likely to meet a great deal of opposition in her choice of a lover, and that her behaviour may make her unpopular.

Sleight of Hand

To dream of practising sleight of hand, or seeing others doing so, signifies you will be placed in a position where your energy and power of planning will be called into strenuous play to extricate yourself.

Sliding

To dream of sliding portends disappointments in affairs and broken promises.

To slide down a hillside covered with green grass foretells that you may be deceived by flattering promises.

Slighted

To dream of slighting any person or friend denotes that you will fail to find happiness, as you will cultivate a morose and repellent bearing.

If you are slighted you will probably have cause to bemoan your unfortunate position.

Slippers

To dream of slippers warns you that you are about to enter into an unfortunate alliance or intrigue. You are likely to find favour with a married person which will result in trouble, if not scandal.

To dream that your slippers are much admired warns that you may be involved in a flirtation, which will end in disgrace.

Smoke

To dream of smoke, foretells that you will be perplexed with doubts and fears.

To be overcome with smoke, denotes that dangerous persons are victimizing you with flattery.

Snail

Snails crawling in your dream signify that unhealthy conditions surround you.

To step on them denotes that you will come in contact with disagreeable people.

Snakes

For a woman to dream that a dead snake is biting her warns that she may suffer from malice of a pretended friend.

To dream of snakes, is a foreboding of evil in its various forms and stages.

To dream of a poisonous snake is unfortunate. Women may lose the respect of honourable and virtuous people. Sweethearts may wrong each other.

To see them wriggling and falling over others foretells struggles with fortune and remorse.

To kill them, you will feel that you have used every opportunity of advancing your own interests, or respecting that of others. You will enjoy victory over enemies.

To walk over them, you will worry about of the prospect of

illness. Selfish persons may seek to usurp your place in your companion's life.

If they bite you, you risk succumbing to evil influences.

To dream that a snake coils itself around you and darts its tongue out at you is a warning that you may be placed in a position where you will be powerless in the hands of enemies.

To handle them, you will use strategy to aid in overthrowing opposition.

To see hairs turn into snakes foretells that seemingly insignificant incidents will make distressing cares for you.

If snakes turn into unnatural shapes, you will have troubles which will be dispelled if treated with indifference, calmness and willpower.

To see or step on snakes while wading or bathing denotes that there may be trouble where unalloyed pleasure was anticipated.

To see them bite others warns that some friend may be injured and criticized by you.

To see little snakes warns that you may entertain persons with friendly hospitality who will secretly defame you and work to overthrow your growing prospects.

To see children playing with them, is a sign that you will find it hard to distinguish your friends from your enemies.

For a woman to think a child places one on the back of her head, and she hears the snake's hisses, foretells that she may be persuaded to yield up some possession.

To see snakes raising up their heads in a path just behind your friend, denotes that you will uncover a conspiracy which has been formed to injure your friend and also yourself. To think your friend has them under control, denotes that some powerful agency will be employed in your favour to ward off evil influences.

For a woman to hypnotize a snake denotes that your rights will be assailed, but you will be protected by law and influential friends.

*See also **Adder, Reptile, Viper**.*

Sneeze

To dream that you sneeze denotes that hasty tidings will cause you to change your plans.

To see or hear others sneeze, some people will bore you with visits.

Snouts

To dream of snouts warns of dangerous seasons for you. Enemies are surrounding you, and difficulties will be numerous.

Snow

To see snow in your dreams denotes that while you have no real misfortune, there will be the appearance of illness and unsatisfactory enterprises.

To find yourself in a snow storm denotes sorrow and disappointment in failure to enjoy some long-expected pleasure. There always follows more or less discouragement after this dream.

If you eat snow, you will fail to realize ideals.

To see dirty snow foretells that your pride will be humbled, and you will seek reconciliation with some person whom you held in haughty contempt.

To see it melt, your fears will turn into joy.

To see large, white snowflakes falling while looking through a window foretells angry words with your sweetheart, and financial depression.

To see the sun shining through landscapes of snow foretells that you will conquer adverse fortune and possess yourself of power.

If snowbound or lost, ill luck is portended.

Snowball

To dream of throwing snowballs denotes that you will probably have to struggle with distasteful issues; if your judgment is not well-grounded, you will face defeat.

Snuff

To dream of snuff warns that your enemies are insinuating themselves into the confidence of your friends. For a woman to use it in her dreams foretells complications which may involve her separation from a favoured friend.

Soap

To dream of soap foretells that friendships will reveal interesting entertainment. Farmers will have success in their varied affairs.

For a young woman to be making soap predicts that a substantial and satisfactory income will be hers.

Socialist

To see a socialist in your dreams, your unenvied position among friends and acquaintances is predicted.

Sold

To dream that you have sold anything denotes that unfavourable business will worry you.

Soldiers

To see soldiers marching in your dreams foretells for you a period of flagrant excesses, but at the same time you will be promoted to elevations above rivals.

To see wounded soldiers is a sign of the misfortune of others causing you serious complications in your affairs. Your sympathy may outstrip your judgment.

To dream that you are a worthy soldier, you will have literal fulfilment of ideals. Women are in danger of disrepute if they find themselves dreaming of soldiers.

See also Army.

Son

To dream of your son, if you have one, as being handsome and dutiful, foretells that he will afford you proud satisfaction, and will aspire to high honours.

For a mother to dream that her son has fallen to the bottom of a well, and she hears cries, it is a warning of losses and sickness. If she rescues him, threatened danger will pass away unexpectedly.

Soot

If you see soot in your dreams, it warns that you may meet with ill success in your affairs. Lovers will be quarrelsome and hard to please.

Sorcerer

To dream of a sorcerer foretells that your ambitions will undergo strange disappointments and change.

Sores

To dream of seeing sores warns that illness may cause you loss stress.

To dress a sore foretells that your personal wishes and desires will give place to the pleasure of others.

Soul

To dream of seeing your soul leaving your body signifies that you are in danger of sacrificing yourself to useless designs, which will dwarf your sense of honour and cause you to become mercenary and uncharitable.

For an artist to see his soul in another foretells that he will gain distinction if he applies himself to his work and avoids sentimentality.

To imagine another's soul is in you denotes you will derive solace and benefit from some stranger who is yet to come into your life.

For a young woman musician to dream that she sees another young woman on the stage clothed in sheer robes, and imagining it is her own soul in the other person denotes that she will be outrivalled in some great undertaking.

To dream that you are discussing the immortality of your soul denotes you will have opportunities which will aid you in gaining desired knowledge and pleasure of intercourse with intellectual people.

Soup

To dream of soup is a forerunner of good tidings and comfort.

To see others taking soup foretells that you will have many good chances to marry.

For a young woman to make soup signifies that she will not be compelled to do menial work in her household, as she will marry a wealthy man.

To drink oyster soup made of sweet milk, there will be quarrels with some bad luck, but reconciliations will follow.

See also **Broth**.

Sovereign

To dream of a gold sovereign denotes increasing prosperity and new friends.

Sowing

To dream that you are sowing seed foretells good harvests for a farmer, if he sows in new ploughed soil.

To see others sowing, much business activity is portended, which will bring gain to all.

Spade

To dream of a spade denotes that you will have work to complete, which will give you much annoyance in superintending.

If you dream of the suit of cards named spades, you risk being enticed into follies which will bring you grief and misfortune.

For a gambler to dream that spades are trumps means that unfortunate deals will deplete his winnings.

Sparrow

To dream of sparrows denotes that you will be surrounded with love and comfort. This will cause you to listen with kindly interest to tales of woe, and your benevolence will gain you popularity.

To see them distressed or wounded foretells sadness.

Spectacles *see* Glasses

Spice

To dream of spice foretells you risk damaging your own reputation in search of pleasure. For a young woman to dream of eating spice is an omen of deceitful appearances winning her confidence.

Spider

To dream of a spider denotes that you will be careful and energetic in your labours, and that fortune will be amassed to pleasing proportions.

To see one building its web foretells that you will be happy and secure in your own home.

To kill one signifies quarrels with your wife or sweetheart.

If one bites you, you may be the victim of unfaithfulness and suffer from enemies in your business.

To dream that you see many spiders hanging in their webs around you foretells most favourable conditions, fortune, good health and friends.

To dream of a large spider confronting you signifies that your elevation to fortune will be swift unless you and it are in dangerous contact.

To dream of a white spider betokens purity and deliverance from danger.

To dream that you see a very large spider and a small one coming towards you denotes that you will be prosperous, and that you will feel for a time that you are immensely successful; but if the large one bites you, enemies may steal away your good fortune. If the little one bites you, you will be harassed with little spites and jealousies.

To imagine that you are running from a large spider notes that you will lose fortune if you ignore opportunities. If you kill the spider you will eventually come into some property or wealth.

For a young woman to dream she sees gold spiders crawling around her foretells that her fortune and prospect for happiness will improve, and new friends will surround her.

See also **Tarantula**.

Spider's web

To see spider's webs, denotes pleasant associations and fortunate ventures. *See also* **Web**.

Spinning

To dream that you are spinning means that you will engage in some enterprise which will be all you could wish.

Spirit

To see spirits in a dream warns that some unexpected trouble could confront you. If they are white-robed, business speculation will be disapproving. If they are robed in black, beware of treachery and disloyalty.

If a spirit speaks, there is some evil near you, which you might avert if you listen to wise advice.

To dream that you hear spirits knocking on doors or walls denotes that trouble may arise unexpectedly.

To see them moving draperies, or moving behind them, is a warning to hold control over your feelings, as you are likely to commit indiscretions. Quarrels are also threatened.

To see the spirit of your friend floating in your room warns of disappointment and insecurity.

To hear music supposedly coming from spirits warns of unfavourable changes in the household.

See also **Ghost**.

Spitting

To dream of spitting denotes unhappy terminations of seemingly auspicious undertakings. For someone to spit on you foretells disagreements and alienation of affections.

Splendour

To dream that you live in splendour denotes that you will succeed to elevations, and will reside in a different state to the one you now occupy.

To see others thus living signifies pleasure derived from the interest that friends take in your welfare.

Splinter

To dream of splinters sticking into your flesh warns that you are likely to have many vexations from members of your family or from jealous rivals.

If while you are visiting you stick a splinter in your foot you will soon make, or receive, a visit which is likely to prove extremely unpleasant. Your affairs will go slightly wrong through your continued neglect.

Sponges

Sponges seen in a dream warn that deception is being practised upon you.

To use one in erasing, you risk being the victim of folly.

Spools

To dream of spools of thread indicates some long and arduous tasks, which when completed will meet your highest expectations. If they are empty, there will be disappointments for you.

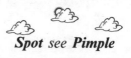

Spoons

To see, or use, spoons in a dream, denotes favourable signs of advancement. Domestic affairs will afford contentment.

To think a spoon is lost denotes that you will be suspicious of wrongdoing.

To steal one is a sign that you will deserve censure for your contemptible meanness in your home.

To dream of broken or soiled spoons signifies loss and trouble.

Spot *see* Pimple

Spring

To dream that spring is advancing is a sign of fortunate undertakings and cheerful companions.

To see spring appearing unnaturally is a foreboding of disquiet and losses.

Spur

To dream of wearing spurs denotes that you may engage in some unpleasant controversy.

To see others with them on warns that enmity is working you trouble.

Spy

To dream that spies are harassing you warns of dangerous quarrels and uneasiness.

To dream that you are a spy denotes that you may be involved in unfortunate ventures.

Squall

To dream of squalls foretells disappointing business and unhappiness.

Square

To dream of a square can signify stability and inner health. A negative dream of a square signifies a sense of imprisonment.

Squinting

To dream that you see some person with squinting eyes, denotes that you will be annoyed with unpleasant people.

For a man to dream that his sweetheart, or some good-looking girl, squints her eyes at him, foretells that he is threatened with loss by seeking the favours of women. For a young woman to have this dream about men, her good reputation may be in jeopardy.

Squirrel

To dream of seeing squirrels denotes that pleasant friends will soon visit you. You will see advancement in your business also.

To kill a squirrel denotes that you will be unfriendly and disliked.

To pet one signifies family joy.

To see a dog chasing one foretells disagreements and unpleasantness among friends.

Stable

To dream of a stable is a sign of fortune and advantageous surroundings.

To see a stable burning denotes successful changes, or it may be seen in actual life.

Stables appear only rarely in dreams.

Stag

To see stags in your dream foretells that you will have honest and true friends, and will enjoy delightful entertainments.

See also **Deer**.

Stain

To see a stain on your hands, or clothing, while dreaming, foretells that trouble over small matters will assail you.

To see a stain on the garments of others, or on their flesh, warns that some person may betray you.

Staircase

To dream of climbing a staircase signifies an emotional and spiritual search. This dream foretells good fortune and much happiness.

Descending a staircase generally signifies a voyage into your unconscious. It may signify misfortune in your affairs.

If you fall down stairs you risk being the object of hatred and envy.

To see broad, handsome stairs foretells approaching riches and honours.

To see others going down stairs warns that unpleasant conditions may take the place of pleasure.

To sit on stair steps denotes a gradual rise in fortune and delight.

Stake

To dream of seeing wood piled up to burn you at the stake signifies that you are threatened with loss but, if you escape, you will enjoy a long and prosperous life

Stall

To dream of a stall denotes that you will expect impossible results from some enterprise.

Stallion

To dream of a stallion foretells that prosperous conditions are approaching you, in which you will hold a position which will confer honour upon you.

To dream that you ride a fine stallion denotes that you will rise to position and affluence in a phenomenal way; however, your success may warp your morality and sense of justice.

See also **Horse**.

Stammer

To dream that you stammer in your conversation denotes that worry and illness may threaten your enjoyment.

To hear others stammer warns that unfriendly persons may delight in annoying you and giving you needless worry.

Stamps

To dream of postage stamps denotes system and remuneration in business.

If you try to use cancelled stamps, you may fall into disrepute.

To receive stamps signifies a rapid rise to distinction.

To see torn stamps denotes that there are obstacles in your way.

Standard-bearer

To dream that you are a standard-bearer denotes that your occupation will be pleasant and varied.

To see others acting as standard-bearers foretells that you will be jealous and envious of some friend.

Stars

To dream of looking upon clear, shining stars foretells good health and prosperity. If they are dull or red, there is trouble and misfortune ahead.

To see a shooting or falling star warns of sadness and grief.

To see stars appearing and vanishing mysteriously, there will be some strange changes and happenings in your near future.

To see them rolling around on the earth is a sign of formidable danger and trying times.

Starving

To dream of being in a starving condition warns of unfruitful labours and a dearth of friends.

To see others in this condition omens dissatisfaction with present companions and employment.

Statues

To see statues in dreams warns of estrangement from a loved one. Lack of energy will cause you disappointment in realizing wishes.

To dream of yourself as a statue indicates transformation in your waking life.

To dream of seeing someone you know as a statue indicates that you are putting this person on a pedestal, possibly without good reason. Or it could signify that you perceive this person as cold, hard and aloof. The interpretation depends on your emotions during the dream.

Stealing

To dream of stealing, or of seeing others commit this act, foretells bad luck and loss of character.

To be accused of stealing warns that you may be misunderstood in some affair, and suffer therefrom, but you will eventually find that this will bring you favour.

To accuse others denotes that you will treat some person with hasty inconsideration.

Steeple

To see a steeple rising from a church is a harbinger of sickness and reverses.

To climb a steeple foretells that you will have serious difficulties, but will surmount them.

To fall from one warns of losses in trade and ill health.

Stepping Stones

To dream of crossing a clear stream of water using stepping stones denotes pleasant employment and profit. If the water is thick and muddy, it indicates loss and temporary disturbance. For a woman this dream indicates either a quarrelsome husband, or one of mild temper and regular habits, as the water is muddy or clear.

Steps

To dream that you ascend steps denotes that fair prospects will relieve former anxiety.

To decend them, you may look for misfortune.

To fall down them, you are threatened with unexpected failure in your affairs.

See also **Ascent**.

Stepsister

To dream of a stepsister denotes that you may have unavoidable care and annoyance thrust upon you.

Stethoscope

To dream of a stethoscope warns of troubles and recriminations in love.

Sticks

To dream of sticks is generally an unlucky omen.

Stilts

To dream of walking on stilts, denotes that your fortune is in an insecure condition.

To fall from them, or feel them break beneath you, you may be precipitated into embarrassments by trusting your affairs to the care of others.

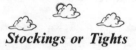

Sting

To feel that any insect stings you in a dream is a foreboding of unhappiness.

For a young woman to dream that she is stung is ominous of sorrow and remorse from over-confidence in men.

Stockings or Tights

To dream of stockings or tights denotes that you may derive pleasure from dissolute companionship

For a young woman to see her stockings or tights ragged or worn foretells that she will be guilty of unwise conduct. To dream that she puts on fancy stockings or tights, she will be fond of the attention of men, and she should be careful to whom she shows preference. If white ones appear to be on her feet, she is threatened with disappointment or illness.

Stone

To see stones in your dreams warns of perplexities and failures.

To walk among rocks or stones omens that an uneven and rough pathway will be yours for at least a while.

To make deals in ore-bearing rock lands, you will be successful in business after many lines have been tried. If you fail to profit by the deal, you will have disappointments. If anxiety is greatly felt in closing the trade, you will succeed in buying or selling something that will prove profitable to you.

Small stones or pebbles imply that little worries and vexations will irritate you.

If you throw a stone, you will have cause to admonish a person.

If you design to throw a pebble or stone at some belligerent person, it denotes that some evil feared by you will pass because of your untiring attention to right principles.

See also **Rock**.

Stone Mason

To see stone masons at work while dreaming foretells disappointment.

To dream that you are a stone mason warns that your labours may be unfruitful. and your companions dull and uncongenial.

Store

See also **Department Store, Shop**

Storm

To see and hear a storm approaching warns of sickness, unfavourable business, and separation from friends. If the storm passes, your affliction will not be so heavy.

Stranger

To dream of a stranger pleasing you denotes good health and pleasant surroundings; if he displeases you, look for disappointments.

To dream that you are a stranger denotes abiding friendship.

Straw

If you dream of straw, you are threatened with emptiness and failure.

To see straw piles burning is a signal of prosperous times.

To feed straw to stock foretells that you will make poor provisions for those depending upon you.

Strawberries

To dream of strawberries is favourable to advancement and pleasure. You will obtain some long wished-for object.

To eat them denotes required love.

To deal in them denotes abundant harvest and happiness.

Street

To dream that you are walking in a street warns of ill luck and worries. You will almost despair of reaching the goal you have set up in your aspirations.

To be in a familiar street in a distant city, if it appears dark, you will make a journey soon, which will not afford the profit or pleasure contemplated. If the street is brilliantly lighted you will engage in pleasure, but this will quickly pass.

To pass down a street and feel alarmed lest a thug attack you, denotes that you are venturing upon dangerous ground in advancing your pleasure or business.

Struggling

To dream of struggling foretells that you will encounter serious difficulties. If you gain the victory in your struggle, you will also surmount present obstacles.

Stumble

If you stumble in a dream while walking or running, you will meet with disfavour, and obstructions will bar your path to success, but you will eventually surmount them, if you do not fall.

Stumps

To dream of a stump, foretells that you are to have reverses and will depart from your usual mode of living. To see fields of stumps signifies that you will find it hard to defend yourself from the encroachments of adversity. To dig or pull them up is sign that you will extricate yourself from poverty by throwing off sentiment and pride and meeting the realities of life with a determination to overcome whatever opposition you may meet.

Suffocating

To dream that you are suffocating warns that you may experience deep sorrow and mortification at the conduct of some one you love. You should be careful of your health after this dream.

Sugar

To dream of sugar denotes that you will be hard to please in your domestic life and may entertain jealousy while seeing no cause for anything but satisfaction and secure joys. There may be worries, and your strength and temper taxed after this dream.

To eat sugar in your dreams, you will have unpleasant matters to contend with for a while, but they will result better than expected.

To price sugar denotes that you are menaced by enemies.

To deal in sugar and see large quantities of it being delivered to you, you will narrowly escape a serious loss.

To see a cask of sugar burst and the sugar spilling out foretells a slight loss.

To hear someone singing while unloading sugar, some seemingly insignificant affair will bring you great benefit, either in business or social states.

Suicide

To commit suicide in a dream warns of misfortune.

To dream that a friend commits suicide indicates that you will have trouble in deciding a very important question.

To see or hear others committing this deed foretells that the failure of others may affect your interests.

For a young woman to dream that her lover commits suicide, her disappointment in the disloyalty of her lover is accentuated.

461

Sulphur

To dream of sulphur warns you to use much discretion in your dealings, as you are threatened with foul play.

To see sulphur burning is ominous of great care attendant upon your wealth.

To eat sulphur indicates good health and consequent pleasure.

Sun

To dream of seeing a clear, shining sunrise foretells joyous events and prosperity, which give delightful promises.

To dream that you are shrivelling under a scorching sun signifies that you will neglect the emotional side of your life to your detriment.

To see the sun at noontide denotes the maturity of ambitions and signals unbounded satisfaction.

To see the sun set is prognostic of joys and wealth passing their zenith, and warns you to care for your interests with renewed vigilance.

To see the sun obscured by clouds indicates a lack of spiritual direction on the part of the dreamer.

A sun shining through clouds denotes that troubles and difficulties are losing their hold on you, and prosperity is nearing you.

If the sun appears weird, or in an eclipse, there will be stormy and dangerous times, but these will eventually pass, leaving your business and domestic affairs in better forms than before.

Sunshade

To dream of seeing young girls carrying sunshades foretells prosperity and exquisite delights.

Surgeon

To dream of a surgeon warns that you are threatened by enemies who are close to you in business.

Surgical Instruments

To see surgical instruments in a dream foretells that you will feel dissatisfaction at the indiscreet manner a friend manifests toward you.

Swallow

To dream of swallows is a sign of peace and domestic harmony.

To see a wounded or dead one signifies unavoidable sadness.

Swamp

To walk through swampy places in dreams foretells that you may be the object of adverse circumstances and undergo keen disappointments in your love matters

To go through a swamp where you see clear water and green growths, you will take hold on prosperity and singular pleasures, the obtaining of which will be attended with danger and intriguing.

Swan

To dream of seeing white swans floating upon placid waters foretells prosperous outlooks and delightful experiences.

To see a black swan denotes illicit pleasure, if near clear water.

A dead swan foretells satiety and discontentment.

To see them flying, pleasant anticipations will be realized soon.

Swearing

To dream of swearing denotes some unpleasant obstructions in business. A lover may have cause to suspect the faithfulness of his affianced after this dream.

To dream that you are swearing before your family denotes that disagreements may be brought about by your unloyal conduct.

Sweat

To dream that you are sweating foretells that you will come out of some difficulty, which has caused much gossip, with new honours.

Sweeping

To dream of sweeping denotes that you will gain favour in the eyes of your family, and children will find pleasure in the home.

If you think the floors need sweeping, and you for some reason neglect them, there will be disappointments awaiting you in the approaching days.

Sweetheart

To dream that your sweetheart is affable and of pleasing physique foretells that you will woo a woman who will prove a joy to your pride and will bring you a good inheritance. If she appears otherwise, you may become discontented with her. To dream of her as being sick or in distress denotes that sadness will be mixed with joy.

Sweets

To dream of making sweets denotes profit accruing from industry.

To dream of eating crisp, new sweets implies social pleasures and much lovemaking among the young and old. Sour sweets are a sign of illness or that disgusting annoyances will grow out of confidences too long kept.

To receive a box of bonbons signifies to a young person that he or she will be the recipient of much adulation. It generally means prosperity. If you send a box you will make a proposition, but will meet with disappointment.

Sweet Taste

To dream of any kind of a sweet taste in your mouth denotes that you will be praised for your pleasing conversation and calm demeanour in a time of commotion and distress.

To dream that you are trying to get rid of a sweet taste, foretells that you will oppress and deride your friends, and will incur their displeasure.

Swelling

To dream that you see yourself swollen denotes that you will amass fortune, but your egotism will interfere with your enjoyment.

To see others swollen foretells that advancement will meet with envious obstructions.

Swimming

To dream of swimming is an augury of success if you find no discomfort in the act. If you feel yourself going down, dissatisfaction may present itself to you.

For a young woman to dream that she is swimming with a girlfriend who is an artist in swimming foretells that she will be loved for her charming disposition, and her little love affairs will be condoned by her friends.

To swim under water foretells struggles and anxieties.

Switch

To dream of a switch warns of changes and misfortune.

A broken switch warns of disgrace and trouble.

Sword

To dream that you wear a sword indicates that you will fill some public position with honour.

To have your sword taken from you warns of your vanquishment in rivalry.

To see others bearing swords foretells that altercations will be attended with danger.

Symphony

To dream of symphonies, heralds delightful occupations.

Synagogue

To dream of a synagogue, foretells that you have enemies powerfully barricading your entrance into fortune's realms. If you climb to the top on the outside, you will overcome oppositions and be successful.

If you read the Hebrew inscription on a synagogue, you will meet disaster, but will eventually rebuild your fortunes with renewed splendour.

Syringe

To dream of a syringe denotes that false alarm of the gravity of a relative's condition will reach you. To see a broken one warns that you are approaching a period of ill health or worry over slight mistakes in business.

T

'And it was so, when Gideon heard the telling of the dream, and the interpretation thereof, that he worshiped, and returned into the host of Israel, and said, "Arise; for the Lord hath delivered into your hand the host of Midian."'

—Judges vii, 15.

Table

To dream of setting a table before a meal foretells happy unions and prosperous circumstances.

To see empty tables signifies poverty or disagreements.

To clear the table denotes that pleasure may soon assume the form of trouble and indifference.

To eat from a table without a cloth foretells that you will be possessed of an independent disposition.

To see a table walking or moving in some mysterious way foretells that dissatisfaction will soon enter your life, and you will seek relief in change.

To dream of a soiled cloth on a table warns that quarrelling will follow pleasure.

To see a broken table is ominous of decaying fortune.

To see one standing or sitting on a table foretells that to obtain their desires they may be guilty of indiscretions.

Tacks

To dream of tacks means many vexations and quarrels to you.

For a woman to hammer in a tack foretells that she will master unpleasant rivalry.

If she mashes her finger while driving it in, she will become distressed over unpleasant tasks.

Tadpole

To dream of tadpoles foretells that uncertain speculation will bring cause for uneasiness in business. For a young woman to see them in clear water foretells that she may form a relation with a wealthy but immoral man.

Tail

To dream of seeing only the tail of a beast, unusual annoyance is indicated where pleasures seemed assured.

To cut off the tail of an animal denotes that you will suffer misfortune through your own carelessness.

To dream that you have the tail of a beast grown on you denotes that strange events will cause you perplexity.

Tailor

To dream of a tailor denotes that worries may arise on account of some journey to be made.

To have a misunderstanding with one shows that you will be disappointed in the outcome of some scheme.

For one to take your measure warns that you may have quarrels and disagreements.

Talisman

To dream that you wear a talisman implies that you will have pleasant companions and enjoy favours from the rich. For a young woman to dream her lover gives her one denotes that she will obtain her wishes concerning marriage.

Talking

To dream of talking warns that there may be worries in your affairs.

To hear others talking loudly foretells that you may be accused of interfering in the affairs of others. To think they are talking about you warns that you are menaced with illness and disfavour.

Tallow

To dream of tallow forebodes that your possessions of love and wealth may vanish.

Tambourine

To dream of a tambourine, signifies you will have enjoyment in some unusual event which will soon take place.

Tank

To dream of a tank foretells that you will be prosperous and satisfied beyond your expectations. To see a leaking tank denotes loss in your affairs.

Tape

To dream of tape denotes that your work will be wearisome and unprofitable. For a woman to buy it warns that she may find misfortune laying oppression upon her.

Taper

To dream of lighting wax tapers denotes that some pleasing occurrence will bring you into association with friends long absent.

To blow them out signals disappointing times. Sickness may forestall expected opportunities of meeting distinguished friends.

Tapestry

To dream of seeing rich tapestry foretells that luxurious living will be to your liking. If the tapestries are not worn or ragged, you will be able to gratify your inclinations.

If a young woman dreams that her rooms are hung with tapestry, she will soon wed someone who is rich and above her in standing.

Tar

If you see tar in dreams, it warns you against pitfalls and designs of treacherous enemies.

To have tar on your hands or clothing warns of sickness and grief.

Tarantula

To see a tarantula in your dream signifies enemies are attempting to overwhelm you with loss. To kill one, denotes that you will be successful after much ill luck.

Target

To dream of a target foretells that some affair will divert your attention from other more pleasant ones. For a young woman to think she is a target denotes that her reputation is in danger through the envy of friendly associates.

Tassels

To see tassels in a dream denotes that you will reach the height of your desires and ambition. For a young woman to lose them denotes that she may undergo some unpleasant experience.

Tattoo

To see your body appearing tattooed foretells that some difficulty may cause you to make a long and tedious absence from your home.

To see tattooes on others warns that strange loves may make you an object of jealousy.

To dream you are a tattooist is a warning that you may estrange yourself from friends because of your fancy for some strange experience.

Taxes

To dream that you pay your taxes foretells that you will succeed in destroying evil influences rising around you. If others pay them, you may be forced to ask aid of friends. If you are unable to pay them, you will be unfortunate in experiments you are making.

Taxi

To ride in a taxi in dreams is significant of pleasant avocations, and average prosperity you will enjoy.

To ride in a taxi at night, with others, indicates that you will have a secret that you will endeavour to keep from your friends.

To ride in a taxi with a woman, scandal will couple your name with others of bad repute.

To dream of driving a taxi denotes manual labour, with little chance of advancement.

Tea

To dream that you are brewing tea warns that you may be guilty of indiscreet actions feel deeply remorseful as a consequence.

To see your friends drinking tea with you denotes that social pleasures may pall on you, and that you may seek to change your feelings by serving others in their sorrows.

To see leaves in your tea warns you of trouble in love and your social life.

To spill tea is a sign of domestic confusion and grief.

To find your tea caddy empty portends disagreeable gossip and news.

To dream that you are thirsty for tea denotes that you will be surprised with uninvited guests.

Teacher

To dream of a teacher denotes that you are likely to enjoy learning and amusements in a quiet way. If you are one, you are likely to reach desired success in literary and other works.

To dream of being praised by a teacher in front of the rest of the class indicates that you have belief in your own abilities. Being castigated by the teacher denotes feelings of guilt over an action in waking life.

Teacups

To dream of teacups foretells enjoyable outings. For a woman to break or see them broken warns that her pleasure and good fortune may be marred by sudden trouble. To drink wine from one foretells that fortune and pleasure will be combined in the near future.

Tears

To dream that you are in tears warns that some affliction may envelop you.

To see others shedding tears foretells that your sorrows will affect the happiness of others.

See also **Crying, Weeping**.

Teasing

To find yourself teasing any person while dreaming denotes that you will be loved and sought after because of your cheerful and amiable manners. Your business will be eventually successful.

To dream of being teased denotes that you will win the love of merry and well-to-do persons.

For a young woman to dream of being teased foretells that she may form a hasty attachment.

Teeth

An ordinary dream of teeth warns of an unpleasant contact with sickness, or disquieting people.

If you dream that your teeth are loose, there may be failures and gloomy tidings.

If the doctor pulls your tooth, you are likely to be unwell.

To have them filled, you will recover lost valuables after much uneasiness.

To clean or wash your teeth foretells that some great struggle will be demanded of you in order to preserve your fortune.

To dream that you are having a set of false teeth made denotes that severe difficulties may fall upon you, and you will strive to throw them aside.

If you lose your teeth, you are likely have heavy burdens.

To dream that you have your teeth knocked out warns of sudden misfortune.

To examine your teeth warns you to be careful of your affairs, as enemies are lurking near you.

If they appear decayed and snaggled, your business or health may suffer due to stress.

To dream of spitting out teeth portends sickness.

Imperfect teeth is a dream full of mishaps for the dreamer.

For one tooth to fall out foretells disagreeable news; if two, it denotes unhappy states that the dreamer may be plunged into.

For a man to dream about rotten, ripped-out, or wobbly teeth signifies his fear of diminution and powerlessness.

To dream of tartar or any deposit falling off of the teeth and leaving them sound and white, is a sign of temporary indisposition, which will pass, leaving you wiser in regard to conduct, and you will find enjoyment in the discharge of duty.

To admire your teeth for their whiteness and beauty foretells that pleasant occupations and much happiness will be experienced through the fulfilment of wishes.

Telegram

To dream that you receive a telegram denotes that you will soon receive tidings, probably of an unpleasant character. Some friend is likely to misrepresent matters which are of much concern to you.

To send a telegram is a sign that you may be estranged from someone holding a place near you, or that business may disappoint you.

If you are the operator sending these messages, you will be affected by them only through the interest of others.

To see or be in a telegraph office foretells unfortunate engagements.

See also **Cable**.

Telephone

To dream of a telephone warns that you may meet strangers who harass and bewilder you in your affairs. For a woman to dream of talking on the phone denotes that she may have much jealous rivalry, but will overcome all evil influences. If she cannot hear well over the phone, she is threatened by malicious gossip.

Telescope

To dream of a telescope warns of unfavourable seasons for love and domestic affairs. Business is likely to be changeable and uncertain.

To look at planets and stars through one portends for journeys you which will afford you much pleasure, but later cause you much financial loss.

To dream that you are looking through a telescope warns of imminent changes which may put you at a disadvantage.

To see one broken, or out of use, indicates that matters may go awry for you. Trouble is likely.

Tempest see Storm

Temptation

It is always good to dream that you have successfully resisted any temptation. To yield to temptation is bad.

To dream that you are surrounded by temptations, denotes that you will be involved in some trouble with an envious person who is trying to displace you in the confidence of friends. If you resist them, you will be successful in some affair in which you have much opposition.

Tenant

For a landlord to see his tenant in a dream warns of business trouble and vexation. To imagine you are a tenant foretells that you may suffer loss in experiments of a business character. If a tenant pays you money, you will be successful in some engagements.

Ten Commandments

To read the Ten Commandments, or to hear them read, denotes that you risk falling into errors from which you will escape only with great difficulty, even with the advice of friends or wise and unerring judgment.

Tenpin Bowling

If you dream at playing at tenpin bowling, you may soon engage in some affair which will bring discredit upon your name, and lose you money and true friendship.

To see others engaged in this dream foretells that you may pleasure in frivolous people and even lose employment.

For a young woman to play a successful game of tenpins, is an omen of light pleasures, but sorrow may attend her later.

See also **Bowling**.

Tent

To dream of being in a tent foretells a change in your affairs.

To see a number of tents denotes journeys with unpleasant companions.

If the tents are torn or otherwise dilapidated, there is likely to be trouble for you.

Terror

To dream that you feel terror at any object or happening warns of disappointments and loss.

To see others in terror means that the unhappiness of friends will seriously affect you.

Tetanus

To dream that you have tetanus signifies trouble ahead for you, as some person is likely to betray your confidence. For a woman to see others with lockjaw, foretells her friends may unconsciously detract from her happiness by assigning her unpleasant tasks. If livestock have it, you may lose a friend.

Text

To dream of hearing a minister reading his text warns that quarrels may lead to separation with a friend.

To dream that you are in a dispute about a text foretells unfortunate adventures for you.

If you try to recall a text, you may meet with unexpected difficulties.

If you are repeating and pondering over one, you will have great obstacles to overcome if you are to gain your desires.

Thatch

To dream that you thatch a roof with any quickly perishable material denotes that sorrow and discomfort are likely to surround you.

If you find that a roof which you have thatched with straw is leaking, there will be threatenings of danger, but by your rightly directed energy they may be averted.

Thaw

To dream of seeing ice thawing foretells that some affair which has caused you much worry will soon give you profit and pleasure.

To see the ground thawing after a long freeze foretells prosperous circumstances.

Theatre

To dream of being at a theatre denotes that you will have much pleasure in the company of new friends. Your affairs will be satisfactory after this dream. If you are one of the players, your pleasures will be of short duration.

If you attend a music hall, you are in danger of losing property through silly pleasures. If it is a grand opera, you will succeed in your wishes and aspirations.

If you applaud and laugh at a theatre, you will sacrifice duty to the gratification of fancy.

To dream of trying to escape from one during a fire or other excitement foretells that you will engage in some enterprise which will be hazardous.

Thermometer

To dream of looking at a thermometer warns of unsatisfactory business, and disagreements in the home.

To see a broken one foreshadows illness. If the mercury seems to be falling, your affairs may assume a distressing shape. If it is rising, you may be able to throw off bad conditions in your business.

Thief

To dream of being a thief pursued by the police is a sign of reverses in business, and unpleasantness in social relations.

If you pursue or capture a thief, you will overcome your enemies.

Thigh

To dream of seeing your thigh smooth and white denotes unusual good luck and pleasure.

To see wounded thighs warns of illness and treachery.

For a young woman to admire her thigh signifies willingness to engage in adventures: she should heed this as a warning to be careful of her conduct.

Thimble

If you use a thimble in your dreams, you will have many others to please besides yourself. If a woman, you will have your own position to make.

To lose one warns of poverty and trouble. To see an old or broken one denotes that you are about to act unwisely in some momentous affair.

To receive or buy a new thimble portends new associations in which you will find contentment.

Thirst

To dream of being thirsty shows that you are aspiring to things beyond your present reach; if your thirst is quenched with pleasing drinks, you will obtain your wishes.

To see others thirsty and drinking to slake it, you will enjoy many favours at the hands of wealthy people.

Thorns

To dream of thorns is an omen of dissatisfaction; evil will surround every effort at advancement.

If the thorns are hidden beneath green foliage, your prosperity may be interfered with by secret enemies.

Thread

To dream of thread denotes that your fortune lies along intricate paths.

To see broken threads, you will suffer loss through the disloyalty of friends.

Three

To dream of the number three, or symbols thereof such as the triangle, signifies order, harmony and perfection.

Threshing

To dream of threshing grain denotes great advancement in business and happiness among families. But if there is an abundance of straw and little grain, unsuccessful enterprises will be undertaken.

To break down or have an accident while threshing, you are likely to have some great sorrow in the midst of prosperity.

Throat

To dream of seeing a well-developed and graceful throat portends a rise in position.

If you feel that your throat is sore, you may be deceived in your estimation of a friend, and will have anxiety over the discovery.

Throne

If you dream of sitting on a throne, you will rapidly rise to favour and fortune.

To descend from one, there is much disappointment for you.

To see others on a throne, you will succeed to wealth through the favour of others.

Thumb

To dream of seeing a thumb foretells that you will be the favourite of artful persons and uncertain fortune.

If you are suffering from a sore thumb, you may lose in business, and your companions may prove disagreeable. To dream that you have no thumb implies destitution and loneliness. If it seems unnaturally small, you will enjoy pleasure for a time. If abnormally large, your success will be rapid and brilliant.

If the thumb has a very long nail, you are at risk of falling into evil through seeking exotic pleasures.

Thunder

To dream of hearing thunder foretells that you may soon be threatened with reverses in your business.

To be in a thunderstorm denotes that trouble and grief are close to you.

To hear the terrific peals of thunder, which make the earth quake, portends great loss and disappointment.

Ticket Collector

To dream of a ticket collector denotes that a time of reckoning is at hand.

Tickle

To dream of being tickled denotes worries and illness.

If you tickle others, you will throw away much enjoyment through weakness and folly.

Ticks

To mash a tick on you denotes that you may be annoyed be enemies.

To see in your dreams large ticks on stock warns that enemies are endeavouring to get possession of your property by foul means.

Tiger

To dream of a tiger advancing towards you, you risk being tormented and persecuted by enemies. If it attacks you, failure will bury you in gloom. If you succeed in warding it off, or killing it, you will be extremely successful in all your undertakings.

To see one running away from you is a sign that you will overcome opposition, and rise to high positions.

To see them in cages foretells that you will foil your adversaries.

To see rugs of tiger skins denotes that you are on the way to enjoy luxurious ease and pleasure.

Tightrope

To walk a tightrope signifies that you will engage in hazardous speculation but will succeed against the odds.

To see others walking a tightrope, you will benefit from the fortunate ventures of others.

Tights** see **Stockings and Tights

Till

To dream of seeing money and valuables in a till foretells coming success. Your love affairs will be exceedingly favourable. An empty one denotes disappointed expectations.

Timber

To dream of timber denotes many difficult tasks but little remuneration or pleasure.

To see piles of timber burning indicates profit from an unexpected source.

To dream of sawing timber denotes unwise transactions and unhappiness.

Tipsy

To dream that you are tipsy denotes that you will cultivate a jovial disposition, and that the cares of life will make no serious inroads into your conscience.

To see others tipsy shows that you are careless as to the demeanour of your associates.

See also **Drunk, Intoxication**.

Toad

To dream of toads signifies unfortunate adventures. If a woman, your good name is threatened with scandal.

To kill a toad foretells that your judgment is likely to be harshly criticised.

To put your hands on them, you will be instrumental in causing the downfall of a friend.

Tobacco

To dream of tobacco denotes success in business affairs, but poor returns in love.

To use it warns you against enemies and extravagance.

To see it growing foretells successful enterprises. To see it dry in the leaf ensures good crops to farmers, and consequent gain to traders.

To smoke tobacco denotes amiable friendships.

Tomatoes

To dream of eating tomatoes signals the approach of good health. To see them growing denotes domestic enjoyment and happiness.

For a young woman to see ripe ones foretells her happiness in the married state.

Tomb

To dream of seeing tombs warns of sadness and disappointments in business.

To read the inscription on tombs, foretells unpleasant duties.

Tongue

To dream of seeing your own tongue denotes that you may be looked upon with disfavour by your acquaintances.

To see the tongue of another foretells that scandal may villify you.

To dream that your tongue is affected in any way denotes that your carelessness in talking will get you into trouble

Tools

To dream of tools denotes unsatisfactory means of accomplishing some work. If the tools are broken, you will be threatened with illness or failure in business.

Toothless

To dream that you are toothless denotes your inability to advance your interests. Ill health may cast gloom over your prospects.

To see others toothless foretells that enemies are trying in vain to slander you.

Toothpicks

To dream of toothpicks foretells that small anxieties, and spites will harass you unnecessarily if you give them your attention.

If you use one, you may be a party to a friend's injury.

Top

To dream of a top denotes that you will be involved in frivolous difficulties.

To see one spinning foretells that you will waste your means in childish pleasures.

To see a top foretells that indiscriminate friendships will involve you in difficulty.

Topaz

To see topaz in a dream signifies that fortune will be liberal in her favours, and you will have very pleasing companions. For a woman to lose topaz ornaments foretells that she may be injured by jealous friends who court her position. To receive one from another beside a relative foretells that an interesting love affair will occupy her attention.

Torch

To dream of seeing torches foretells pleasant amusement and favourable business.

To carry a torch denotes success in lovemaking or intricate affairs. For one to go out warns of failure and distress.

Tornado

If you dream that you are in a tornado, you are likely to be filled with disappointment and perplexity over the miscarriage of studied plans for swift attainment of fortune.

See also **Hurricane, Whirlwind.**

Torrent

To dream that you are looking upon a rushing torrent warns of unusual trouble and anxiety.

Torture

To dream of being tortured warns that you may undergo disappointment and grief through the machination of false friends.

If you are torturing others, you will fail to carry out well-laid plans for increasing your fortune.

If you are trying to alleviate the torture of others, you will succeed after a struggle in business and love.

Tourist

To dream that you are a tourist denotes that you will engage in some pleasurable affair which will take you away from your usual residence.

To see tourists indicates brisk but unsettled business and anxiety in love.

Tower

To dream of seeing a tower denotes that you will aspire to high elevations. If you climb one, you will succeed in your wishes, but if the tower crumbles as you descend, you will be disappointed in your hopes.

Town

To dream of a town that is busy and friendly signifies the dreamer's active and happy involvement in waking life. If the town is empty and cold, the dreamer feels lonely and cut off.

See also **City**.

Town Hall

To dream of a town hall denotes contentions and threatened lawsuits.

To a young woman this dream is a foreboding of unhappy estrangement from her lover by her failure to keep virtue inviolate.

Toys

To see toys in dreams foretells family joys. especially if new.

To see children at play with toys, marriage of a happy nature is indicated.

To dream of playing with toys yourself, if you are an adult, denotes that you are not taking life seriously and need to face up to reality.

To give away toys in your dreams foretells that you will be ignored in a social way by an acquaintance.

Trade

To dream of trading denotes fair success in your enterprise. If you fail, trouble and annoyances are likely to overtake you.

Train

To see a train moving in your dreams, you will soon have cause to make a journey.

To be on a train and it appears to move smoothly along, though there is no track, denotes that you will be much worried over some affair which will eventually prove a source of profit to you.

To see freight trains in your dreams is an omen of changes which will tend to your elevation.

To miss a train foretells that you are likely to be foiled in an attempt to forward your prospects.

To be unable to get onto a crowded train for lack of space denotes that you are overwilling to drop back in the face of competition.

To dream of seeing a train crash in which you are not a participant portends trouble of a business character.

Traitor

To see a traitor in your dream warns that you have enemies working against you. If someone calls you one, or if you imagine yourself one, there may be unfavourable prospects before you.

Tram

To see trams in your dreams warns that some malicious person is actively interested in causing you trouble and disquiet.

To ride on a tram foretells that rivalry and jealousy will get in the way of your happiness.

To stand on the platform of a tram while it is running denotes that you will attempt to carry on an affair which may be extremely dangerous; but if you ride without accident, you will be successful. If the platform is up high, your danger will be more apparent, but if low, you will just manage to accomplish your purpose.

Tramp

To dream of tramps signifies the contempt which the dreamer feels for himself at having missed out on the adventures of life, and his anxiety in facing the future.

Trap

To dream of setting a trap denotes that you are willing to use intrigue to carry out your designs

If you are caught in a trap, you will be outwitted by your opponents.

If you catch game in a trap, you will flourish in whatever vocation you may choose.

To see an empty trap, there may be misfortune in the immediate future. An old or broken trap warns of failure.

Travel

To dream of travel signifies profit and pleasure combined. To dream of travelling through rough unknown places portends dangerous enemies, and perhaps sickness. Over bare or rocky steeps, signifies apparent gain, but loss and disappointment will swiftly follow. If the hills or mountains are fertile and green, you will be eminently prosperous and happy.

To dream you travel alone in a car denotes that you may possibly make an eventful journey, and affairs may be worrying. To travel in a crowded train foretells fortunate adventures, and new and entertaining companions.

Dreams of travel may also signify your personal and professional growth, and the achievement of aspirations. The ease of travelling denotes the ease, or difficulty, with which this is achieved.

See also **Journey**.

Tray

To see trays in your dream warns that your wealth may be foolishly wasted, and surprises of an unpleasant nature may shock you. If the trays seem to be filled with valuables, surprises will come in the shape of good fortune.

Treasures

To dream that you find treasures denotes that you will be greatly aided in your pursuit of fortune by some unexpected generosity.

If you lose treasures, bad luck in business and the inconstancy of friends is indicated.

Trees

Dreams of trees signify permanence, rebirth and inner vitality.

To dream of trees in new foliage foretells a happy consummation of hopes and desires. Dead trees signal sorrow and loss.

To climb a tree is a sign of swift elevation and preferment.

To cut one down, or pull it up by the roots, denotes that you will waste your energies and wealth foolishly.

To see green trees newly felled portends unhappiness coming unexpectedly upon scenes of enjoyment or prosperity.

See also **Forest, Woods**.

Trenches

To see trenches in dreams warns you of distant treachery. You may sustain loss if not careful in undertaking new enterprises, or associating with strangers.

To see filled trenches warns that many anxieties are gathering around you.

Triangle

To dream of a triangle, if the dream is pleasant, signifies order, harmony and perfection. If the dream is unpleasant, separation from friends and love affairs end in disagreement.

Tripe

To see tripe in a dream warns of sickness and danger.

To eat tripe denotes that you may be disappointed in some serious matter.

Triplets

To dream of seeing triplets foretells success in affairs where failure was feared.

For a man to dream that his wife has them signifies a pleasant termination to some affair which has been long in dispute.

To hear newly-born triplets crying signifies disagreements which will be hastily reconciled to your pleasure.

For a young woman to dream that she has triplets denotes that she may suffer loss and disappointment in love, but will succeed to wealth.

Trophy

To see trophies in a dream signifies that some pleasure or fortune will come to you through the endeavours of mere acquaintances. For a woman to give away a trophy implies doubtful pleasures and fortune.

Trousers

To dream of trousers foretells that you will be tempted to dishonourable deeds.

If you put them on inside out, you will find that a fascination is fastening its hold upon you.

Trout

To dream of seeing trout is significant of growing prosperity. To eat some denotes that you will be happily conditioned.

To catch one with a hook foretells assured pleasure. If it falls back into the water, you will have a short season of happiness.

To catch them with a net is a sign of unparalleled prosperity.

To see them in muddy water warns that your success in love may bring you to grief and disappointments.

Trowel

To dream of a trowel denotes you will vanquish poverty. To see one rusty or broken, ill luck is approaching.

Trumpet

To dream of a trumpet denotes that something of unusual interest is about to befall you.

To blow a trumpet signifies that you will gain your wishes.

Trunk

To dream of trunks foretells journeys and ill luck. To pack your trunk denotes that you will soon go on a pleasant trip.

To see the contents of a trunk thrown about in disorder foretells quarrels, and a hasty journey from which only dissatisfaction will accrue.

Empty trunks warn of disappointment in love and marriage.

For a drummer to check his trunk is an omen of advancement and comfort. If he finds that his trunk is too small for his wares, he will soon hear of his promotion, and his desires will reach gratification. For a young woman to dream that she tries to unlock her trunk and can't, signifies that she will make an effort to win some wealthy person, but by a misadventure she will lose her chance. If she fails to lock her trunk, she may be disappointed in making a desired trip.

Trusts

To dream of trusts foretells indifferent success in trade or law.

If you imagine that you are a member of a trust, you will be successful in designs of a speculative nature.

Tub

To dream of seeing a tub full of water denotes domestic contentment. An empty tub proclaims unhappiness and waning of fortune.

A broken tub foretells family disagreements and quarrels.

Tumble

To dream that you tumble off of anything denotes that you are given to carelessness, and should strive to be prompt with your affairs.

To see others tumbling is a sign that you will profit by the negligence of others.

Tunnel

To dream of going through a tunnel is bad for those in business and in love.

To see a train coming towards you while in a tunnel foretells ill health and change in occupation.

To pass through a tunnel in a car denotes unsatisfactory business, and much unpleasant and expensive travel.

To see a tunnel caving in portends failure and malignant enemies.

To look into one denotes that you will soon be compelled to face a desperate issue.

Turf

To dream of a racing turf signifies that you will have pleasure and wealth at your command, but your morals will be questioned by your most intimate friends.

To see a green turf indicates that interesting affairs will hold your attention.

Turkey

To dream of seeing turkeys signifies abundant gain in business, and favourable crops to the farmer.

To see them dressed for the market denotes improvement in your affairs.

To see them sick, or dead, foretells that stringent circumstances may cause your pride to suffer.

To dream you eat turkey foretells some joyful occasion approaching.

To see them flying denotes a rapid transit from obscurity to prominence. To shoot them as game is a sign that you will unscrupulously amass wealth.

Turkish Baths

To dream of taking a Turkish bath foretells that you will seek health far from your home and friends, but you will have much pleasurable enjoyment.

To see others take a Turkish bath signifies that pleasant companions will occupy your attention.

Turnips

To see turnips growing denotes that your prospects will brighten, and that you will be much elated over your success.

To eat them is a warning of ill health. To pull them up denotes that you will improve your opportunities and your fortune thereby.

To eat turnip greens is a sign of bitter disappointment. Turnip seed is a sign of future advancement.

For a young woman to sow turnip seed foretells that she will inherit good property and win a handsome husband.

Turpentine

To dream of turpentine foretells that your near future holds unprofitable and discouraging engagements. For a woman to dream that she binds turpentine to the wound of another shows she will gain friendships and favour through her benevolent acts.

Turquoise

To dream of a turquoise foretells that you are soon to realize some desire which will greatly please your relatives. For a woman to have one stolen foretells she will meet with obstacles in love. If she comes by it dishonestly, she will suffer for yielding to hasty susceptibility in love.

Turtle

To dream of seeing turtles signifies that an unusual incident will cause you enjoyment and improve your business conditions.

To drink turtle soup denotes that you will find pleasure in compromising intrigue.

Tweezers

To see tweezers in a dream denotes that uncomfortable situations will fill you with discontent, and your companions may abuse you.

Twine

To see twine in your dream warns you that your business is assuming complications which will be hard to overcome.

Twins

To dream of twins foretells security in business, and faithful and loving contentment in the home.

Two

To dream of the number two, or symbols thereof such as couples or objects occurring in pairs, signifies an inner conflict which you need to look into and resolve.

U

UFOs *see Flying Saucer*

Ugly

To dream that you are ugly denotes that you may have a difficulty with your sweetheart, and that your prospects may assume a depressed shade.

If a young woman thinks herself ugly, she may conduct herself offensively toward her lover, which will probably cause a break in their pleasant associations.

Ulcer

To see an ulcer in your dream warns of loss of friends and removal from loved ones. Affairs may be unsatisfactory.

To dream that you have ulcers warns that you will become unpopular with your friends if you give yourself up to foolish pleasures.

Umbrella

To dream of carrying an umbrella warns that trouble and annoyances are likely to beset you.

To see others carrying them foretells that you will be appealed to for aid by charity.

494

To borrow one, you may have a misunderstanding, perhaps with a warm friend.

To lend one portends injury from false friends. To lose one denotes trouble with someone who holds your confidence.

To see one torn to pieces, or broken, foretells that you may be misrepresented and maligned.

To carry a leaky one denotes that pain and displeasure may be felt by you towards your sweetheart or companions.

To carry a new umbrella over you in a clear shower, or sunshine, omens exquisite pleasure and prosperity.

Uncle

If you see your uncle in a dream, you are likely to have news of a sad character soon.

To dream repeatedly that you see your uncle troubled in mind, you may have trouble with your relations which results in estrangement, at least for a time.

To see your uncle dead denotes that you have formidable enemies.

To have a misunderstanding with your uncle denotes that your family relations may be unpleasant. Illness may be present.

Underground

To dream of being in an underground habitation, you are in danger of losing reputation and fortune.

To dream of riding on an underground railway foretells that you may engage in some peculiar speculation which will contribute to your stress and anxiety.

Underwear

To dream that you are wearing underwear which you are ashamed to reveal indicates that you hold inner prejudices of which you are unaware.

Undress

To dream that you are undressing foretells that scandalous gossip will overshadow you.

For a woman to dream that she sees the ruler of her country undressed warns that sadness may overtake anticipated pleasures. She may suffer pain through the apprehension of evil to those dear to her.

To see others undressed is an omen of stolen pleasures, which will rebound with grief.

Unfortunate

To dream that you are unfortunate warns of loss to yourself and trouble for others.

Uniform

To see a uniform in your dream denotes that you will have influential friends to aid you in obtaining your desires.

Dreaming about divesting yourself of a uniform is a warning to you about the uselessness of adhering to false or meaningless values.

For a young woman to dream that she wears a uniform foretells that she will luckily confer her favours upon a man who returns love for passion. If she discards it, she will be in danger of public scandal as a result of her notorious love for adventure.

To see people arrayed in strange uniforms foretells the disruption of friendly relations with some other power by your own government. This may also apply to families or friends. To see a friend or relative looking sad while dressed in uniform, or as a soldier, predicts ill fortune or continued absence.

United States Mailbox

To see a United States mailbox, in a dream, denotes that you may be about to enter into transactions which will be claimed to be illegal.

To put a letter in one denotes you will probably be held responsible for some irregularity of another.

Unknown

To dream of meeting unknown persons foretells change for good or bad depending in whether the person is pleasant or disagreeable.

To feel that you are unknown denotes that strange things may cast a shadow of ill luck over you.

Urgent

To dream that you are supporting an urgent petition is a sign that you will engage in some affair which will need fine financiering to carry it through successfully.

Urn

To dream of an urn foretells that you will prosper in some respects, but that in others disfavour will be apparent. To see broken urns, unhappiness is likely to confront you.

Usurper

To dream that you are a usurper, foretells you will have trouble in establishing a good title to property.

If others are trying to usurp your rights, there will be a struggle between you and your competitors, but you will eventually win.

For a young woman to have this dream, she will be a party to a spicy rivalry, in which she will win.

V

'Where there is no vision, the people perish; but he that keepeth the law, happy is he.'

—Proverbs xxix., 18.

Vaccinate

To dream of being vaccinated foretells that your susceptibility to the charms of the opposite sex may be played upon to your sorrow.

To dream that others are vaccinated denotes that you will find it difficult to find contentment.

For a young woman to be vaccinated on her leg warns of treachery.

Vagrant

To dream that you are a vagrant warns of poverty and misery. To give to a vagrant, denotes that your generosity will be applauded.

Valentine

To dream that you are sending valentines warns that you may lose opportunities of enriching yourself.

For a young woman to receive one suggests that she will marry her lover against the counsels of her guardians.

Valley

To find yourself walking through green and pleasant valleys foretells great improvements in business. Lovers will be happy and congenial.

If the valley is barren, the reverse is predicted. If marshy, illness or vexations may follow.

A fertile valley signifies spirituality, inner transformation and contemplation.

Vapour Bath

To dream of a vapour bath, you will have fretful people for companions, unless you dream of emerging from one, and then you will find that your cares will be temporary.

Varnishing

To dream of varnishing anything denotes that you may seek to win distinction by fraudulent means.

To see others varnishing warns that you are threatened with danger from the endeavour of friends to add to their own possessions.

Vase

To dream of a vase denotes that you will enjoy the sweetest pleasure and contentment in your home life.

To drink from a vase, you will soon thrill with the delights of stolen love.

To see a broken vase warns of early sorrow. For a young woman to receive one, signifies that she will soon obtain her dearest wish.

Vat

To see a vat in your dreams warns of suffering from the hands of cruel persons.

Vatican

To dream of the Vatican signifies that unexpected favours may fall within your grasp.

Vault

To dream of a vault warns of bereavement or other misfortune. To see a vault for valuables signifies that your fortune will surprise many, as your circumstances will appear to be meagre. To see the doors of a vault open warns of the loss and treachery of people whom you trust.

Vegetables

To dream of eating vegetables is an omen of strange luck. You will think for a time that you are tremendously successful, but will find to your sorrow that you have been grossly imposed upon.

Withered or decayed vegetables bring sadness.

For a young woman to dream that she is preparing vegetables for dinner foretells that she will lose a man whom she desired through pique, but win a well-meaning and faithful husband. Her engagements will be somewhat disappointing.

Vehicle

To ride in a vehicle while dreaming, warns of threatened loss or illness.

To be thrown from one foretells hasty and unpleasant news. To see a broken one signals failure in important affairs.

To buy one, you will reinstate yourself in your former position. To sell one denotes unfavourable change in affairs.

Veil

To dream that you wear a veil denotes that you may not be perfectly sincere with your lover, and will as a result be forced to use stratagem to retain him.

To see others wearing veils, you may be maligned and defamed by apparent friends.

An old, or torn veil, warns you that deceit is being thrown around you with sinister design.

For a young woman to dream that she loses her veil denotes that her lover sees through her deceitful ways and is likely to retaliate with the same.

To dream of seeing a bridal veil foretells that you will make a successful change in the immediate future, with much happiness in your position.

For a young woman to dream that she wears a bridal veil denotes that she will engage in some affair which will afford her lasting profit and enjoyment. If it gets loose, or any accident befalls it, she may be burdened with sadness and pain.

To throw a veil aside warns of separation or disgrace.

Vein

To see your veins in a dream ensures that you will not be slandered, if they are normal

To see them bleeding denotes great sorrow.

To see them swollen, you will rise hastily to distinction and places of trust.

Velvet

To dream of velvet portends very successful enterprises. If you wear it, some distinction will be conferred upon you.

To see old velvet means that your prosperity will suffer from your extreme pride.

If a young woman dreams that she is clothed in velvet garments, it denotes that she will have honours bestowed upon her, and the choice between several wealthy lovers.

Veneer

To dream that you are veneering denotes that you may systematically deceive your friends. Your speculations may be of a misleading nature.

Ventriloquist

To dream of a ventriloquist denotes that some affair is going to prove detrimental to your interest.

If you think yourself one, you may not conduct yourself honourably towards people who trust you.

For a young woman to dream she is mystified by the voice of a ventriloquist warns that she may be deceived into illicit adventures.

Veranda

To dream of being on a veranda denotes that you will be successful in some affair which is giving you anxiety.

For a young woman to be with her lover on a veranda denotes her early and happy marriage.

To see an old veranda denotes the decline of hopes and disappointment in business and love.

Vermin

Vermin crawling in your dreams signifies trouble. If you succeed in ridding yourself of them, you will be fairly successful.

Vertigo

To dream that you have vertigo foretells loss of domestic happiness.

Vessels

To dream of vessels denotes labour and activity.
See also **Boat, Ship**.

Vexed

If you are vexed in your dreams, you will find many worries scattered through your early awakening.

If you think some person is vexed with you, it is a sign that you will have difficulty in reconciling some slight misunderstanding.

Vicar

To dream of a vicar foretells that you may do foolish things while furious with jealousy and envy.

For a young woman to dream she marries a vicar, foretells that she may fail to awake reciprocal affection in the man she desires.

See also Clergyman, Minister, Preacher, Priest.

Vice

To dream that you are favouring any vice warns that you are about to endanger your reputation by letting evil persuasions entice you.

If you see others indulging in vice, some ill fortune may engulf the interest of a relative or associate.

Victim

To dream that you are the victim of any scheme warns that you will be oppressed by your enemies. Your family relations may also be strained.

To victimize others denotes that you will amass wealth dishonourably and prefer illicit relations, to the sorrow of your companions.

Victory

To dream that you win a victory foretells that you will successfully resist the attacks of enemies, and will have the love of others for the asking.

Village

To dream that you are in a village denotes that you will enjoy good health and find yourself fortunately provided for.

To revisit the village home of your youth denotes that you will have pleasant surprises in store and favourable news from absent friends.

If the village looks dilapidated, or the dream indistinct, it foretells trouble and sadness.

Vine

To dream of vines is propitious of success and happiness. Good health is in store for those who see flowering vines. If they are dead, you are likely to fail in some momentous enterprise.

To see poisonous vines foretells that you may be the victim of a plausible scheme.

Vinegar

To dream of drinking vinegar denotes that you may be exasperated and worried into assenting to some engagement which will fill you with evil foreboding.

To use vinegar on vegetables warns of a deepening of already distressing affairs.

To dream of vinegar, at all times, denotes inharmonious and unfavourable aspects.

Vineyard

To dream of a vineyard denotes favourable speculations and auspicious lovemaking.

To visit a vineyard which is not well-kept and is filled with bad odours denotes that disappointment may overshadow your anticipations.

Violence

To dream that any person does you violence, denotes that you will be overcome by enemies.

If you do some other persons violence, you will lose fortune and favour as a result of your reprehensible way of conducting your affairs.

It is interesting to note that many people who are violent by nature do not have violent dreams, whereas some people who could not imagine causing pain or suffering to others count dreams of violence among their most common dreams.

Violet

To see violets in your dreams, or gather them, brings joyous occasions on which you will find favour with some superior person.

For a young woman to gather them denotes that she will soon meet her future husband.

To see them dry, or withered, denotes that her love will be scorned and thrown aside.

To dream of or in the colour violet betokens sadness, spiritual repentance and even inner grieving.

Violin

To see or hear a violin in dreams foretells harmony and peace in the family, and many joyful occasions abroad; financial affairs will cause no apprehension.

For a young woman to play one in her dreams denotes that she will be honoured and receive lavish gifts.

If her attempt to play is unsuccessful, she may lose favour, and aspire to things she never can possess.

A broken violin indicates or bereavement separation.

Viper

To dream of a viper warns that calamities are threatening you. To dream that a many-hued viper, capable of throwing itself into many pieces, or unjointing itself, attacks you, denotes that your enemies are bent on your ruin and will work unitedly, yet apart, to displace you.

Virgin

To dream of a virgin denotes that you will be relatively lucky in your speculations. For a married woman to dream that she is a virgin warns that she may suffer remorse over her past.

Visit

If you visit in your dreams, you will shortly have some pleasant occasion in your life.

If your visit is unpleasant, your enjoyment will be marred by the action of malicious persons.

For a friend to visit you denotes that news of a favourable nature will soon reach you. If the friend appears sad and travel-worn, there will be a note of displeasure growing out of the visit, or other slight disappointments may follow.

Visions

To dream that you have a strange vision warns that you are likely to be unfortunate in your dealings.

If persons appear to you in visions, it foretells uprising and strife of families or state.

If your friend is near dissolution and you are warned in a vision, he may appear suddenly before you, usually in white garments. Visions of death and trouble have such close resemblance that they are sometimes mistaken one for the other.

To see visions of any order in your dreams, you may look for unusual developments in your business, and a different atmosphere and surroundings in private life. Things may be reversed for a while with you. You will have changes in your business and private life seemingly bad, but eventually good for all concerned.

Vitriol

If you see vitriol in your dreams, it is a token of some innocent person being censured by you.

To throw it on people shows you will bear malice towards parties who seek to favour you.

For a young woman to have a jealous rival throw it in her face warns that she may be the innocent object of some person's hatred. This dream, for a businessperson, denotes enemies and much persecution.

Voice

To dream of hearing voices denotes pleasant reconciliations, if they are calm and pleasing; high-pitched and angry voices signify disappointments and unfavourable situations.

To hear weeping voices, shows that sudden anger may cause you to inflict injury upon a friend.

If you hear the voice of God, you will make a noble effort to rise higher in unselfish and honourable principles, and will justly hold the admiration of high-minded people.

For a mother to hear the voice of her child is a sign of approaching perplexity and doubt.

To hear the voice of distress, or a warning one calling to you, implies your own serious misfortune or that of some one close to you. If the voice is recognized, it is often ominous of accident or illness

Volcano

To see a volcano in your dreams signifies that you may be involved in violent disputes, which threaten your reputation as a fair dealing and honest citizen.

For a young woman, it means that her selfishness and greed will lead her into intricate adventures.

Vomit

To dream of vomiting, is a sign that you will be afflicted with a malady, or you will be connected with a racy scandal.

To see others vomiting denotes that you will be made aware of the false pretences of persons who are trying to engage your aid.

For a woman to dream that she vomits a chicken, and it hops off, denotes that she will be disappointed in some pleasure by the illness of some relative. Unfavourable business and discontent are also portended.

If it is blood you vomit, you will find illness a hurried and unexpected visitor. You will be cast down with gloomy forebodings, and children and domesticity in general will ally to work you discomfort.

Vote

If you dream of casting a vote on any measure, you are likely to be engulfed in a commotion which affects your community.

To vote fraudulently foretells that you may let your dishonesty overcome your better inclinations.

Voucher

To dream of vouchers foretells that patient toil will defeat idle scheming to arrest fortune from you.

To sign one denotes that you have the aid and confidence of those around you, despite the evil workings of enemies.

To lose one signifies that you will have a struggle for your rights with relatives.

Vow

To dream that you are making or listening to vows, foretells that complaint may be made against you of disloyalty in business, or some love contract. To take the vows of a church denotes that you will bear yourself with unswerving integrity through some difficulty.

To break or ignore a vow warns that disastrous consequences may attend your dealings.

Voyage

To make a voyage in your dreams foretells that you will receive some inheritance besides that which your labours win for you.

A disastrous voyage brings incompetence and false loves.

Vultures

To dream of vultures signifies that some scheming person is bent on injuring you, and will not succeed unless you see the vulture wounded or dead.

For a woman to dream of a vulture warns that she may be the victim of slander and gossip.

W

'Therefore night shall be unto you, that ye shall not have a vision, and it shall be dark unto you, that ye shall not divine; and the sun shall go down over the prophets, and the day shall be dark over them.'

—Micah iii,6.

Wading

If you wade in clear water while dreaming, you will partake of fleeting but exquisite joys. If the water is muddy, you are in danger of illness, or some sorrowful experience.

To see children wading in clear water is a happy prognostication, as you will be favoured in your enterprises.

For a young woman to dream of wading in clear foaming water, she will soon gain the desire nearest her heart.

Wadding

Wadding, if seen in a dream, brings consolation to the sorrowing, and indifference to unfriendly criticism.

Wafer

Wafers, if seen in a dream, purport an encounter with enemies. To eat one, suggests impoverished fortune.

For a young woman to bake them denotes that she may be tormented and distressed by fears of remaining single.

Wager see Bet

Wages

Wages, if received in dreams, bring unlooked-for good to persons engaging in new enterprises.

To pay out wages denotes that you will be confounded by dissatisfaction.

To have your wages reduced warns you of unfriendly interest that is being taken against you.

An increase of wages suggests unusual profit in any undertaking.

Wagon

To dream of a wagon warns that you may be unhappily partnered.

To drive one down a hill is ominous of proceedings which may fill you with disquiet and cause you loss

To drive one uphill improves your worldly affairs.

To drive a heavily loaded wagon denotes that duty will hold you in a particular moral position, despite your efforts to throw it off.

To drive into muddy water warns of unhappiness and foreboding.

To see a covered wagon warns of treachery, which may hold up your advancement.

For a young woman to dream that she drives a wagon near a dangerous embankment portends that she may be involved in an illicit entanglement. If she drives across a clear stream of water, she will enjoy adventure without bringing opprobrium upon herself.

A broken wagon represents distress and failure.

Wagtail

To see a wagtail in a dream warns that you may be the victim of unpleasant gossip, and your affairs may develop unmistakable loss.

Waif

To dream of a waif denotes personal difficulties, and warns of bad luck in business.

Waist

To dream of a round full waist denotes that you will be favoured by an agreeable dispensation of fortune.

An unnaturally tiny waist warns of displeasing success and recriminating disputes.

Waiter or waitress

To dream of a waiter or waitress signifies that you will be pleasantly entertained by a friend. To see one cross or disorderly means that offensive people will thrust themselves upon your hospitality.

To find yourself waiting on others denotes that you may be too subservient in waking life.

If the waiter or waitress spills food or drink, the dreamer's carelessness is indicated.

Wake

To dream that you attend a wake denotes that you will sacrifice an important engagement to enjoy some ill-favoured assignation.

For a young woman to see her lover at a wake foretells that she will listen to the entreaties of passion.

Walking

To dream of walking through rough, briar-entangled paths denotes that you may be distressed by business complications, and that disagreeable misunderstandings may produce coldness and indifference.

To walk in pleasant places, you will be the possessor of fortune and favour.

To walk in the night brings misadventure and struggle for contentment.

For a young woman to find herself walking rapidly in her dreams denotes that she will inherit some property, and will possess a much desired object.

Walking Stick

To see a walking stick in a dream foretells that you may enter into contracts without proper deliberation and consequently suffer reverses. If you use one in walking, you will be dependent upon the advice of others. To admire handsome ones, you will entrust your interest to others, but they will be faithful.

Wallet

To see wallets in a dream, foretells that burdens of a pleasant nature will await your discretion as to assuming them. An old or soiled one implies unfavourable results from your labours.

To find a wallet filled with money in your dreams, you will be quite lucky, gaining your desire in nearly every instance. If it is empty, you risk being disappointed in some big hope.

If you lose your wallet, you are likely to disagree with a good friend.

Walls

Dreaming of being surrounded by walls may denote a need for privacy or secrecy, or to be alone, on the part of the dreamer.

To dream that you find a wall obstructing your progress, you risk succumbing to ill-favoured influences and losing important victories in your affairs.

To jump over it, you will overcome obstacles and win your desires. To force a breach in a wall, you will succeed in the attainment of your wishes by sheer tenacity of purpose.

To demolish one you will overthrow your enemies. To build one foretells that you will carefully lay plans and will solidify your fortune to the exclusion of failure, or designing enemies.

For a young woman to walk on top of a wall shows that her future happiness will soon be made secure. For her to hide behind a wall denotes that she is likely to form connections that she will be ashamed to acknowledge.

Walnut

To dream of walnuts is an omen significant of prolific joys and favours.

To dream that you crack a decayed walnut denotes that your expectations are likely to end in bitterness and regrettable collapse.

For a young woman to dream that she has walnut stains on her hands foretells that she may see her lover turn his attention to another; if so, she will entertain regrets for her past indiscreet conduct.

Waltz

To see the waltz danced foretells that you will have pleasant relations with a cheerful and adventuresome person.

For a young woman to waltz with her lover denotes that she will be the object of much admiration. If she sees her lover waltzing with a rival, she will overcome obstacles to her desires with strategy. If she waltzes with a woman, she will be loved for her virtues and winning ways. If she sees persons whirling in the waltz as if intoxicated, she will be engulfed in desire and pleasure.

Want

To dream that you are in want denotes that you have unfortunately ignored the realities of life, and chased folly to her stronghold of sorrow and adversity.

If you find yourself contented in a state of want, you will bear the misfortune which threatens you with heroism, and will see the clouds of misery disperse.

To relieve want signifies that you will be esteemed for your disinterested kindness, but you will feel no pleasure in good deeds.

War

To dream of war foretells unfortunate conditions in business, and much disorder and strife in domestic affairs. Such dreams can also denote the dreamer's internal conflict.

For a young woman to dream that her lover goes to war denotes that she is likely to hear of something detrimental to her lover's character.

To dream that your country is defeated in war is a sign that it will suffer revolution of a business and political nature. Personal interest will sustain a blow either way.

If you dream of victory, there will be brisk activity along business lines and domesticity will be harmonious.

Wardrobe

To dream of your wardrobe denotes that your fortune will be endangered by your attempts to appear richer than you are.

If you imagine that you have a scant wardrobe, you will seek association with strangers.

Warehouse

To dream of a warehouse denotes for you a successful enterprise. To see an empty one is a sign that you may be cheated and foiled in some plan which you have given much thought.

Warrant

To dream that a warrant is being served on you denotes that you will engage in some important work which will give you great uneasiness as to its standing and profits.

To see a warrant served on someone else there will be danger of your actions bringing you into serious quarrels or misunderstandings. You are likely to be justly indignant with the wantonness of some friend.

Warts

If you are troubled with warts on your person, in dreams, you will find it difficult to parry the thrusts made at your honour.

To see them leaving your hands foretells that you will overcome disagreeable obstructions to fortune.

To see them on others shows that you have bitter enemies near you. If you doctor them, you will struggle with energy to ward off threatened danger to you and yours.

Washboard

To see a washboard in your dreams is indicative of embarrassment. If you see a woman using one, it warns that you are likely to let women rob you of energy and fortune.

A broken one warns that you will come to grief through fast living.

Washerwoman

A washerwoman seen in dreams represents infidelity and a strange adventure. For the businessperson, or farmer, this dream indicates expanding trade and fine crops. For a woman to dream that she is a washerwoman denotes that she may throw decorum aside in her persistent effort to gain the favour of men.

Washing

To dream that you are washing yourself, signifies that you pride yourself on the numberless liaisons you maintain.

Washing-up Bowl

To dream of a washing-up bowl signifies that new cares will interest you, and afford much enjoyment to others.

To bathe your face and hands in a bowl of clear water denotes that you will soon consummate passionate wishes which will bind you closely to someone who interested you before passion enveloped you.

If the bowl is soiled, or broken, you may rue an illicit engagement, which will give others pain, and afford you small pleasure.

Wasp

Wasps, if seen in dreams warn that enemies may scourge and spitefully villify you.

If one stings you, you are likely to feel the effect of envy and hatred. To kill them, you will be able to subdue your enemies, and fearlessly maintain your rights.

Waste

To dream of wandering through waste places foreshadows doubt and failure, where promise of success was bright before you.

To dream of wasting your fortune denotes that you will be unpleasantly encumbered with domestic cares.

Watch

To dream of a watch denotes that you will be prosperous in well-directed speculations. To look at the time of one, your efforts risk being defeated by rivalry. To break one, distress and loss will threaten you.

To drop the glass of one foretells carelessness, or unpleasant companionship. For a woman to lose a watch signifies that domestic disturbances will produce unhappiness. To imagine that you steal one, you will have a violent enemy who may attack your reputation.

To make a present of one denotes that you may let your own interests suffer in the pursuit of undignified recreations.

Water

To dream of clear water foretells that you will joyfully realize prosperity and pleasure.

If the water is muddy, you may be in danger and gloom may occupy pleasure's seat.

If you see it rise up in your house, you will struggle to resist evil but, unless you see it subside, you are likely to succumb to dangerous influences.

If you find yourself baling it out, but your feet are getting wet, trouble, sickness, and misery will hit you hard, but you will forestall them by your watchfulness. The same may be applied to muddy water rising in vessels.

To fall into muddy water is a warning that you are likely to make many bitter mistakes, and suffer poignant grief therefrom.

To drink muddy water portends sickness, but drinking clear and refreshing water brings favourable consummation of fair hopes.

To sport with water denotes a sudden awakening to love and passion.

To have it sprayed on your head denotes that your passionate awakening to love will meet reciprocal consummation.

The following dream and its allegorical occurrence in actual life is related by a young woman student of dreams:

'Without knowing how, I was (in my dream) on a boat, I waded through clear blue water to a wharfboat, which I found to be snow white, but rough and splintry. The next evening I had a delightful male caller, but he remained beyond the time prescribed by mothers and I was severely censured for it.' The blue water and roughness of the boat were the disappointing prospects in the symbol.

Water-carrier

To see water-carriers passing in your dreams denotes that your prospects will be favourable and that love will prove no laggard in your chase for pleasure.

If you think you are a water-carrier, you will rise above your present position.

Waterfall

To dream of a waterfall foretells that you will secure your wildest desire, and fortune will be exceedingly favourable to your progress.

Water Lily

To dream of a water lily, or to see them growing, foretells there will be a close commingling of prosperity and sorrow or bereavement.

Waves

To dream of waves is a sign that you hold some vital step in contemplation, which may yield much knowledge if the waves are clear; but you will make a fatal error if you see them muddy or lashed by a storm.

Way

To dream of losing your way warns you to disabuse your mind of lucky speculations: your enterprises threaten failure unless you are painstaking in your management of affairs.

Wealth

To dream that you are possessed of much wealth foretells that you will energetically nerve yourself to meet the problems of life with that forcefulness which compels success.

To see others wealthy foretells that you have friends who will come to your rescue in perilous times.

For a young woman to dream that she is associated with wealthy people denotes that she will have high aspirations and will manage to enlist someone who is able to further them.

See also **Affluence, Opulence, Riches**.

Weasel

To see a weasel bent on a marauding expedition in your dreams warns you to beware of the friendships of former enemies, as they will try to devour you when you least expect it.

If you get rid of it, you will succeed in foiling deep schemes laid for your defeat.

Weather

To dream of the weather foretells fluctuating tendencies in fortune. One minute you are progressing immensely, the next you are suddenly confronted with doubts and rumblings of failure.

To think you are reading weather forecasts indicates that you will change your place of abode, after much weary deliberation, but will be benefited by the change.

Weaving

To dream that you are weaving denotes that you will baffle any attempt to defeat you in your struggle to build up an honourable fortune.

To see others weaving shows that you will be surrounded by healthy and energetic conditions.

Web

To dream of webs warns that deceitful friends may cause you loss and displeasure. If the web is non-elastic, you will remain firm in withstanding the attacks of envious persons who are seeking to obtain favours from you.

See also **Spider's Web**.

Wedding

To attend a wedding in your dream, you will speedily find that there is approaching you an occasion which is likely to cause you bitterness and delayed success

For a young woman to dream of her wedding foretells that she will soon enter upon new engagements, which will afford her distinction, pleasure and harmony.

For a young woman to dream that her wedding is a secret is decidedly unfavourable to character.

If she contracts a worldly or approved marriage, this signifies that she will rise in the estimation of those about her, and anticipated promises and joys will not be withheld.

If she thinks in her dream that there are parental objections, she will find that her engagement will create dissatisfaction among her relatives. For her to dream that her lover weds another foretells that she will be distressed with needless fears, as her lover will faithfully carry out his promises.

Wedding Clothes

To see wedding clothes signifies that you will participate in pleasing works and will meet new friends. To see them soiled or in disorder warns you may lose close relations with some much-admired person.

Wedding Ring

For a woman to dream that her wedding ring is bright and shining, foretells that she will be shielded from cares and infidelity.

If it should be lost or broken, much sadness may come into her life through death and uncongeniality.

To see a wedding ring on the hand of a friend, or some other person, denotes that you are likely to hold your vows lightly and court illicit pleasure.

Wedge

To dream of a wedge warns of trouble in business arrangements which may cause your separation from relatives.

Separation of lovers or friends may also be implied.

Wedlock

To dream that you are in the bonds of an unwelcome wedlock denotes that you may be unfortunately implicated in a disagreeable affair.

For a young woman to dream that she is dissatisfied with wedlock denotes that her inclinations may persuade her into scandalous escapades.

For a married woman to dream of her wedding day warns her to fortify her strength and feelings against disappointment. She may also be involved in secret quarrels and jealousies. For a woman to imagine she is pleased and securely cared for in wedlock, is a propitious dream.

See also **Marriage**.

Weeding

To dream that you are weeding foretells that you may have difficulty in proceeding with some work which will bring you distinction.

To see others weeding, you will be fearful that enemies will upset your plans.

Weeping

Weeping in your dreams warns of ill tidings and disturbances in your family.

To see others weeping signals pleasant reunion after periods of saddened estrangements. This dream for a young woman is ominous of lovers' quarrels, which can only reach reconciliation by self-abnegation.

For the trader, it foretells temporary discouragement and reverses.

See also **Crying, Tears**.

Weevil

To dream of weevils portends loss in trade and falseness in love.

Weighing

To dream of weighing denotes that you are approaching a prosperous period. If you aim determinedly for success you will victoriously reap the fruits of your labours.

To weigh others, you will be able to subordinate them to your interest.

For a young woman to weigh herself with her lover foretells that he will be ready at all times to comply with her demands.

Weight

To dream of losing weight signifies that the dreamer risks becoming diminished in business or love, or fears becoming less important to close friends and family.

Welcome

To dream that you receive a warm welcome into any society foretells that you will become distinguished among your acquaintances and will have deference shown you by strangers. Your fortune will approximate anticipation.

To accord others welcome denotes that your congeniality and warm nature will be your passport to anywhere you desire to go.

Well

To dream that you are working down a well warns that you may succumb to adversity through your misapplied energies. You will let strange elements direct your course.

To fall into a well warns of overwhelming despair. For one to cave in warns that enemies' schemes may overthrow your own.

To see an empty well denotes that you may be robbed of fortune if you allow strangers to share your confidence.

To see one with a pump in it shows that you will have opportunities to advance your prospects.

To dream of an artesian well foretells that your splendid resources will gain you admittance into the realms of knowledge and pleasure.

To draw water from a well denotes the fulfilment of ardent desires. If the water is impure, there will be unpleasantness.

Welsh Rarebit

To dream of preparing or eating Welsh rarebit denotes that your affairs will assume a complicated state, owing to your attention being absorbed by artful people and enjoyment of neutral fancies.

Wet

To dream that you are wet warns that a possible pleasure may involve you in loss and disease. You are warned to avoid the blandishments of seemingly well-meaning people.

For a young woman to dream that she is soaking wet warns that she may be embarrassingly implicated in an affair with a married man.

Whale

To dream of seeing a whale approaching a ship denotes that you will have a struggle between duties, and will be threatened with loss of property.

If the whale swims away, you will happily decide between right and inclination, and will encounter pleasing successes.

To see a whale overturn a ship warns of a whirlpool of disasters.

Whalebone

To see or work with whalebone in your dreams, you will form an alliance which will afford you solid benefit.

Wheat

To see large fields of growing wheat in your dreams denotes that your interest will take on encouraging prospects.

If the wheat is ripe, your fortune will be assured and love will be your joyous companion.

To see large clear grains of wheat running through the thresher foretells that prosperity has opened her portals to the fullest for you.

To see it in sacks or barrels, your determination to reach the apex of success is soon to be crowned with victory and your love matters will be firmly grounded.

To see that your granary is not well covered and its contents getting wet foretells that while you have amassed a fortune, you have not secured your rights and you risk seeing your interests diminishing at the hand of enemies.

If you rub wheat from the head into your hand and eat it, you will labour hard for success and will obtain and make sure of your rights.

To dream that you climb a steep hill covered with wheat and think you are pulling yourself up by the stalks of wheat denotes that you will enjoy great prosperity and thus be able to distinguish yourself in any chosen pursuit.

Wheels

To see swiftly rotating wheels in your dreams foretells that you will be thrifty and energetic in your business, and successful in pursuits of domestic bliss.

To see idle or broken wheels proclaims problems in your household.

Whetstone

To dream of a whetstone is significant of sharp worries. Close attention is needed in your own affairs, if you want to avoid difficulties.

You are likely to be forced into an uncomfortable journey.

Whip

To dream of a whip signifies unhappy dissensions and unfortunate and formidable friendships.

To dream that someone is using a whip on you indicates that you are harbouring guilt and feel that you deserve punishment.

Whirlpool

To dream of a whirlpool warns that great danger is imminent in your business and that, unless you are extremely careful, your reputation will be seriously blackened by some disgraceful intrigue.

Whirlwind

To dream that you are in the path of a whirlwind foretells that you are confronting a change which threatens to overwhelm you with loss and calamity.

For a young woman to dream that she is caught in a whirlwind and has trouble to keep her skirts from blowing up and entangling her waist, denotes that she will carry on a secret flirtation and will be horrified to find that she has become the subject of scandal.

See also **Hurricane, Tornado**.

Whisky

To dream of whisky in bottles denotes that you will be careful of your interests, protecting them with energy and watchfulness, thereby adding to their proportion.

To drink it alone foretells that you may sacrifice your friends to your selfishness.

To destroy whisky, you may lose your friends by your ungenerous conduct.

Whisky is not fraught with much good. Disappointment in some form will most likely appear.

To see or drink it is to strive and reach a desired object after many disappointments. If you only see it, you are highly unlikely to obtain the result hoped and worked for.

Whispering

To dream of whispering warns that you may be disturbed by the evil gossiping of people near you.

To hear a whisper coming to you as advice or warning foretells that you stand in need of aid and counsel.

Whistle

To hear a whistle in your dream denotes that you may be shocked by some sad news, which will change your plans for innocent pleasure.

To dream that you are whistling foretells a merry occasion in which you expect to figure largely. This dream for a young woman indicates indiscreet conduct and failure to obtain wishes.

White

To dream of the colour white can signify either purity and hope or, by contrast, desolation and mourning.

To see yourself or others garbed in white denotes eventful changes; you will nearly always find that these bring sadness.

To walk with a person wearing white proclaims that person's illness or distress, unless it is a young woman or child, in which case you will have pleasing surroundings for a season at least.

Whitewash

To dream that you are whitewashing foretells that you will seek to reinstate yourself with friends by ridding yourself of offensive habits and companions.

For a young woman, this dream is significant of well-laid plans to deceive others and gain back her lover who has been estranged by her insinuating bearing toward him.

Widow or Widower

To dream that you are a widow or widower foretells that you may have many troubles through malicious persons.

For a man to dream that he marries a widow denotes that he may see some cherished undertaking crumble down in disappointment.

Wife

To dream of your wife warns of unsettled affairs and discord at home.

To dream that your wife is unusually affable denotes that you will receive profit from some important venture in trade.

Wig

To dream you wear a wig warns that you may soon make an unpropitious change.

To lose a wig, you will incur the derision and contempt of enemies. To see others wearing wigs is a sign of treachery entangling you.

Wild

To dream that you are running about wild warns that you may sustain a serious fall or accident.

To see others doing so denotes that unfavourable prospects will cause you worry and excitement.

Wild Man

To see a wild man in your dream denotes that enemies will openly oppose you in your enterprises. To think you are one foretells that you may be unlucky in following out your designs.

Will

To dream you are making your will is significant of momentous trials and speculations.

For anyone to think a will is against them, portends that they will have disputes and disorderly proceedings to combat in some event soon to transpire.

If you fail to prove a will, you are in danger of libellous slander. To lose one is unfortunate for your business.

To destroy one warns you that you are about to be a party to treachery and deceit.

Willow

To dream of willows foretells that you will soon make a sad journey, but you will be consoled in your grief by faithful friends.

Wind

Dreaming of the wind signifies that change is under way. This may be positive or negative.

To dream of the wind blowing softly and sadly upon you signifies that great fortune will come to you through bereavement.

To walk briskly against a brisk wind foretells that you will courageously resist temptation and pursue fortune with a determination not easily put aside. For the wind to blow you along against your wishes portends failure in business undertakings and disappointments in love. If the wind blows you in the direction you wish to go, you will find unexpected and helpful allies, or that you have natural advantages over a rival or competitor.

Windmill

To see a windmill in operation in your dreams foretells abundant accumulation of fortune and marked contentment.

To see one broken or idle signifies adversity coming unawares.

Window

To see windows in your dreams is an augury of fateful culmination to bright hopes. Your fairest wish will probably go down in despair. Fruitless endeavours will most likely be your portion.

To see closed windows is a representation of desertion. If they are broken, you will probably be hounded by miserable suspicions of disloyalty from those you love.

To sit in a window denotes that you may be the victim of folly. To enter a house through a window denotes that you will be found out if you use dishonourable means to consummate a seemingly honourable purpose.

To escape by one indicates that you may fall into trouble whose toils will hold you unmercifully close.

To look through a window when passing, if strange objects appear, foretells that you are likely to fail in your chosen vocation.

Wine

To dream of drinking wine forebodes joy and consequent friendships.

To dream of breaking bottles of wine foretells that your love and passion will border on excess.

To see barrels of wine prognosticates great luxury. To pour it from one vessel into another signifies that your enjoyments will be varied and you will journey to many notable places.

To dream of dealing in wine denotes that your occupation will be remunerative.

For a young woman to dream of drinking wine indicates she will marry a gentleman who is both wealthy and honourable.

See also **Claret**.

Wine Cellar

To dream of a wine cellar foretells that superior amusements or pleasure will come your way, to be disposed of at your bidding.

Wineglass

To dream of a wineglass foretells that a disappointment will affect you seriously, as you will fail to see anything pleasing until shocked into the realization of trouble.

Wings

To dream that you have wings warns that you may experience grave fears for the safety of someone gone on a long journey away from you.

To see the wings of fowls or birds denotes that you will finally overcome adversity and rise to wealthy degrees and honour.

Winning

To dream of winning always signifies good, unless you cheat in order to succeed.

Narrowly failing to win may indicate a fear of success.

Winter

To dream of winter is a prognostication of ill health and dreary prospects for the favourable progress of fortune. After this dream your efforts are unlikely to yield satisfactory results.

Wire

To dream of wire denotes that you will make frequent but short journeys which may be to your disparagement.

Old or rusty wire signifies that you will be possessed of a bad temper, which will give troubles to your kindred.

To see a wire fence in your dreams foretells that you may be cheated in some trade you have in view.

Wisdom

To dream you are possessed of wisdom signifies that your spirit will be brave under trying circumstances, and you will be able to overcome these trials and rise to prosperous living. If you think you lack wisdom, it implies you are wasting your native talents.

Witch

To dream of witches denotes that you, with others, will seek adventures which will afford hilarious enjoyment, but may eventually rebound to your mortification. Business may suffer prostration if witches advance upon you; home affairs may be disappointing.

Witness

To dream that you bear witness against others signifies you may have great oppression through slight causes. If others bear witness against you, you may be compelled to refuse favours to friends in order to protect your own interest. If you are a witness for a guilty person, you may be implicated in a shameful affair.

Wizard

To dream of a wizard denotes that you are going to have a big family, which will cause you much inconvenience as well as pleasure. For young people, this dream warns of loss and broken engagements.

Wolf

To dream of a wolf warns that you have a thieving person in your employ, who may also betray secrets.

To kill one denotes that you will defeat sly enemies who seek to overshadow you with disgrace. To hear the howl of a wolf signifies that you will uncover a secret alliance to defeat you in honest competition.

Women

To dream of women foreshadows intrigue.

To argue with one foretells that you will be outwitted and foiled.

To see a dark-haired woman, with blue eyes and a pug nose, definitely determines your withdrawal from a race in which you stood a showing for victory. If she has brown eyes and a Roman nose, you will be cajoled into a dangerous speculation. If she has auburn hair with this combination, it adds to your perplexity and anxiety. If she is blonde, you will find that all your engagements will be pleasant and favourable to your inclinations.

Wood

To see wood in your dreams is an augury of prosperous times and peaceful surroundings.

If the wood is dead, there is disappointment in store for you.

Wooden Shoe

To dream of a wooden shoe, is significant of lonely wanderings and penniless circumstances. Those in love may suffer from unfaithfulness.

Woodpile

To dream of a woodpile warns of unsatisfactory business and misunderstandings in love.

Woods

To dream of woods brings a natural change in your affairs. If the woods appear green, the change will be lucky. If stripped of verdure, it will prove unlucky.

To see woods on fire denotes that your plans will reach satisfactory maturity. Prosperity will beam with favour upon you.

See also **Forest, Trees**.

Wool

To dream of wool is a pleasing sign of prosperous opportunities to expand your interests.

To see soiled, or dirty wool foretells that you will seek employment with those who detest your principles.

Work

To dream that you are hard at work denotes that you will win merited success by concentration of energy.

To see others at work denotes that hopeful conditions will surround you.

To look for work means that you will benefit by some unaccountable occurrence.

Workhouse

To dream that you are in a workhouse warns that some event will cause you harm and loss.

Workshop

To see workshops in your dreams foretells that you will use extraordinary schemes to undermine your enmies.

Worms

To dream of worms warns that you may be oppressed by the low intriguing of disreputable persons.

To use them in your dreams as fish bait foretells that by your ingenuity you will use your enemies to good advantage.

Wound

To dream that you are wounded signals distress an an unfavourable turn in business.

To see others wounded denotes that injustice will be accorded you by your friends.

To relieve or dress a wound signifies that you will have occasion to congratulate yourself on your good fortune.

Wreath

To dream that you see a wreath of fresh flowers denotes that great opportunities for enriching yourself will soon present themselves before you.

A withered wreath bears sickness and wounded love.

To see a bridal wreath foretells a happy ending to uncertain engagements.

Wreck

To see a wreck in your dream, foretells that you will be harassed with fears of destitution or sudden failure in business.

See also **Shipwreck**.

Writing

To dream that you are writing foretells that you will make a mistake which will almost prove your undoing.

To see writing denotes that you may be upbraided for your careless conduct and a lawsuit may cause you embarrassment.

To try to read strange writing signifies that you will escape enemies only by making no new speculation after this dream.

Y

'The prophet that hath a dream, let him tell a dream.'

—Jereniah xxiii., 28.

Yacht

To see a yacht in a dream denotes happy recreation away from business and troublesome encumbrances. A stranded one represents miscarriage of entertaining engagements.

Yardstick

To dream of a yardstick foretells that much anxiety may possess you, though your affairs assume unusual activity.

Yarn

To dream of yarn denotes success in your business and an industrious companion in your home.

For a young woman to dream that she works with yarn foretells that she will be proudly recognized by a worthy man as his wife.

Yawning

If you yawn in your dreams, you will search in vain for health and contentment.

To see others yawning foretells that you may see some of your friends in a miserable state. Sickness may prevent them from their usual labours.

Yearn

To feel in a dream that you are yearning for the presence of someone denotes that you will soon hear comforting tidings from your absent friends.

For a young woman to think her lover is yearning for her, she will have the pleasure of soon hearing some one making a long-wished-for proposal. If she lets him know that she is yearning for him, she is likely to be left alone and her longings will grow apace.

Yellow

To dream of or in yellow signifies eternity and religiosity.

To dream of or in pale yellow warns of sorrow, sickness, or deception.

To see yellow apparel foretells approaching joy and financial progress. Seen as a flitting spectre, in an unnatural light, the reverse may be expected.

You will be fortunate if you dream of yellow cloth.

To see a yellow bird fluttering about warns that some great event will fill you with fear for the future.

Yew Tree

To dream of a yew tree is a forerunner of illness and disappointment. If a young woman sits under one, she is likely to have many fears over her fortune and the faithfulness of her lover. If she sees her lover standing by one, she may expect to hear of his illness or misfortune. To admire one, she will estrange herself from her relatives by an unfortunate alliance.

Yield

To dream you yield to another's wishes denotes that you will throw away by weak indecision a great opportunity to elevate yourself.

If others yield to you, exclusive privileges will be accorded you and you will be elevated above your associates.

535

To receive poor yield for your labours, you may expect cares and worries.

Yoke

To dream of seeing a yoke denotes that you will unwillingly conform to the customs and wishes of others.

To yoke oxen in your dreams, signifies that your judgment and counsels will be accepted submissively by those dependent upon you. To fail to yoke them, you will be anxious over some prodigal friend.

Young

To dream of seeing young people is a prognostication of reconciliation of family disagreements and favourable times for planning new enterprises.

To dream that you are young again foretells that you will make mighty efforts to recall lost opportunities, but will nevertheless fail.

For a mother to see her son an infant or small child again, foretells that old wounds will be healed and she will take on her youthful hopes and cheerfulness.

To see the young at school foretells that prosperity and usefulness will envelope you with favours.

Yule Log

To dream of a yule log foretells that your joyous anticipations will be realized by your attendance at great festivities.

Z

Zebra

To dream of a zebra denotes that you will be interested in varying and fleeting enterprises.

To see one wild in his native country foretells that you will pursue a chimerical fancy which will return you unsatisfactory pleasure upon possession.

Zenith

To dream of the zenith foretells elaborate prosperity, and that your choice of suitors will be successful.

Zinc

To work with or to see zinc in your dreams indicates substantial and energetic progress. Business will assume a brisk tone in its varying departments.

To dream of zinc ore promises the approach of eventful success.

Zodiac

To dream of the zodiac is a prognostication of unparalleled rise in material worth, but also indicates alloyed peace and happiness.

To study the zodiac in your dreams denotes that you will gain distinction and favour by your dealings with strangers.

If you approach it or it approaches you, foretells that you will succeed in your speculations to the wonderment of others and beyond your wildest imagination.

To draw a map of it signifies future gain.

Zoo

To dream of visiting a zoo denotes that you will have a varied fortune. Sometimes it seems that enemies will overpower you and again you stand in the front rank of success. You will also gain knowledge by travel and sojourn in foreign countries.